THRO' THE VISION
OF THE NIGHT

Now a thing was secretly brought to me, and
mine ear received a little thereof. In thoughts
from the visions of the night, when deep
sleep falleth on men.

Job 4 : 13–14

Lancelot, whom the Lady of the Lake
Caught from his mother's arms – the wondrous
  one
Who passes thro' the vision of the night –

Lancelot and Elaine 1393–5

*

THRO' THE VISION
OF THE NIGHT

A Study of Source,
Evolution and Structure
in Tennyson's
Idylls of the King

*

J·M·GRAY

McGill–Queen's University Press
Montreal

© J. M. Gray 1980
Edinburgh University Press
22 George Square, Edinburgh

Published simultaneously in Canada by
McGill–Queen's University Press
1020 Pine Avenue West, Montreal H3A 1A2

ISBN 0–7735–0519–9

Legal Deposit 3rd quarter 1980
Bibliothèque nationale du Québec

Printed in Great Britain by
Clark Constable Ltd
Edinburgh

*

Preface

In this study my intention is *not* to present a critical judgement of the *Idylls*, whether in comparison with other works in the same genre, or in relationship to the rest of Tennyson's poetry. Mine is essentially an enquiry into the *poetic process* – the miraculous creative synthesis – as exemplified in narrative poems that re-embody literary traditions in unique forms.

My task involves close *explication* and *analysis* of the texts, severally and collectively, but precludes *comparison* with works outside the chosen corpus. I trace the aesthetic and cognitive structure of the sealed system – the Idyll-world.

Until recently, the automatic critical response to the *Idylls* has been condemnatory. I must therefore ask my readers to accept, at the outset, my conviction that these are fine poems and the work of a master-craftsman. My book is an attempt to demonstrate this craftsmanship, in some detail, much as a musicologist might conduct a demonstration, note-by-note, of the craftsmanship of a sonata or a quartet.

This does *not* mean asking my reader to believe that every line of the *Idylls* is perfect, that every passage is stamped with power, that each Idyll is the equal of its fellows in conception and artistic design. There *are* points at which Tennyson falters – what else would one expect? – and there *are* some poems that are weak in comparison with others. This I take for granted – as also the principle that for every lapse of power there will be, sooner or later, a compensatory gain; the whole work, with its strengths and weaknesses, is brought into as good a balance as human imperfection can devise. It is not, however, my business to dwell on the weaknesses of the *Idylls*; that would be to frustrate or at least obscure my intention to show the creative mind at work.

For help, assistance, comfort, encouragement of many kinds during this undertaking I would like to thank the following: Professor Jerome Buckley; Dr Arthur Melville Clark; my parents, Alfred Williams Gray and Annie Hughes Gray; Professor Donald Hair; Mr Gordon Howie; Melvin and Gilda Katz; Dr George Kay; Sandy McKenzie; my uncle, Mr James Martin; Professor Christopher Ricks; Professor John Rosenberg; Professor Malcolm Ross.

My greatest debt is to Rev. Dr Alexander King and Mrs Magda

King, for reading the whole work line by line, and suggesting many improvements, and to Dr Walter Nash, without whose linguistic insights into Tennyson's language this study could not have been written. Nor could it have been, certainly never completed, without the help of my wife, Hilary, and the forbearance of my daughters, Kirstie and Marion.

For excellent research facilities I am indebted to the National Library of Scotland, Edinburgh, Edinburgh University Library, the McLaughlin Library of University of Guelph, University of Nottingham Library, and the Tennyson Research Centre, Lincoln. A little of this material has appeared in *Explicator*, *Notes and Queries*, *Renaissance and Modern Studies*, *Tennyson Research Bulletin*, *Victorian Poetry*. This book has been published with the help of a grant from the Canadian Federation for the Humanities, using funds provided by the Social Sciences and Humanities Research Council of Canada.

J.M.G.

Contents

Abbreviations

Aen.	Virgil's *Aeneid*
FQ	Spenser's *The Faerie Queene*
Il.	Homer's *Iliad*
Met.	Ovid's *Metamorphoses*
Od.	Homer's *Odyssey*
PL	Milton's *Paradise Lost*
PR	Milton's *Paradise Regained*
Prel.	Wordsworth's *Prelude*
TC	Chaucer's *Troylus and Cressida*

TENNYSON'S IDYLLS

BB	*Balin and Balan*
CA	*The Coming of Arthur*
G	*Guinevere*
GE	*Geraint and Enid*
GL	*Gareth and Lynette*
HG	*The Holy Grail*
LE	*Lancelot and Elaine*
LT	*The Last Tournament*
MG	*The Marriage of Geraint*
MV	*Merlin and Vivien*
PA	*The Passing of Arthur*
PE	*Pelleas and Ettarre*

TO HILARY

Introduction

The aim of this book is a reappraisal of Tennyson's *Idylls of the King*. Poetry of this depth and complexity cannot be dismissed merely as 'a collection of fragments united by threads'.[1] Admittedly, to examine the *Idylls* in the scope and perspective they demand is a daunting task. The poet took decades to evolve the work, holding back each segment of the serial and cyclic design until it assumed its correct place and emphasis within the whole. At every stage the poet is in control of his material. Each part is narratively self-contained, but each gains enormously as it locks into the others. The interlocking process develops in various ways: cyclic strategies, repeated heroic and narrative formulae, and composite characterisation (shared characters, and characters who show one aspect of their personality in one idyll, a different in another). The inner logic of the poem's development is discussed in my opening chapter, and remains a theme throughout. I shall try to show that the serial poem has a coherent structure from beginning to end.

Of course, the long, mysterious periods of gestation between publishing segments of the cycle, exposed Tennyson to the all too ready ridicule of critics. However, uncertainty over the poem's composition at different stages does not prove that the completed poem is 'not an organic whole'.[2] No one attacks Balzac, Proust, Joyce, Pound or Anthony Powell for taking years to complete a comprehensive design, so why single out Tennyson? The only pertinent point is whether these serial works develop systematically. Tennyson was well aware of pressures and temptations: 'The age gives an author no time to mature his works'.[3] To write maturely of men and things one must be mature oneself. It is greatly to the poet's credit that he had the patience and responsibility to wait till the time was ripe. He well knew the long gestation of perfection.[4] Then, when everything had fallen into place, Tennyson was capable of incredible virtuosity, as in the realisation of *The Holy Grail* in ten days during August 1868. But behind this rapidity lie years of brooding over the whole theme.

Years were needed to develop Tennyson's Arthurian scheme because it is encyclopaedic. It draws on the best of Arthurian tradition. In addition, Tennyson selects elements from a great range of other heroic literature. A detailed understanding of Malory is the key

1

to understanding the *Idylls*. My aim is not simply to dismiss the common charge that Tennyson, in his changes and adjustments, is attempting 'to degrade noble material'.[5] Rather, it is to show that the poet makes consummate use of it. He creates an Arthurian world of his own, and a style to express that world.

Tennyson's recourse to Malory, the *Mabinogion*, and other forms of the Arthurian legend is traced in detail in my second chapter, and is afterwards referred to, where relevant. Subsequent chapters deal with the range of Tennyson's allusion, his descriptions of natural and man-made settings, and the serial development of motifs such as songs and dreams. A central chapter is devoted to linguistic innovation and word creation, and the last chapter to a study of characters. I attempt to show that Tennyson's serial poem has a descriptive, a stylistic and a dramatic unity. Above all, its psychological unity is profound. The 'compacted and vertebrate poem'[6] to which Tennyson aspired, is embodied in the finished work. *Idylls of the King*, so long relegated to a critical limbo, is a poem of consummate art. I have no hesitation in placing the *Idylls* with Chaucer's *Troilus and Criseyde*, Spenser's *The Faerie Queene*, Milton's *Paradise Lost*, Wordsworth's *The Prelude*, and Browning's *The Ring and the Book* as one of the six great long poems in our literature.

Serial Evolution

In recent years, and traditionally, there have been few arguments for and many against the artistic integrity and structural unity of Tennyson's *Idylls of the King*. It is regarded as a structurally variable serial poem that exploits a body of conflicting and often fragmentary legendary material. It sets, therefore, a difficult task to critical assessment. Further, the serial's dates of composition are widespread: 1856–9, 1868–72, incorporating an episode composed already during 1833–4, and the last idyll written in 1872–4, but not published until 1885. All this has been taken as evidence of sporadic inspiration and uneven design. Such evidence does little to inspire confidence. Reading the poem in its narrative order exposes seemingly incompatible styles and methods; the approach is at times symbolic, at times allegoric, and at times mixed. Everything suggests that what Tennyson has achieved, whatever his intention, is unsatisfactory. However, other nineteenth-century cyclic works previously unappreciated have since been hailed as consummate art, as, for example, Wagner's *Ring*. Here an awareness of subtle repetition and variation of themes and motifs within an overall cyclic design is very important for understanding its meaning. If *Idylls of the King* is regarded as a cycle of a similar kind, its meaning becomes much clearer. But the serial poem is best approached through examining the relative size and shape of its separate poems in the order in which Tennyson composed them. Such an examination suggests a great many strategies for appraising the work as a whole.

The most general indication of an ordering design is how Tennyson begins, how he develops the central theme, and how he terminates the cycle. Among all possible orders in which the serial poem could have been developed, Tennyson chose to leave himself free by first composing a final episode, *Morte d'Arthur*. Then he set about a full series in earnest, beginning and ending precisely in the centre, with *Merlin and Vivien* and *Balin and Balan*. Half-way through the evolution he composed *The Holy Grail*, in some ways the hardest idyll to write. This was immediately followed by the two terminal or outer framing poems, *The Coming of Arthur* and *The Passing of Arthur*, containing the *Morte d'Arthur* unchanged. This, in itself, argues for greater artistic order and control than have so far been accorded to the scheme. There is some evidence to show that the twelve books of Virgil's masterpiece, the *Aeneid*, were composed in a similar order.[1]

Organic unity and diversity in the *Idylls* is suggested by the fact that *The Holy Grail*, the sixth of twelve poems to be composed, is counterbalanced by *Balin and Balan* in the design. In the narrative order these poems are the eighth and fifth respectively. The poem *Enid*, later split into *The Marriage of Geraint* and *Geraint and Enid*, was created immediately after *Merlin and Vivien*, but preceded it in the narrative order. Similarly, the last poem to be composed, *Balin and Balan*, found its appropriate place between *Geraint and Enid* and *Merlin and Vivien*.

Much can be learned also from the length of each poem in the finished work. What Goethe called a *systole-diastole* movement, an alternating organic expansion and contraction in terms of themes and treatment, clearly emerges. The alternation in length (successive poems being approximately half or double their predecessors) is clearly evident in poems otherwise different in treatment and structure. *Morte d'Arthur* is 262 lines long, barely half the epic book length. Then, after a seventeen-year interval, the first set of *Idylls* (1859) contains four poems of respectively 822, 1818, 691, and 1418 lines.

At the resumption of the serial poem in 1868–70 the same shaping development is evident. This time there are poems of 916, 437, 440 (169 of which were added to complete *Morte d'Arthur*) and 578 lines. The two middle poems of this phase are more compressed than usual (437, 440 lines) because they are designed to be terminal frames in the finished narrative. They also have deliberate stylistic and thematic similarities. Both length and style help to set a measure for the poem as a whole. The second full phase of the design, like the first, is worked out in four poems.

Three poems, composed between 1870 and 1874, complete the last phase of the design. In a significant departure from his normal practice Tennyson published the first of these, *The Last Tournament*, in a journal a year before issuing it with *Gareth and Lynette*. No critic then or since has commented on how different in style or structure were these two poems.[2] With the resolving perspectives of *Balin and Balan*, held back over a decade until publication in 1885, these three poems comprise an intricate internal frame for the entire cycle. The poems of this final phase of composition show a graded reduction in length (1394, 756, and 620 lines), revealing growing compression and subtlety in Tennyson's treatment of his theme.

The way in which four poems were expanded and another split into two during 1873–5 points again to an ordering and controlling

4

sensibility. The poem that was split into two was the 1859 *Enid* (see p. 4), receiving the final titles *The Marriage of Geraint* and *Geraint and Enid* in 1886. These two poems are twice the usual length of a book in a long poetic narrative (1818 lines). They are originally one story, woven into two strands that complement and contrast with each other.

After the climactic *The Holy Grail* Tennyson created the three shortest poems: *The Coming of Arthur*, *The Passing of Arthur*, and *Pelleas and Ettarre*. In a parallel development, after composing *Gareth and Lynette* and *The Last Tournament*, he wrote the brief and particularly compressed *Balin and Balan*. The whole of the work thus shows an inner proportion between its component parts, giving evidence that the cycle possesses an imaginative logic of its own.

A comparison between the order of composition and the place that each idyll finds in the finished work suggests a narrative drive or progression in the overall design.[3] The evidence for this will be found in the summary at the end of this chapter.

The preceding investigations help us to understand how different elements of the Arthurian legend are combined by Tennyson. Half the *Idylls* owe markedly less to traditional sources than the other half. They are, in the order of composition, *Merlin and Vivien* (2), *Guinevere* (5), *The Holy Grail* (7), *The Coming of Arthur* (8), *The Last Tournament* (10), and *Balin and Balan* (12). The other half shows, at least on first inspection, much more verbal or substantival borrowing. They are *Morte d'Arthur* as the centre of *The Passing of Arthur* (1), *The Marriage of Geraint* and *Geraint and Enid* (3 and 4), *Lancelot and Elaine* (6), *Pelleas and Ettarre* (9), and *Gareth and Lynette* (11). The movement from closer borrowing to freer invention, and back again, shows something important about the working of the poet's imagination.

I believe and hope to demonstrate later, that by 1856 Tennyson had worked out both a rough scheme and a method by which he could implement it. The scheme envisaged twelve poems, but this number, symbolising a perfect whole, had to be induced by design. Interweaving of themes, imagery and characters is the method. Every poem becomes interwoven with every other, constantly deepening and expanding their meaning as the work unfolds; and the method itself takes root and grows within the legend. The Arthurian legend itself regulates the order in which its episodes are worked into the scheme.

Clearly, as the scheme becomes older, it becomes increasingly difficult to ring the changes. As the more attractive and approachable tales are exhausted (*The Marriage of Geraint, Geraint and Enid,*

Lancelot and Elaine), or are used up because they are essential for the moral and dramatic basis of the cycle (*Merlin and Vivien, Guinevere*), Tennyson is left with material so graphic and challenging as the Grail, or so repetitious as the Tristram theme, or refractory, like Arthur's coming, or the profound and disturbingly tragic tale of Balin and his brother.

Nowhere is Tennyson's growing skill in interweaving characters and incidents more in evidence than in the poems that complete his design. But, illuminating as its development may be, it does not guarantee that the intended result will be actually achieved. The ultimate test for the success of the design is the finished work. I shall therefore conclude with a short summary of Tennyson's narrative.

The rise, decline and fall of Arthur's kingdom

The young Arthur does not enter his kingdom by hereditary right – his descent is wrapped in mist and legend – but wins it by extraordinary ability both as an individual fighter and as commander in the field. He establishes and consolidates his rule with the help of renowned knights, who gather round him, attracted by his military and personal excellence. The best of them Arthur forms into the select corps of the Knights of the Round Table. They are bound to the king and to the service of the realm by vowing to keep a code that Arthur lays down for their conduct. The code is inspired by his idealistic, but well-balanced and practical aspiration to meet the most crying needs of the time: first, to bring peace and secure order to a war-torn land, and second, to raise the standards of a people sunk into the savagery of a savage age. The vow of 'purity' enjoins strict monogamy on the knights: it is devised for the protection of women and for overcoming the double standard of morality common since ancient times, which demands purity from women and grants licence to men (Idyll 1).

Like many an actual historical movement aspiring to improve the human lot, Arthur's is at first borne onwards and upwards on a springtide of inspired heroism, in which a certain ascetic streak is not yet carried to the extreme of visionary fanaticism. The knights are lifted up beyond themselves, both on the battlefield and in combat with individual enemies of the realm: they do mightier deeds than is in them to do. So the young 'kitchen-knave' Gareth sallies forth to defeat three formidable knights in single combat, and finally to take on Death himself (Idyll 2). So young Geraint comes to Caerleon to enter the service of the king (Idyll 3). The springtide of Arthur's rule is fittingly presented through the deeds of untried youths rather than in those of long-proved knights.

But, as history shows, men are as a rule lifted beyond themselves only in short spurts; they cannot maintain the effort for good. Movements of practical idealism are exposed to two dangers. One is slackness, loss of faith and inspiration, leading to a sliding from unusually high standards into self-indulgence; the other is the perversion of the idealistic element into fanaticism and a chase after visionary perfection. In other words, when the original balance and stability of the movement is disturbed, it falls apart into two extreme elements: a disillusioned cynicism on one hand, and an unrealistic fanaticism on the other hand.

In the poetical-mythical Arthurian world, the crack appears in the break in the originally single story of Geraint. After his marriage to Enid, this attractive but unstable youth pursues an erratic course, going from one extreme to the other, until after false starts and tribulations, the warring elements in his nature find a new balance, and his story concludes in a fairy-tale happy ending (Idyll 4).

Geraint's story dramatically presents the dangers inherent in Arthur's enterprise. Alas, the crack in a movement is not so easily closed as in a single individual, especially when it is deliberately widened from within. Two women are largely instrumental in bringing about the decline and fall of Arthur's kingdom: Guinevere and Vivien. Ironically, what they attack is the vow of 'purity', specially devised for the protection of women. Guinevere's adultery with the chief knight, Lancelot, at first an ugly rumour and suspicion, is later spread abroad by Vivien, the emissary of the hostile King Mark, the slayer of Isolt's former lover, Tristram. First Guinevere by deed, then Vivien by cunning machinations, bring into disrepute the code of 'purity'. With it, the whole edifice begins to crumble.

The first tragic victim of disillusionment and intrigue is Balin, the shy, savage creature of the woods, together with his better self, his twin brother Balan (Idyll 5). Merlin, the star-gazer, reputedly possessing magic powers, who built Camelot 'to music', is Vivien's most important victim (Idyll 6). The undignified and indeed grotesque end of this wise man is an irreparable blow to Arthur's aspirations. So is Lancelot's ineradicable passion for the Queen. For a moment, there is a gleam of hope that Elaine's love might save Lancelot, but his heart is closed to all women but one (Idyll 7).

The promise of a renewal of waning inspiration seems to come to Camelot with the coming of the Grail. But the promise is illusory. It brings to the surface the other danger inherent in idealistic and religious movements: the chasing after a visionary perfection, the turning of a healthy religion into a fanatical religiosity. The knights scatter on their quest of the Grail, abandoning their service to the realm. Only a fraction of them return (Idyll 8). In reality, the Grail quest seals the doom of Arthur's enterprise, more tragically than disillusionment and backsliding into the weaknesses of human nature, for it arises from man's longing for unattainable perfection.

The approaching doom is dramatically presented in the fate of the simple young innocent, Pelleas, the sombre counterpart of the lighthearted Gareth. Unlike Gareth, who comes to Camelot in the springtide of its inspired youth, Pelleas comes in its declining autumn. His dewy-eyed idealism cannot cope with disillusionment; in his bitterness he turns into the cruel Red Knight (Idyll 9).

It is on a punitive expedition against the Red Knight that Arthur leads his young knights on the day when the last tournament to be held at Camelot takes place. The breakdown of his rule is at hand when his authority and control fail on the field; after Arthur kills the Red Knight, his young knights run amok, paying no heed to his commands. At the same time, the last tournament turns into an ignoble shambles. When Arthur comes back from his expedition, he finds his hall deserted, except by his weeping fool (Idyll 10).

With the remnant of his forces, Arthur now has to face a formidable attack mounted by Modred, rumoured to be his bastard son, though Arthur denies the charge. Modred allies himself with the old enemy, the heathen Saxon invaders. On his way to the battlefield, Arthur visits Guinevere in the nunnery to which she has fled, repenting the past and discovering Arthur's merits when it is too late (Idyll 11). On leaving her, Arthur goes straight to his last battle, in which he kills Modred, but only after being grievously wounded by him. At his behest, Bedivere throws Excalibur into the lake, then Arthur is carried away on a barge, tended by three black-clad queens. His legendary beginning leads to a no less mysterious end, as 'from the great deep to the great deep he goes'.

This simple outline, the backbone of a 'compacted and vertebrate poem', demonstrates that all the main characters, their doings and sayings, and what is done and said to them, contribute in some way to the unfolding of the plot or scheme: the rise, decline and fall of Arthur's kingdom. There may be other ways of demonstrating the wholeness of a work and the coherence of its contributory parts, but I don't know of a better way.

Admittedly, the simple outline is difficult to see at a glance. It is obscured by the very richness and variety of incidents, the turns and twists of the story and the number of protagonists who make their entries and exits. The difficulty is aggravated by time-lags and flashbacks: what happens at the beginning is often told only much later, and even then in a fragmentary way. There is one real 'time-lock' in the sequence of the *Idylls*: in *Balin and Balan*, the fifth Idyll, Vivien is already on her way to Camelot, while in the sixth Idyll, *Merlin and Vivien*, she is still at King Mark's court, getting ready to set out for Arthur's capital in order to destroy him.

In spite of these admittedly confusing details, the clear outline of the *Idylls* shows that Tennyson has achieved a whole and coherent work, and in so doing has created an Arthurian world of his own. He has used the existing body of Arthurian legend with great skill, as we shall see in a detailed investigation in the next chapter.

Arthurian Legend

Tennyson drew widely on Arthurian chronicles, legends, and romances, deliberately choosing 'from mythology and legend, which had been before but imperfectly treated, or of which the stories were slight, so that he might have scope for his imagination'.[1] An artist's way with legend is not that of a scholar. Tennyson read and leafed through Malory's prose chapters (a convenient pocket edition accompanying him on all his Arthurian journeys) storing in his memory words and phrases, images, gestures, episodes, characters, stories. In weaving together his Arthurian series, Tennyson gave it range, depth, perspective, and above all unity. Of course, the unity of a long serial work cannot grow solely from the plot. It must be sustained by, among other things, certain technical devices, which I call 'frames'. These are, for instance, the recurrence of the same characters in various situations; similarities in events; similar features of events that are in themselves different; even single images or phrases that recall an earlier image or phrase.

A single sentence in Malory provides Tennyson with a basic frame for his first poem, the *Morte d'Arthur*:

> And thus they fought all the long day, and never stinted till the noble knights were laid to the cold earth; and ever they fought still till it was near night, and by that time there was an hundred thousand laid dead upon the down.[2]

Malory's occasional use of 'so' to open earlier books, and his phrases 'all the long day' and the alliterative 'laid dead upon the down' provided Tennyson with the three main terms for his famous opening:[3]

> So all day long the noise of battle roll'd
> Among the mountains by the winter sea ...

Here Tennyson expands a single 'down' to many mountains and transposes 'all the long day' to 'all day long'. What Tennyson does not find in Malory is winter, though the noble knights being laid 'to the cold earth' may have helped to suggest it. We are at the inception of the seasonal frame, the year cycle which encloses decay and growth, woven in from the opening image of 'the winter sea'. Winter extends across the poem in architecturally designed sequence. It is amplified and reflected in the jewels of Excalibur's hilt (*Morte*

49–58). At the exact centre of the poem is the next winter image, the epic simile of the Aurora Borealis. This brings a release of tension as Excalibur turns over and over on being thrown by Bedivere (*Morte* 139–42). The poem is divided into two movements round this centrally located simile. Emphasis on winter is renewed when Bedivere bears Arthur to the shore where the barge waits (*Morte* 181–92). Round the central and most extended simile the poem is structured like an arch.

Simultaneous simplification and expansion is another aspect of Tennyson's 'interweaving' method. In Malory, Lucan and Bedivere 'led (Arthur) betwixt them both, to a little chapel not far from the seaside'.[4] Tennyson omits Lucan and amplifies the little chapel 'to a chapel nigh the field, / A broken chancel with a broken cross' (*Morte* 8–9). Tennyson could not have devised a stronger terminal symbol for his series than this broken chancel with its broken cross.[5]

Tennyson expands Arthur's few words into a speech. Malory has '"Ah, traitor untrue," said King Arthur . . . "And but if thou do now as I bid thee, if ever I may see thee, I shall slay thee with mine own hands".'[6] In Tennyson this becomes:

> To whom replied King Arthur, much in wrath:
> 'Ah, miserable and unkind, untrue,
> Unknightly, traitor-hearted . . .
> But, if thou spare to fling Excalibur,
> I will arise and slay thee with my hands.
> (*Morte* 118–20, 131–2)

First Tennyson expands Malory's 'said' into the heroic or Miltonic 'To whom replied . . . much in wrath'.[7] Then, by selecting a Malory term ('unknightly') along with imitating Milton's use of two or more words with the same negative prefix, and by expanding Malory's 'traitor' into a hyphenated compound of his own, Tennyson extends 'Ah, traitor untrue' into 'Ah, miserable and unkind, untrue, / Unknightly, traitor-hearted'.[8] Lastly, Malory's 'I shall slay thee' is amplified by 'I will arise and . . .', a resolution with a Biblical resonance.[9]

Even in a simple line such as Arthur's admission 'yet I fear / My wound hath taken cold, and I shall die' (*Morte* 165–6) two elements in Malory are effectively interwoven; the king's words 'for thy long tarrying putteth me in great jeopardy of my life, for I have taken cold' and the queen's words 'Ah, dear brother, why have ye tarried so long from me? alas this wound on your head hath caught overmuch cold'.[10]

Among the mourning ladies who receive Arthur in the funeral barge Malory names one queen. (With a slight inconsistency, three queens appear in the following chapter.) Thus Malory:

when they were at the water's side, even fast by the bank, hoved a little barge, with many fair ladies in it, and among them all was a Queen, and all they had black hoods, and they wept and shrieked when they saw King Arthur.

This passage is transformed by Tennyson:

> Then saw they how there hove a dusky barge,
> Dark as a funeral scarf from stem to stern,
> Beneath them; and descending they were ware
> That all the decks were dense with stately forms
> Black-stoled, black-hooded, like a dream – by these
> Three Queens with crowns of gold – and from them rose
> A cry that shiver'd to the tingling stars,
> And, as it were one voice, an agony
> Of lamentation, like a wind, that shrills
> All night in a waste land, where no one comes,
> Or hath come, since the making of the world.
>   (*Morte* 193–203)

The lament of Tennyson's queens recalls the *Aeneid*: 'The echoing halls resounded through and through with a keening of women, whose wails and shrieks beat at the golden stars'.[11] Tennyson's image of death beyond any mourning and utter desolation 'like a wind . . . All night in a waste land, where no one comes' stems from the potent name of the Queen that Malory has deliberately placed third, the 'Queen of the Waste Lands'.[12]

In Malory Arthur says to Bedivere:

> Comfort thyself . . . and do as well as thou mayest, for in me is no trust for to trust in, for I will into the vale of Avilion, for to heal me of my grievous wound. And if thou never hear more of me, pray for my soul.[13]

Tennyson greatly expands this into the well-known lines that include 'Comfort thyself: what comfort is in me' and that end with a Homeric heaven 'where I will heal me of my grievous wound' (*Morte* 243–64).[14] Malory provides a framework for the rest of the passage.

These examples show how subtly Tennyson interwove Malory with elements from Homer, Virgil, and Milton to create and sustain an effect wholly his own.

In *Merlin and Vivien* also Tennyson makes subtle and varied recourse to Malory's tale. He echoes Malory's account of Merlin's seduction and bases the behaviour of certain characters on what he finds in his source.

Malory tells us that Nimue (the origin of Tennyson's Vivien):

was ever passing weary of him [Merlin], and fain would have been delivered of him. So by her subtle working she made Merlin to go under that stone to let her wit of the marvels there, but she wrought so there for him that he never came out for all the craft he could do.[15]

The act of having 'wrought' something on someone echoes throughout the idyll. In the first place Vivien 'would fain have wrought upon (Arthur's) cloudy mood' (*MV* 154).[16] So potent was this charm that 'if any wrought on anyone' with the magic formula, 'the man so wrought on ever seem'd to lie' within the four walls of a hollow tower, 'Nor could he see but him who wrought the charm' (*MV* 204, 206, 210). Those who have 'wrought' a charm are instanced half way through the poem (*MV* 548, 582, 641). In lines added eighteen years later this pattern, now enriched with Biblical resonance, recurs: Guinevere is led to ask of Vivien, 'What evil have ye wrought? Rise!' only to have the harlot reply, 'None wrought, but suffer'd much, an orphan maid!' (*MV* 65, 67). But the tale does not bear out the truth of this reply. At the end, when Vivien 'wrought upon his mood and hugg'd him close' (*MV* 946) Merlin could do nothing but submit to the spell.

The spellbinding theme is indeed present from the very beginning both in the original romance and in the idyll. But an interesting departure is made by Tennyson when he splits Vivien into two strongly contrasting characters. One is now called the Lady of the Lake while the other retains the name of Vivien.[17] Bedivere, envisaging himself as Excalibur's curator, relates how the sword was made by the lonely maiden of the Lake: 'Nine years she wrought it, sitting in the deeps / Upon the hidden bases of the hills' (*Morte* 105–6).[18]

On the other hand Vivien's attempt to seduce Arthur (*MV* 150–62) is not Tennyson's addition to the legend, but is drawn from an episode in Malory when a similar enchantress, Annowre, tries hard to seduce the king.[19]

Tennyson's recreation of Malory may also be seen in Vivien's comment on the four knights, whose experience with women, she suggests, shows the depth of corruption at Camelot. These knights are Valence, Sagramore, Percivale, and Lancelot (*MV* 702–75). The knight Valence is not mentioned by Malory, but in Arthurian legend.[20] The episode, on the other hand, is of Tennyson's creation. The next knight, Sagramore, does come from Malory, but the experience that Vivien ascribes to him is again Tennyson's invention. It gives substance to Camelot as a court where the profoundest human relationship, enduring love between man and woman, arises as it were from Arthur's love. The whole invented episode may have been evoked by Sagramore's cognomen in Malory, *le desirous*. If so, then Vivien's reference to him as 'that ardent man' (*MV* 720) is an interweaving of modern and ancient, 'desirous' originally having no sexual connotation.[21] Paul Turner suggests that this episode, though Tennyson's invention, is consonant with his source:

> Malory is full of humour, often fairly crude, as when Lancelot . . . innocently goes to sleep in what turns out to be a young lady's bed, and awakes to feel her lover's 'rough beard kissing him'. This type of humour is allowed into the *Idylls* when Sir Sagramore, like Pickwick, goes to bed in the wrong room by mistake, and sleeps all night 'A stainless man beside a stainless maid'; but the joke is functional in a condemnation of Vivien's habit of always thinking the worst of other people.[22]

What happens to Percivale 'fluster'd with new wine' in the church-yard, assailed by 'one of Satan's shepherdesses' (*MV* 754, 756) is also modelled on an experience of Malory's Percivale. While on Grail quest, after drinking 'the strongest wine that ever he drank . . . there-with he was a little chafed more than he ought to be', he tried to make love to what seemed a gentlewoman. Fortunately before any harm was done he caught sight of a cross-shaped sword hilt where-upon the damsel vanished.[23] Merlin has no difficulty in refuting Vivien's charge concerning Percivale, but when she raises the question of Lancelot's 'commerce' with Guinevere (*MV* 768) he is forced to admit that their love has its origin with the kingdom:

> Sir Lancelot went ambassador, at first,
> To fetch her, and she watch'd him from her walls.
> A rumour runs, she took him for the King,
> So fixt her fancy on him: let them be.
>   (*MV* 772–5)

Merlin may be considered to have special authority here because in Malory it was he who escorted Guinevere to Arthur.[24]

From the outset Tennyson's 'interweaving' method involves other sources as well as Malory. The hart that Arthur's knights chase at the time of the Round Table's foundation stems from Malory, but where it vanishes comes from the *Mabinogion*:

> vanish'd by the fairy well
> That laughs at iron – as our warriors did –
> Where children cast their pins and nails, and cry,
> 'Laugh, little well!' but touch it with a sword,
> It buzzes fiercely round the point; and there
> We lost him: (*MV* 426–31)

Here Tennyson echoes a note in *Mabinogion*:

The fountain of Baranton is supplied by a mineral spring, and it bubbles up on a piece of iron or copper being thrown into it.

'Les enfans s'amusent à y jeter des épingles, et disent par commun proverbe: "Ris donc, fontaine de Berendon, et je te donnerai une épingle".'[25]

In contrast to *Merlin and Vivien*, where an evil woman debases a wise man, in *The Marriage of Geraint* and *Geraint and Enid* a modest and constant woman is portrayed in relation to a proud and unstable man. Two points of interest about these poems may be noted. First, they are entirely based on a Welsh source, the *Mabinogion*. Second, they belong among the 1859 *Idylls* which Tennyson revealingly subtitled: the True and the False. These *Idylls*, as the subtitle indicates, deal pre-eminently with the theme of appearance and reality.

One of the first, most eye-catching features of appearance is apparel. Descriptions of dress are prominent in the Welsh source, the *Mabinogion*, but it is developed and modified by Tennyson. Appearance is not always a false or deceptive appearance. It can also reveal reality. Accordingly, both *Mabinogion* and Tennyson often use external appearance to dramatise the real character of the *dramatis personae*. So, for instance, when Geraint appears on horseback before Guinevere:

> of princely mien, and a golden-hilted sword was at his side . . . and around him was a scarf of blue-purple, at each corner of which was a golden apple. And his horse stepped stately, and swift, and proud.[26]

His whole attire, including his horse, gives an immediate picture of Geraint's true nature. Similarly, in Tennyson, Geraint

> wearing neither hunting-dress
> Nor weapon, save a golden-hilted brand,
> Came quickly flashing thro' the shallow ford
> Behind them . . . (*MG* 165–68)

As this passage shows, Tennyson further amplifies and dramatises the description in the original.

Particular pieces of dress may also provide a motif that links various episodes together. In *Mabinogion* a dwarf who rides with a haughty knight strikes both at Guinevere's maidservant and at Geraint: 'until the blood flowed forth . . . so that the blood coloured the scarf that Geraint wore'.[27] Tennyson curtails the first detail to: 'struck at her with his whip' in order to heighten the second: 'struck at him with his whip, and cut his cheek. / The Prince's blood spirted upon the scarf, / Dyeing it' (*MG* 201, 207–9). By the same item of apparel Tennyson gives a humorous touch to Geraint's response to Enid:

'the Prince, as Enid past him, fain / To follow, strode a stride, but Yniol caught / His purple scarf, and held' (*MG*375–7).

The slightly exaggerated emphasis on dress continues with Earl Yniol. In the original he is first viewed on a bridge, 'a hoary-headed man, upon whom were tattered garments'.[28] Tennyson expands this into 'There musing sat the hoary-headed Earl, / (His dress a suit of fray'd magnificence, / Once fit for feasts of ceremony)' (*MG*295–7). In Yniol's ruined palace Geraint

> beheld an old decrepit woman, sitting on a cushion, with old tattered garments of satin upon her; and it seemed to him that he had never seen a woman fairer than she must have been, when in the fulness of youth. And beside her there was a maiden, upon whom were a vest and a veil, that were old, and beginning to be worn out. And truly, he never saw a maiden more full of comeliness, and grace, and beauty than she.[29]

Tennyson omits Geraint's admiration for Yniol's wife and transforms the clothing:

> He found an ancient dame in dim brocade;
> And near her, like a blossom vermeil-white,
> That lightly breaks a faded flower-sheath,
> Moved the fair Enid, all in faded silk,
> Her daughter ... (*MG*363–7)

Here the outward appearance, presented by dress, is misleading and distorting. Geraint, however, had already fallen in love with Enid's singing even before catching sight of her. The unspoken suggestion of the passage is that Geraint's love penetrates through the mean appearance to Enid's true beauty. Her poor attire is reflected in the rusty armour Geraint wears in his fight with Edyrn:

> Yniol's rusted arms
> Were on his princely person, but thro' these
> Princelike his bearing shone.
> (*MG*543–5)

Here again reality breaks through the distorting appearance. Since this detail is Tennyson's own invention, without parallel in *Mabinogion*, it once again shows his constant concern with appearance and reality.

In the Welsh tale, after defeating Edyrn, Geraint commands:

> 'Let not the damsel array herself ... except in her vest and veil, until she come to the court of Arthur, to be clad by Gwenhywvar as she may choose.' So the maiden did not array herself.[30]

The parallel passage in Tennyson, is slightly amplified:

> ... live to wed with her whom first you love:
> But ere you wed with any, bring your bride,

And I, were she the daughter of a king,
Yea, tho' she were a beggar from the hedge,
Will clothe her for her bridals like the sun.
　(*MG*227–31)

Tennyson, however, modifies the original by finding another source for Enid's attire: 'Enid fell in longing for a dress / All branch'd and flower'd with gold' (*MG*630–1).[31] Such a dress had in fact been made by Enid's mother and secretly preserved from the sack of their palace. Enid's wish is fulfilled and she can now travel to court suitably clothed. To complete the episode in fairy-tale fashion, Guinevere also carries out her promise and as matron of honour 'clothed her for her bridals like the sun' (*MG*836).

But Enid ever kept the faded silk,
Remembering how first he came upon her,
Drest in that dress, and how he loved her in it,
And all her foolish fears about the dress . . .
　(*MG*841–4)

This passage again recalls the suggestion that love penetrates through false appearance to reality. In Enid's case the exaggerated importance her fears ascribed to dress dissolves in the light of Geraint's love for her.

Later in the tale *Mabinogion* relates that Geraint commands Enid to clothe herself 'in the worst riding dress that thou hast in thy possession'.[32] In the parallel passage of the *Idylls*, on the other hand, Tennyson specifically names the 'faded silk', bending back the end to the beginning.

To our modern taste, Tennyson's emphasis on dress is apt to become wearisome. Our immediate feeling is to sympathise with the Victorian critic who declared: 'And here we are treated to an amount of millinery against which not all our reverence for Tennyson's genius shall stay us from protesting.'[33] At the same time, we must keep in view Tennyson's own intention: apparel plays an essential part in the drama of appearances. It 'displays' the actors in the drama, it helps to motivate them, and to make their Arthurian character more authentic.

In *The Marriage of Geraint* the most important addition Tennyson makes to his Welsh source relates to the incident of the chase. In the original, Queen Guinevere asks Arthur for permission to view the hunt, which he grants. But on the day

Arthur wondered that Gwenhwyvar did not awake, and did not move in her bed; and the attendants wished to awaken her. 'Disturb her not,' said Arthur, 'for she had rather sleep than go to see the hunting.'[34]

Mabinogion tells us the bare fact that Guinevere overslept. Though the bare fact of what a person does is not a 'false appearance', it may effectively hide the truth, namely the real motive that gave rise to the action. This is what Tennyson reveals in his treatment of the incident:

> But Guinevere lay late into the morn,
> Lost in sweet dreams, and dreaming of her love
> For Lancelot, and forgetful of the hunt
> (*MG*157–9)

At a stroke, Tennyson has integrated the *Mabinogion* episode with the largely Malory-based cycle. At the same time, in revealing the queen's hidden motive, this episode shows one of Tennyson's ways of penetrating to reality through the appearance.

Tennyson's preoccupation with this theme is strikingly displayed at the point where he breaks the originally single tale he found in *Mabinogion* into two. Critics have long remarked on this seemingly arbitrary procedure, some of them ascribing it to the extraneous reason that the poem is inordinately long.[35] I have argued, on the contrary, that Tennyson had already conceived the scheme of his *Idylls* before he came to write the twin poems (see ch. 1, p. 5 ff.).

The beginning of the second poem, *Geraint and Enid*, is unique in the whole cycle. Here Tennyson interrupts the narrative with an invocation:

> O purblind race of miserable men,
> How many among us at this very hour
> Do forge a life-long trouble for ourselves,
> By taking true for false, or false for true.

The True and the False, (the subtitle of the so-called 1859 *Idylls*) has so far been considered in its wider meaning, namely the contrast between appearance and reality. We shall now be concerned with its narrower meaning, which Tennyson has primarily in mind: the true and the false embodied in persons and in their relations to each other. This theme is well illustrated by the second of the twin poems, *Geraint and Enid*. Geraint's unstable nature, vacillating between two extremes, is largely responsible for his cruelly unjust treatment of Enid, and throws her true, steadfast and faithful character all the more sharply into relief. Most important, and in many respects most revealing, is their meeting with the Earls of Limours and Doorm.

These two subsidiary characters appear in *Mabinogion* merely as villainous bandits. Tennyson recreates them into far more striking figures, over life size in one way, and under life size in another way, both being incomplete, exaggeratedly one-sided, moral cripples. Tennyson presents an affected Limours who is 'femininely fair and dissolutely pale' and a brutal, overtly masculine Doorm, called 'the Bull' by his vassals (*GE*275, 439).[36]

In these two enlarged, yet crippled figures, Geraint confronts the extremes of his own nature. In fighting and overcoming them, he symbolically overcomes the division in himself. Tennyson thus re-creates the unremarkable *Mabinogion* characters not only by investing them with a more and a less than ordinary dimension, but also with a symbolic meaning that is entirely absent from the original.

His treatment of the marvellous and the supernatural, which pervades the Welsh tale, is revealing. The world of the fairy-tale stands on its own, and has its own truth and falsehood, which fall outside our commonly understood appearance and reality. Tennyson omits many marvellous elements (giants, men with supernatural powers), yet preserves something of the fairy-tale atmosphere. So, after many false starts, follies and mistakes, trials and sufferings, Geraint is cleansed of the dross and regains his early nobility. He lives with Enid 'happily ever after' in a long and fruitful companionship. They found a dynasty of, as Tennyson charmingly says, 'Enids and Geraints / Of times to be' (*GE*964–5). Even the happy ending is heightened by comparison with the subsequent eight idylls, each of which has a tragic outcome. Even Geraint's long life does not end on an unhappy note. It ends worthily, in a real historical incident in which Geraint[37]

> ... fell
> Against the heathen of the Northern Sea
> In battle, fighting for the blameless King.

Immediately after *Geraint and Enid* Tennyson composed the core of the next idyll, Arthur's meeting with Guinevere before the last battle.[38] *Guinevere* differs from Malory's romance, where the queen enters a nunnery only after Arthur's death. Tennyson follows Geoffrey of Monmouth in having Guinevere enter a nunnery before the last battle.[39] It is vital for his design to make Arthur meet the queen on his way to the battle in the seclusion of a religious order. Round the meeting Tennyson interweaves elements from Malory, such as Modred's discovery of Lancelot and Guinevere together, and the description of the queen as nun and abbess.

Malory gives a graphic account of the discovery. Agravaine and Modred with twelve other Round Table knights came and

> said with crying voice: Traitor knight, Sir Launcelot du Lake, now art thou taken. And thus they cried with loud voice, that all

the court might hear it; and they all fourteen were armed at all points as they should fight in a battle.

When Lancelot does issue forth, he first slays Agravaine then twelve others. Modred is wounded, and then 'he fled with all his might'.[40] Tennyson echoes the challenge but changes everything else. As the repeated word 'creatures' suggests, the only Round Table member present is their leader, Modred:[41]

> and Modred brought
> His creatures to the basement of the tower
> For testimony; and crying with full voice
> 'Traitor, come out, ye are trapt at last,' aroused
> Lancelot, who rushing outward lionlike
> Leapt on him, and hurl'd him headlong, and he fell
> Stunn'd, and his creatures took and bare him off,
> And all was still ... (G102-9)

In dramatising the scene, Tennyson has changed the place of discovery from the queen's chamber to a tower.[42]

Tennyson also makes other alterations. In Malory, after Arthur's death, Lancelot visits Guinevere in the nunnery at Almesbury and vows penance. Before leaving, however, he asks a farewell kiss:

> Wherefore, madam, I pray you kiss me and never no more.
> Nay, said the queen, that shall I never do, but abstain you from such works: and they departed.[43]

Their farewell in Tennyson, before the last battle, is more tender:

> And then they rode to the divided way,
> There kiss'd, and parted weeping.
>   (G123-4)

This is not mere sentimentality. The artistry of the cycle prescribes that their relationship should close as it opened, with a kiss.

Into his closing frame Tennyson weaves Malory's description of Guinevere in the nunnery:

> and there she let make herself a nun, and ware white clothes and black, and great penance she took, as ever did sinful lady in this land, and never creature could make her merry; but lived in fasting, prayers, and alms-deeds, that all manner of people marvelled how virtuously she was changed ... and there she was abbess and ruler as reason would.[44]

This becomes Guinevere's request to the nuns to join their order:

> So let me, if you do not shudder at me,
> Nor shun to call me sister, dwell with you;
> Wear black and white, and be a nun like you,
> Fast with your fasts, not feasting with your feasts

and so

> ... for the power of ministration in her,
> And likewise for the high rank she had borne,
> Was chosen Abbess, there, an Abbess, lived
> For three brief years, and there, an Abbess, past
> To where beyond these voices there is peace. (*G*669–92)

Many elements from Malory's tale of Elaine are richly interwoven in *Lancelot and Elaine* as part of the design and style at the centre of the year cycle in high summer. In Malory Arthur is present at Astolat when Lancelot walks in its garden, and so the king knows from the start his greatest knight is practising a stratagem.[45] In Malory's narrative Astolat is adjacent to Camelot, whereas in Tennyson they become worlds apart so that they complement one another in the design as a whole.

Tennyson casts a symbolic spell over his narrative. In Malory when Lancelot first comes to Astolat 'and there it happed him in the eventide he came to an old baron's place that hight Sir Bernard of Astolat'.[46] From the moment Tennyson's Lancelot sees Astolat it seems fated:

> Till as he traced a faintly-shadow'd track
> That all in loops and links among the dales
> Ran to the Castle of Astolat, he saw
> Fired from the west, far on a hill, the towers.
> Thither he made, and blew the gateway horn.
> (*LE*164–8)

From the outset Elaine is as fated as her prototype, the Lady of Shalott.[47] Even the hornblowing adds to the atmosphere of fate that surrounds the castle.

When it helps to authenticate his own account, Tennyson echoes Malory. In Malory Guinevere tells Lancelot

> Sir Launcelot, ye are greatly to blame thus to hold you behind my lord; what trow ye what will your enemies and mine say and deem? nought else but, See how Sir Launcelot holdeth him ever behind the king, and so doth the queen, for that they would have their pleasure together.[48]

Tennyson renders this:

> To blame, my lord Sir Lancelot, much to blame!
> Why go ye not to these fair jousts? the knights
> Are half of them our enemies, and the crowd
> Will murmur, 'Lo the shameless ones, who take
> Their pastime now the trustful King is gone!'
> (*LE*97–101)

Tennyson's incidental lead in to the above passage: 'No sooner gone than suddenly she began' shows marvellous sound control to make a smooth transition to the Malory, and the line that follows our passage achieves its power through alliterating vowel and consonant: 'Then Lancelot vext at having lied in vain' (*LE*96, 102).

Whereas Malory simply relates why Sir Torre's shield was blank: 'and the eldest hight Sir Tirre, and he was hurt the same day he was made knight, that he may not ride, and his shield ye may have', Tennyson weaves it into a conversation between Lancelot, the Lord of Astolat, Torre and Lavaine, thus bringing all the characters together (*LE*194–221).[49]

A composite perspective is an essential means of integrating the serial poem, and Tennyson is a master of it. Arthur, through his nature and constancy, is the pivotal character, so that the events that take place in his presence are chiefly seen through his eyes. Other characters are often reflected through each other's eyes. So, for instance, we first see Lancelot in this poem as he appears to Elaine. His initial effect on her is devastating. To achieve this effect, Tennyson weaves together two separate images of Lancelot in Malory: the cheek wound by which a hermit identifies Lancelot mid way through the prose romance, and an image from Ector's lament over the dead Lancelot at the close: 'And thou was the meekest man and the gentlest that ever ate in hall among ladies'.[50] Malory's framing image becomes the smaller frame for Tennyson's

> Marr'd as he was, he seem'd the goodliest man
> That ever among ladies ate in hall,
> And noblest, when she lifted up her eyes.
> However marr'd, of more than twice her years,
> Seam'd with an ancient swordcut on the cheek,
> And bruised and bronzed, she lifted up her eyes
> And loved him, with that love which was her doom
>   (*LE*253–9)

Note the steps in Tennyson's amplification. 'That ever among ladies ate in hall' is given as part of Elaine's impression, hence we are identified with her and see him through her eyes. 'When she lifted up her eyes' is use of a Biblical expression to convey expectation.[51] 'Of more than twice her years' makes for contrast and complement. Malory's 'wound on his cheek' is imaginatively felt by Elaine in its texture and shape: 'Seam'd with an ancient swordcut on the cheek'. Thus Lancelot's scar stands out from the texture of the design.

Various elements in Malory enter into the scene when Elaine comes to court:

> So as fair Elaine came to Winchester she sought there all about, and by fortune Sir Lavaine (her brother) was ridden to play him, to enchafe his horse. And anon as Elaine saw him she knew him.[52]

Into this Tennyson inserts Malory's stylised landscape, 'till they came to a fair meadow full of fair flowers and grass' [53] so that Elaine

> before the city-gates
> Came on her brother with a happy face
> Making a roan horse caper and curvet
> For pleasure all about a field of flowers
> (*LE*785-8)

Several motifs in Malory are interwoven again when Tennyson's Elaine admits to Lancelot: 'Not to be with you, not to see your face – / Alas for me then, my good days are done' (*LE*941-2). Malory has two very different Elaines, one a dame and the other a maid, and both are involved with Lancelot. It is Dame Elaine who says 'O father, now have I need of your help, and but if that ye help me farewell my good days for ever'.[54]

At the climax of Malory's tale when the oarsman who steers Elaine's funeral barge arrives at Camelot, 'no word would he speak'.[55] Tennyson amplifies this detail so the man is dumb because caught and 'reft' of his tongue by the heathen (*LE*169-71, 269-79). This graphic scene is much modified by Tennyson. In Malory, Gawain is present when Elaine's barge reaches Camelot. Tennyson substitutes an angry Guinevere who throws away the diamonds he had won for her, and a Lancelot sick at heart who sees the barge pass (*LE*1225-35). Then Malory's Arthur sends Kay, Brandiles and Agravain to investigate the mysterious arrival of the barge, which Tennyson makes into the occasion for weaving in the two chief Grail knights, Galahad and Percivale. They are appointed as pall-bearers (*LE*1256-7). Their appointment implies that Arthur is not so blind to the prevailing morality in Camelot as has traditionally been maintained. These two Grail knights, Galahad and Percivale, foreshadow *The Holy Grail* written nine years later, 1868, supporting my suggestion that Tennyson was already working to a scheme of the whole cycle.

In Malory, Guinevere spies the letter in the dead Elaine's hand. Because of her misunderstanding with Lancelot, Tennyson's queen is so overwrought that she sees nothing. The stable, all-seeing Arthur does.[56] Further, Malory tells of 'jousts made for a diamond' immediately after the death of Elaine.[57] Tennyson weaves this detail into his poem and expands it to nine diamonds won in nine yearly jousts, thus giving temporal depth to his series.

Other aspects of Tennyson's handling of Malory's Elaine tale will be considered later. When at the poem's close

> So groan'd Sir Lancelot in remorseful pain,
> Not knowing he should die a holy man
> (*LE*1417-18)

this echoes the words of a hermit of Lancelot's during his Grail quest: 'But God knoweth his thought and his unstableness, and yet shall he die right an holy man'.[58]

Tennyson uses his source in *The Holy Grail* with equal skill. By selecting an experience of Malory's Percivale, and by basing the whole outlook of his knight upon this experience, Tennyson transforms him into a Victorian doubter – an example of his interweaving the old with the new.

In Malory, knights quest in pairs or threes. Their experiences are all given the same weight. Tennyson projects the Grail account through the eyes and personality of Percivale. Making the one character narrate the equivalent of a whole epic book is modelled on Milton's Raphael. The angel speaks for the bulk of the seventh book of *Paradise Lost* (line 110 to the end) and his speech is terminated in the first two framing lines of the eighth book. Tennyson takes this method a stage further by expanding it into a whole book and by framing it even more severely in a single line, the very last (*HG*916).

The nucleus of Tennyson's sceptical portrayal of Percivale derives from a brief moment of doubt expressed in his talk with a hermit:

> Sir, said the old man, of whence ye be? Sir, said Sir Percivale, I am of King Arthur's court, and a knight of the Table Round, the which am in the quest of the Sangreal; and here I am in great duresse, and never like to escape out of this wilderness.[59]

Immediately, however, the hermit reassures Percivale, who is subsequently granted the Grail vision and ends his life in a monastery. Tennyson, however, seeking to express basic human types in his knights, singles out Percivale's hesitancy in his otherwise full and successful Grail quest.

Malory writes of the Grail's arrival in Camelot:

> Then anon they heard cracking and crying of thunder, that them thought the place should all to drive. In the midst of this blast entered a sunbeam more clearer by seven times than ever they saw day, and all they were alighted of the grace of the Holy Ghost. Then began every knight to behold other, and either saw other, by their seeming, fairer than ever they saw afore.
>
> Not for then there was no knight might speak one word a great while, and so they looked every man on other as they had been dumb. Then there entered into the hall the Holy Greal covered with white samite, but there was none might see it, nor who bare it. And there was all the hall fulfilled with good odours, and every knight had such meats and drinks as he best loved in

24

this world. And when the Holy Greal had been borne through the hall, then the Holy Vessel departed suddenly, that they wist not where it became: then had they all breath to speak. [60]

Through Percivale's eye-witness Tennyson reproduces this with masterly brevity:

And all at once, as there we sat, we heard
A cracking and a riving of the roofs,
And rending, and a blast, and overhead
Thunder, and in the thunder was a cry.
And in the blast there smote along the hall
A beam of light seven times more clear than day:
And down the long beam stole the Holy Grail
All over cover'd with a luminous cloud,
And none might see who bare it, and it past.
But every knight beheld his fellow's face
As in a glory, and all the knights arose,
And staring each at other like dumb men
Stood, till I found a voice and sware a vow.

(*HG*182–94)

As well as reflecting essential images and phrases, Tennyson attains great compression through a feature of Malory's style, the paratactic use of 'and'. [61] 'And' initially in lines one, three, five, seven, nine and twelve, and internally in lines two, three, four, eleven and thirteen (note how the two sets frame and amplify one another) accomplishes every possible linking function. [62] Tennyson's imaginative use of conjunctions is one of the secrets of his style.

Monosyllables help in this process of amplification. Lines one and thirteen are entirely made up of monosyllabic words and formally frame the entire witness. It is as if the experience compelled Percivale to express himself with the utmost simplicity. Lines six and nine are also made up of monosyllables (given that the word 'seven' in line six is pronounced as a monosyllable) and they effect a kind of slowing up which the long vowels of line seven accentuate: 'And down the long beam stole the Holy Grail'. In this way the Grail seems to suspend time and place for a moment.

As we have seen already, the diffidence respecting his own powers that Tennyson makes central to the character of Percivale is drawn from a single moment of doubt in Malory. [63] *The Holy Grail* has always been misinterpreted. Percivale may appear incomplete and flawed and yet he, like all named questers except Gawain, has his moment of supreme truth:

I saw the spiritual city and all her spires
And gateways in a glory like one pearl –

No larger, tho' the goal of all the saints –
Strike from the sea; and from the star there shot
A rose-red sparkle to the city, and there
Dwelt, and I knew it was the Holy Grail,
Which never eyes on earth again shall see.
    (*HG*526–32)

To have had sight of the heavenly city during the quest is surely not to be accorded a failure.[64]

Certain fantasies Percivale experiences before being granted the Grail vision, are drawn from typical quest experiences in Malory. His dreaming of a brook that in his thirst he wished to drink, only to find it gives way to sand and thorns (*HG*379–90) is from Ector's dream about Lancelot.[65] His dream of a golden knight (*HG*409–20) stems from his dreaming that he had to fight 'with the strongest champion of the world'.[66]

Tennyson also borrows from Malory for Galahad's quest:

And then the bishop made semblant as though he would have gone to the sacring of the mass. And then he took an ubblye which was made in likeness of bread. And at the lifting up there came a figure in likeness of a child, and the visage was as red and as bright as any fire, and smote himself into the bread.[67]

This becomes Galahad's personal testimony:

And at the sacring of the mass I saw
The holy elements alone; but he,
'Saw ye no more? I, Galahad, saw the Grail,
The Holy Grail, descend upon the shrine:
I saw the fiery face as of a child
That smote itself into the bread, and went
    (*HG*462–7)

Tennyson's Bors stems also from Malory's presentation of this knight. 'He well had been content / Not to have seen, so Lancelot might have seen' (*HG*650–1) derives from an admission Malory's Bors makes to a hermit:

Sir, said Bors, that were me loth, for wit ye well there is nothing in the world but I had lever do it than to see my lord, Sir Launcelot du Lake, to die in my default.[68]

A single, vivid gesture in Malory: 'Then Sir Bors smiled and did off his helm' is Tennyson's source[69] for a detailed description of Bors – too detailed, perhaps, compared with the simplicity and strength of the source:

A square-set man and honest; and his eyes
An out-door sign of all the warmth within,

Smiled with his lips – a smile beneath a cloud,
But heaven had meant it for a sunny one
  (*HG*700–03)

Tennyson's Gawain also closely follows Malory. This ambiguous and frivolous knight tells Arthur that the quest was
not for such as I.

Therefore I communed with a saintly man,
Who made me sure the Quest was not for me;
For I was much awearied of the Quest:
But found a silk pavilion in a field,
And merry maidens in it; and then this gale
Tore my pavilion from the tenting-pin,
And blew my merry maidens all about
With all discomfort; yea, and but for this,
My twelvemonth and a day were pleasant to me.
  (*HG*738–47)

Malory's Gawain, having 'lived mischievously many winters', went on quest but 'found none adventure that pleased him'.[70] The adventure with maidens in a pavilion, not in Malory, was perhaps suggested by a like incident in a famous collection concerning the knight.[71]

Lancelot's supposed failure also accords with Malory. Early on in Malory, Lancelot comes to a chapel, but can find no entrance to it; and then he sees a sick knight healed by the Grail, but he cannot himself approach the holy vessel.[72] A hermit enlightens him that on account of his sin, no matter how hard he strives, the Grail will not reveal itself to him.[73] Finally, the people of Carbonek tell him

that never shall ye see more of the Sancgreall than ye have seen.
Now I thank God, said Sir Launcelot, of His great mercy of that
I have seen, for it sufficeth me.[74]

This passage is reflected in Tennyson's description of Lancelot's sight of the Grail:

O, yet methought I saw the Holy Grail,
All pall'd in crimson samite, and around
Great angels, awful shapes, and wings and eyes.
And but for all my madness and my sin,
And then my swooning, I had sworn I saw
That which I saw; but what I saw was veil'd
And cover'd; and this Quest was not for me.
  (*HG*843–9)

Nowhere does Tennyson show greater delicacy and tact than in recounting the Grail quest.[75] It is a master stroke to present the quest sequence through the integrated perspective of Percivale. Arthur's summary of it in the closing speech of the poem is reported by Percivale, ending with the comment 'So spake the King: I knew not all he meant'. It is not in Percivale to understand the king, who sees the task alloted to him in a sane and practical light:

> And some among you held, that if the King
> Had seen the sight he would have sworn the vow:
> Not easily, seeing that the King must guard
> That which he rules, and is but as the hind
> To whom a space of land is given to plow.
>   (*HG*899–903)

In writing this passage, Tennyson may well have had the historical example of Richard Coeur de Lion in mind, who left his land to the misrule of his treacherous brother, John. To be a good and effective ruler, demands a well-balanced, self-contained nature, while the quest demands renunciation of the self. 'If I lose myself, I save myself!' (*HG*178) says Galahad, with a clearly Biblical allusion.[76]

Arthur's final judgment must be taken literally.

> But if indeed there came a sign from heaven,
> Blessèd are Bors, Lancelot and Percivale,
> For these have seen according to their sight
>   (*HG*869–71)

Bors, Lancelot and Percivale have each had a form of the vision. They have achieved the fullest human stature open to them in doing so. Arthur closes with his own testimony of having been granted visions without going far afield. To understand most deeply the interplay between matter and spirit, each man must find a way of his own.

Tennyson makes three major modifications in his source material. The first, as we have seen, is to single out Percivale to narrate the whole. He conveys the meaning of a whole idyll through the undistorting medium of his own guileless person, in the same way as Milton's Raphael. Both characters are heavenly intermediaries, and no doubt it was Raphael who first suggested to Tennyson the choice of Percivale for his narrator. Galahad, who might have been the ideal choice,[77] 'hath had the vision face to face, / And now his chair desires him here in vain' (*HG*896–7). In Malory the narrators are the self-abnegating Bors and Lancelot.[78]

Tennyson creates the homely monk, Ambrosius, as a frame to Percivale's narrative. He tells it to Ambrosius on 'a gustful April morn' while the vision of the Grail comes to the assembled knights at Camelot 'on a summer night' (*HG*14, 179). Percivale relates his story to Ambrosius not long before they both die. In Malory, too, Percivale dies in a hermitage after a year and two months.[79]

An important divergence from the original should be specially noted. In Malory, Arthur is present with his knights when the Grail comes.[80] In the *Idylls*, this is not possible. The Vision of the Grail, according to tradition, is granted only to those who renounce the self. This condition excludes the king of the *Idylls*, whom Tennyson conceives as a self-contained nature, complete in himself. His absence from among his knights strangely enhances the prowess and authority both of the Grail and of the king himself. They are now revealed as, in a certain way, counter forces.

In Malory, the knights 'mounted upon their horses and rode through the streets of Camelot' prior to their departure. Guinevere, however, was not present: 'Then the queen departed into her chamber, so that no man should apperceive her great sorrows'.[81] Tennyson, on the other hand, continues in his own vein: Guinevere rides beside Lancelot through the streets and laments 'This madness has come on us for our sins' (*HG*357).

Both Bedivere and Bellicent give an account of Arthur's origins to Leodogran in *The Coming of Arthur*, and Bedivere's version draws on Malory's tale for most details:

> Sir, for ye know that in King Uther's time
> The prince and warrior Gorloïs, he that held
> Tintagil castle by the Cornish sea,
> Was wedded with a winsome wife, Ygerne . . .
> And Uther cast upon her eyes of love:
> But she, a stainless wife to Gorloïs,
> So loathed the bright dishonour of his love,
> That Gorloïs and King Uther went to war:
> And overthrown was Gorloïs and slain.
> Then Uther in his wrath and heat besieged
> Ygerne within Tintagil, where her men,
> Seeing the mighty swarm about their walls,
> Left her and fled, and Uther enter'd in,
> And there was none to call to but himself.
> So, compass'd by the power of the King,
> Enforced she was to wed him in her tears,
> And with a shameful swiftness: afterward,
> Not many moons, King Uther died himself,
> Moaning and wailing for an heir to rule
> After him, lest the realm should go to wrack.
> And that same night, the night of the new year,

By reason of the bitterness and grief
That vext his mother, all before his time
Was Arthur born, and all as soon as born
Deliver'd at a secret postern-gate
To Merlin . . . wherefore Merlin took the child,
And gave him to Sir Anton, an old knight
And ancient friend of Uther; and his wife
Nursed the young prince, and rear'd him with her own.
   (*CA*184–7, 192–213, 220–3)

Bedivere's account of Arthur's conception and birth follows Malory's version except in two details. First, Tennyson has necessarily omitted the magic shape-changing whereby Merlin's skills enable Uther to change into the guise of Gorloïs after the latter has been killed in battle by him.[82] Also, Tennyson has Uther die before Arthur is born.[83]

The lines added to *Morte d'Arthur* to expand it into *The Passing of Arthur* have framing details drawn from Malory. 'That story which the bold Sir Bedivere . . . Told' (*PA*1–3) stems from Malory: after Arthur's death 'this tale Sir Bedivere, knight of the Table Round, made it to be written'.[84] Then the ghost of Gawain who had been 'killed in Lancelot's war' comes as a dream to Arthur during sleep (*PA*29–49). This experience derives from Gawain's ghostly warning to Arthur in Malory.[85]

Tennyson expands the combat between Arthur and Modred, a bastard son of Arthur's in Malory's tale.[86] Malory has:

God speed you well, said Sir Bedivere. Then the king gat his spear in both his hands, and ran toward Sir Modred, crying: Traitor, now is thy death day come. And when Sir Modred heard Sir Arthur, he ran until him with his sword drawn in his hand. And then King Arthur smote Sir Modred under the shield, with a foin of his spear, throughout the body, more than a fathom. And when Sir Modred felt that he had his death wound he thrust himself with the might that he had up to the bur of King Arthur's spear. And right so he smote his father Arthur, with his sword holden in both his hands, on the side of the head, that the sword pierced the helmet and the brainpan, and therewithal Sir Modred fell stark dead to the earth; and the noble Arthur fell in a swoon to the earth, and there he swooned ofttimes.[87]

Tennyson's Arthur denies the kinship with Modred, 'no kin of mine' (*G*570), and indicates again in the present passage that no close kinship exists:

30

Then spake the bold Sir Bedivere . . .
    '. . . who hates thee, he that brought
The heathen back among us, yonder stands,
Modred, unharm'd, the traitor of thine house.'

    Then spake the King: 'My house hath been my doom.
But call not thou this traitor of my house
Who hath but dwelt beneath one roof with me.
My house are rather they who sware my vows,
Yea, even while they brake them, own'd me King . . .
King am I, whatsoever be their cry;
And one last act of kinghood shalt thou see
Yet, ere I pass.' And uttering this the King
Made at the man: then Modred smote his liege
Hard on that helm which many a heathen sword
Had beaten thin; while Arthur at one blow,
Striking the last stroke with Excalibur,
Slew him, and all but slain himself, he fell.
    (*PA*154–69)

On first meeting Pelleas, Ettarre greets him with the words, 'Youth, we are damsels errant, and we ride . . . to tilt against the knights' (*PE*61–2). The meeting is Tennyson's own invention, but the expression 'damsels errant' comes from Spenser, and the Amazonian touch in the scene has, of course, a classical origin.[88]

    In Malory, Ettarre's relation to Pelleas is dominated by pride:

And so he chose her for his sovran lady, and never to love other but her, and she was so proud that she had scorn of him, and said that she would never love him though he would die for her.[89]

Tennyson dramatises the situation by inserting a meeting between Ettarre and Pelleas before the tournament at Caerleon. After the tournament, however, when he claims her as the victor:

    She that saw him cried,
'Damsels – and yet I should be shamed to say it –
I cannot bide Sir Baby . . . would rather that we had
Some rough old knight who knew the worldly way,
Albeit grizzlier than a bear, to ride
And jest with: take him to you, keep him off,
And pamper him with papmeat . . .
    (*PE*181–7)

Malory does not specify where the tournament takes place. Tennyson, on the other hand, placed it in Arthur's Welsh capital,

Caerleon, which plays a part in *Mabinogion*, but is unknown in Malory. The idyll concludes at the main court, Camelot, which Pelleas reaches in a day's furious ride from Ettarre's castle near Caerleon. So Tennyson skilfully indicates the extent of Arthur's kingdom, while weaving together the background of two Arthurian tales.

The interweaving of Malory with other Arthurian sources continues in the last three idylls of the cycle. *Gareth and Lynette* preserves the wonderful freshness of Malory's tale of Beaumains. A good example of how selectively Tennyson combines elements from Malory is given in the combats Gareth must fight with coloured knights. In the poetic narrative, the number of combats is reduced from eight to four, and each of these is a composite.

To begin with, Lynette warns Gareth's blue-armoured opponent who guards the bridge over a river:

> See that he fall not on thee suddenly,
> And slay thee unarm'd: he is not knight but knave

To which the luminary replies:

> A kitchen knave, and sent in scorn of me!
> Such fight not I, but answer scorn with scorn.
> For this were shame to do him further wrong
> Than set him on his feet, and take his horse
> And arms, and so return him to the King.

Gareth is incensed, and retorts:

> Dog, thou liest.
> I spring from loftier lineage than thine own.

When they clash on the bridge, both are unhorsed and Gareth's shield is cloven in two, but he forces his adversary into submission (*GL*883 ... 948).

Gareth's victory over the nameless knight, the second in Malory's series, is derided by Lynette: 'by mishap thou camest behind him and mishappily thou slew him'.

In his third encounter the Knight of the Black Land disdains the mere boy: 'I shall put him down upon one foot, and his horse and his harness he shall leave with me, for it were shame to me to do him any more harm . . . Thou liest, said Beaumains, I am a gentleman born, and of more high lineage than thou'.

In his fourth combat Gareth fights a green knight anxious to avenge his brother, who 'gave a great stroke of might and clave his shield through'.

But it is the sixth knight, Sir Persant of Inde, bearing splendid dark-blue arms, to whom Malory devotes almost a full chapter of rich description. It is from him that Tennyson chiefly develops the appearance of Morning Star, and of his retinue of matching colours.[90]

Malory's Beaumains tale is one of his best. Its liveliness is well displayed in part of the dialogue between Gareth and Lynette:

> Damosel, said Beaumains, say to me what ye will, I will not go from you whatsomever ye say, for I have undertaken to King Arthur for to achieve your adventure, and so shall I finish it to the end, either I shall die therefor. Fie on thee, kitchen knave, wilt thou finish mine adventure? thou shalt anon be met withal, that thou wouldest not for all the broth that ever thou suppest once look him in the face.[91]

Tennyson effortlessly works the lively tone into his dialogue:

> 'Damsel,' Sir Gareth answer'd gently, 'say
> Whate'er ye will, but whatsoe'er ye say
> I leave not till I finish this fair quest,
> Or die therefore.'
>
>   'Ay, wilt thou finish it?
> Sweet lord, how like a noble knight he talks!
> The listening rogue hath caught the manner of it.
> But, knave, anon thou shalt be met with, knave,
> And then by such a one that thou for all
> The kitchen brewis that was ever supt
> Shalt not once dare to look him in the face.
>
>   (*GL*753–62)

Lancelot participates both in the prose romance and Tennyson's poem, but his relationship to Gareth is not identical. In Malory the two knights fight to a draw, and then Gareth asks for and is granted knighthood by Lancelot.[92] In Tennyson Arthur alone can make men knights. He sends Lancelot to shadow the inexperienced Gareth during his first three encounters. After the third victory, Gareth boasts 'There rides no knight, not Lancelot, his great self, / Hath force to quell me' (*GL*1153–4).[93] Just after, Lancelot appears, and in the ensuing combat Gareth is easily beaten. He takes this defeat with good humour, and in preparation for his final adversary, Death, Lancelot teaches him all the tricks of the trade. Thus Death, though ominous in appearance, is easily overcome. Indeed, he is revealed to be a fresh young boy, sent by his brothers 'To make a horror all about the house, / And stay the world from Lady Lyonors' (*GL*1376–7). So the story ends on a gay and charming note:

> And he that told the tale in older times
> Says that Sir Gareth wedded Lyonors,
> But he, that told it later, says Lynette.

The skilful reorganisation of significant detail is motivated by Tennyson's criticism of Malory's romance: 'There are very fine things in it, but all strung together without Art'.[94] The prevalent taste today may not accept Tennyson's judgment without strong qualifications, but it was in keeping with a poet of such finished artistry as Tennyson.

Taking the *Idylls* in their order of evolution, we note that *The Last Tournament* was written in conjunction with *Gareth and Lynette*, and so shares certain features with it.[95] In the finished cycle, *Gareth and Lynette* comes second, *The Last Tournament* comes tenth, being the two supporting pillars of an arch that spans the distance between the late and early idylls. These two poems have most importantly a common ground in Malory's tale of Beaumains or Gareth. This tale provides not only virtually all the incidents in *Gareth and Lynette* but also a later, vividly described combat of Gareth's with a certain Knight of the Red Laundes. As will now be demonstrated, Tennyson models the Red Knight in *The Last Tournament* on his precursor in Malory.

First, in Malory's tale, Gareth comes to the territory of the Red Knight, who owns a tower 'as white as any snow, well matchecold all about, and double dyked'.[96] After defeating this, and another knight, five chapters later, Gareth

> espied upon great trees, as he rode, how there hung full goodly armed knights by the neck, and their shields about their necks with their swords, and gilt spurs upon their heels.

Such an outrage prompts Gareth to speculate:

> it is a marvel that he endureth so long that none of the noble knights of my lord Arthur's have not dealt with him . . . And also there was fast by a sycamore tree, and there hung a horn . . . that if there came any errant knight, he must blow that horn, and then will he make him ready and come to him to do battle . . . and therewith he spurred his horse straight to the sycamore tree, and blew so the horn eagerly that all the siege and the castle rang thereof . . . Then the red knight of the red laundes armed him hastily, and two barons set on his spurs upon his heels, and all was blood red, his armour, spear and shield. And an earl buckled his helm upon his head, and then they brought him a red spear and a red steed, and so he rode.[97]

When the red knight, talking to Gareth, refers to 'yonder knights that thou sawest hang upon yonder trees' he angers Gareth so much that he answers 'thou shamest thyself and knighthood'.

Tennyson sets the whole episode in a lurid sunset going down over a great marsh, but the Red Knight's tower is 'machicolated' (*LT*423). As the opening line makes plain, we look at this scene through the eyes of someone not unlike the original Gareth:

'Lo there,' said one of Arthur's youth, for there,
High on a grim dead tree before the tower,
A goodly brother of the Table Round
Swung by the neck: and on the boughs a shield
Showing a shower of blood in a field noir,
And therebeside a horn, inflamed the knights
At that dishonour done the gilded spur,
Till each would clash the shield, and blow the horn.
But Arthur waved them back. Alone he rode.
Then at the dry harsh roar of the great horn,
That sent the face of all the marsh aloft
An ever upward-rushing storm and cloud
Of shriek and plume, the Red Knight heard, and all,
Even to tipmost lance and topmost helm,
In blood-red armour sallying . . .
      (*LT*428–41)

Tennyson not only makes the most of the vividly gruesome details in Malory, but even more importantly, he characterises Arthur. The three spare words 'Alone he rode', suggested by the 'so he rode' of the Knight of the Red Laundes, and the 'as he rode' of Gareth, sets off Arthur, who blows the horn and animates the whole lurid landscape. Tennyson devises a horrendous heraldic crest ('a shower of blood in a field noir') as part of the heraldic symbolism which runs through the *Idylls*.[98] Further, in Malory gilt spurs on the heels of the hanged knights become, more effectively, a single pair on the lone figure, one of Arthur's own knights. In Malory it is the youthful and idealistic Gareth who first notes the scene whereas in Tennyson it is 'one of Arthur's youth'. Gareth's speculation in Malory (it is a marvel that he endureth so long that none of the noble knights of my lord Arthur's have not dealt with him') is probably the nucleus for the expedition led by Arthur in *The Last Tournament* (*LT*56–88, 419–77).

Since Arthur has to lead the expedition versus the Red Knight, he is unable to be present at the actual tournament that gives the idyll its title. A similar tournament is found in Malory, but without the disastrous consequences that Tennyson ascribes to the absence of the king.[99] The unseemly and dissolute behaviour that mars the last tournament may be taken for at least a negative evidence that Arthur's personal authority could still impose a restraint on the decaying chivalry of his realm.

In the original tale Gareth defeats the Knight of the Red Laundes after severe combat. The latter then confesses the reason for his shameful actions:

> Sir, I loved once a lady, a fair damsel, and she had her brother slain; and she said it was Sir Launcelot du Lake, or else Sir Gawaine; and she prayed me as that I loved her heartily, that I would make her a promise by the faith of my knighthood for to labour daily in arms unto I met with one of them; and all that I might overcome I should put them unto a villainous death; and this is the cause that I have put all these knights to death, and so I ensured her to do all the villainy unto King Arthur's knights, and that I should take vengeance upon all these knights.[100]

This passage is behind the admission made by Tennyson's Red Knight: 'Slain was the brother of my paramour / By a knight of thine' and he goes on to say: 'I . . . sware by the scorpion-worm that twists in hell . . . To hang whatever knight of thine I fought' (*LT*447–52). Thus Tennyson's Red Knight is not simply a barbaric product of the poet's imagination but is carefully modelled on selected details in Malory.

Tennyson also weaves the tale of Tristram into *The Last Tournament*. On one occasion Malory's Tristram receives a fervent welcome to Camelot:

> Then King Arthur took Sir Tristram by the hand and went to the Table Round. Then came Queen Guenever and many ladies with her, and all the ladies said at one voice: Welcome, Sir Tristram! Welcome, said the damosels. Welcome, said knights. Welcome, said Arthur, for one of the best knights.[101]

In Tennyson such a welcome becomes positively oceanic to Lancelot: 'anon he heard / The voice that billow'd round the barriers roar / An ocean-sounding welcome to one knight' (*LT*166–8).[102] At one point Malory calls Tristram 'the strongest and highest knight of the world; for he was called bigger than Sir Launcelot, but Sir Launcelot was better breathed'.[103] Accordingly, Tennyson specifies Tristram is 'taller than the rest' (*LT*169). But the welcome accorded him is undercut by the exaggerated and ultimately sardonic description of his appearance:

> And armour'd all in forest green, whereon
> There tript a hundred tiny silver deer,
> And wearing but a holly-spray for crest,
> With ever-scattering berries, and on shield
> A spear, a harp, a bugle –   (*LT*170–4)

Although the heraldry is fanciful, the description shows with what imaginative fluency Tennyson could elaborate on Malory, where the knight appears on one occasion in green armour, with green trappings.[104]

Tennyson develops Tristram and King Mark in such a way that Tristram's fate seems deserved, and nothing less than murder can be expected from Mark. Arthur rejects Mark's application for Round Table membership, because

> Mark hath tarnish'd the great name of king,
> As Mark would sully the low state of churl . . .
> Return, and meet, and hold him from our eyes,
> Lest we should lap him up in cloth of lead,
> Silenced for ever – craven – a man of plots,
> Craft, poisonous counsels, wayside ambushings . . .
> Accursed, who strikes nor lets the hand be seen!'
> (*GL*418-27)

Every feature of Arthur's indictment of Mark can be found in Malory.[105] From Malory also, long after Tristram's adventures had been dropped, we hear that 'that traitor king [Mark] slew the noble knight Sir Tristram, as he sat harping afore his lady La Beale Isoud, with a trenchant glaive'.[106] So it is that Tennyson's Tristram meets his fate immediately after having sung a song to Isolt (*LT*725-32), when '"Mark's way", said Mark, and clove him thro' the brain' (*LT*748).[107]

As a comprehensive example of how Tennyson recreates his material, I shall analyse, from its most general aspect, characterisation, an entire idyll and its source, *Balin and Balan*, and Malory's Book 11, the book of Balin le savage. Because it is the last stage in a long development, and its theme is division or fragmentation of personality, this idyll resolves more readily into its archetypal constituents than any other. From this example of 'dreaming the myth onwards', to use a fine formulation of C. G. Jung's, a better understanding of both Malory's tale and the final poem to evolve in Tennyson's cycle should be possible.[108]

One way of approaching both the tale and the poem leads through the frames that help to create or articulate their meaning. As we have seen already, Tennyson's *Idylls* are framed in many ways and at several levels, this being an essential feature not only of individual poems but of the series as a whole. The question of structure will be examined later. At present, the pertinent point to note is that the most likely occurrence of similarities between Malory and Tennyson is at the beginning, the middle, and the end. Malory's tale is at its most vivid and problematic in its central events. Only a detailed comparison can show how far this applies also to Tennyson's idyll.

Poem and tale are most closely akin at the end, where their fate, its fulfilment hastened by their separation, finally overtakes the two brothers. Tennyson intensifies the psychological problem by making Balin and Balan twins: 'We two were born together, and we die / Together' (*BB*617), and by making Balin's adventures fantastic. But his closeness to Malory at the conclusion is a sign that they are dealing with an archetypal pattern or set, and that behind surface differences the story or mythos is the same.

The poem's opening, on the other hand, seems at first to have nothing in common with its medieval predecessor. In the idyll the action begins and ends in the woods. Only later are the brothers brought to court. In Malory, Balan never appears at court. In another of the many changes Tennyson introduces, he eliminates the mysterious business of Balin's winning and keeping, against advice, a fated sword. On the other hand, his own stress on weaponry, especially spears, is noteworthy. Basically, a division or conflict of loyalties in the character of Balin is at the root of both versions. Though the terms of exile decreed before the main action begins may differ slightly (banishment for killing Arthur's servant in Malory; in Tennyson three years of exile from Camelot for half-killing a thrall) the import is the same. An intriguing element in Malory is Balin's poverty, expressed in poor dress:

> Damosel, I pray you of your courtesy, suffer me as well to assay these lords; though that I be so poorly clothed, in my heart meseemeth I am fully assured as some of these others . . . The damosel beheld the poor knight, and saw he was a likely man, but for his poor arrayment she thought he should be of no worship . . . Ah! fair Damosel . . . worthiness, and good tatches (qualities), and good deeds, are not only in arrayment, but manhood and worship is hid within man's person, and many a worshipful knight is not known unto all people, and therefore worship and hardiness is not in arrayment.[109]

Considering the rigid code governing dress and appearance in medieval chivalry, to appear in Balin's poor condition was certain to invite ostracism. Balin is a kind of scapegoat. His unexplained poor dress in Malory has a number of sympathetic correspondences in Tennyson, chief of which is his dependence, his feelings of isolation, his blunt or defective articulation, the poor figure he feels he cuts in Camelot (*BB*55–61, 161–72, 186–90).

Resemblances at the centre of the poem and the tale seem oblique, but it is possible to see how Tennyson modifies, for dramatic effect, the incidents involving Balin with Garlon and Pellam at the Grail castle.

In Malory's central action Garlon, a strange black-faced knight
with the power of invisibility, strikes Balin and is promptly decapi-
tated. When his brother King Pellam chases Balin into a chapel, the
knight impales him on a spear. At this, the castle collapses and the
two lie senseless in its ruins three days, until Merlin releases Balin
from the spell. Pellam is forgotten until the Grail account many
chapters later. Tennyson's spell is apparently much simpler. Although the encounter between Balin and Garlon seems similar,
Pellam makes no appearance in his hall. In his stead, no less than
twenty retainers chase Balin, who runs into a chapel, only to find:
> before a golden altar lie
> The longest lance his eyes had ever seen,
> Point-painted red; and seizing thereupon
> Push'd thro' an open casement down, lean'd on it,
> Leapt in a semicircle, and lit on earth
> (*BB*404–8)

Balin's escape from Pellam's castle in the poem is a dramatic modification of an earlier incident in Malory when, with typical impetuosity,
Balin 'went up into the tower, and leapt over the walls into the ditch,
and hurt him not' when escaping from the Castle of Maidens.[110] The
whole landscape, with Pellam's castle at its centre, expresses the
conflict within Balin.

Pellam's castle in Tennyson is at the heart of the forest. Though
Malory's Grail castle has no specific setting, his tale has much sug-
gestive imagery throughout. Balin slays Lanceor on a mountain, and
his final combat with Balan is on an island only reached by means of
a 'great boat'.[111] This indeed is fairy country. Traditionally, and in
this tale particularly, forest is a feature of fairy-tale. Balin's epithet
'le savage' indicates that he is a *silvaticus*, a 'savage' man or man of
the woods. In the idyll, the character of the savage is maintained and
is strikingly projected on to Balin's shield, whose crest is a 'rough
beast' with 'langued gules' and is 'tooth'd with grinning savagery'
(*BB*192–3). Hence the poignancy of his despairing cry:
> here I dwell
> Savage among the savage woods, here die –
> Die: let the wolves' black maws ensepulchre
> Their brother beast, whose anger was his lord
> (*BB*478–81)

In Malory it is from 'the great forest' that Balin's as yet significantly
unnamed and unannounced brother steps, as if originating from it.[112]
The forest continues to be a motif throughout. 'So Balin and the
damosel rode into a forest' opens one chapter, and midway through
the terminal adventure 'at the last he came into a fair forest'.[113] It

takes little to see in the 'skyless woods' (*BB*288) a reflection of Balin's state of mind.

Although Tennyson and Malory appear to have little in common in the *dramatis personae*, analysis shows profound resemblances. Behind the Balin tale lies the archaic myth of the Celtic divinities or kings, Belinus and Bran (Brennus). Conflict is indicated from the very first sentence of the account given of them in Geoffrey of Monmouth's *Historia*:

> Belinus and Brennius, the two sons of Dunvallo, each of whom was determined to inherit the kingship, now began a great war of attrition against each other. Their object in this struggle was to decide which of the two should be crowned King of the realm.[114]

Conflict on this scale continues for some time. Significantly, the only force that can unite the brothers is their mother. Tennyson, too, envisages a similar occasion, when Balan asserts 'Pure as our own true Mother is our Queen' (*BB*606). As long as Balan remains with Balin he keeps his brother stable, and only when he goes off on the quest does Balin's disintegration begin.

Such in skeletal form is a world-wide primordial tale. Belinus and Brennus represent opposed yet complementary principles on both the human and the cosmic scale. Projected onto the external universe through the medium of myth, they express a whole range of cosmic oppositions and resolutions. The name of the Celtic autumn solstice, Beltane, and its association with ritual sacrifice by fire, is a reminder that the divinities, Belinus and Brennus, divided the solar year between them. One wonders if in Balan's strange origin from the forest a shadowy trace of this elemental opposition is preserved.[115] At the end of the tale, Balin's death at midnight, following the death of his brother, similarly suggests ancient mythical origins. Malory, who rarely specifies time, mentions the precise hour of Balin's death. May not this be a distant, though unconscious echo of the time of admittance to the nether world? The question cannot be answered with any certainty. What is certain is that the latent element of conflict pervading Malory's tale finds a ready response in the poet's Arthurian cycle. In view of its complexity and power, it is not surprising that its treatment is delayed until the very end.

Though my analysis has so far been centred on Balin and Balan, the psychic split they embody is just as prominently displayed in another pair of brothers, Garlon and Pellam. Their characters express dark conflict and paired opposition. In Malory, Garlon with his ominous black face and his slayings while invisible, is clearly a netherworld figure.[116] He is a hidden killer, whereas his brother, in apparent compensation, is the Grail king or custodian. Moreover, it is surely not by accident that Pellam is named after Pwyll, who became a Celtic prince of the underworld.[117] The two figures express archetypally paired psychic powers associated with the Grail itself.

Tennyson transforms Malory's Garlon and Pellam in much the same way as he does Balin and Balan. As we have seen, he makes Balan's independent existence and departure on the mission to slay a 'wood demon' a motive for Balin's regression to forest life. As for Garlon's actions, Tennyson follows Malory fairly closely, but develops Pellam in a somewhat different way. Pellam's relationship to Garlon is that the latter is merely his 'heir' (*BB*114). No longer tied to each other by close kinship, they express contrary extremes: Pellam is ascetic to an unnatural degree; Garlon is licentious (one incident, for instance, which Tennyson invents, is Garlon's meeting with Vivien in the forest).[118] The two characters suggest opposite ways of spiritual death. Interestingly, they never appear simultaneously with one another or to Balin. Instead of chasing Balin from room to room in the castle, as in Malory's version, Pellam is hardly seen at all, and at the close of the episode he fades into a mere feeble voice (*BB*415). Balin, riding in panic from the castle, is come upon by Vivien, who inflicts a new injury on his soul. By a stroke of irony Vivien's name means life (*vivus* – living).[119] Immediately after her meeting with Balin his fatal combat with Balan takes place. In Malory the two knights are matched fairly, so that Balin, although he is bruised early in the combat when his horse falls, rises and battles with his brother till both are mortally wounded. In Malory, spears merely accomplish the unseating of the combatants; swords do the actual slaying.[120] In Tennyson's poem, on the other hand, Balin's spear comes into play:

> the point
> Across the maiden shield of Balan prick'd
> The hauberk to the flesh; and Balin's horse
> Was wearied to the death, and when they clash'd
> Rolling back upon Balin, crush'd the man
> Inward, and either fell, and swoon'd away
> (*BB*549–54)

Balan's blank or 'maiden' shield denotes inexperience, but a further advantage is conferred on Balan by having the 'longest lance' which he has looted from the 'golden altar' of Pellam's castle.[121] Even so, he cannot escape his fate. He dies when his horse rolls backward upon him and crushes him. By a subtle reorganisation, especially of the bruising during combat which Malory mentions, Tennyson shows the knight ironically destroyed, as it were, by his own 'beast' –

41

a fitting end for one who from the first is unable to govern his passion. So in the end the twins are united in death as they were, perhaps, meant to be one person in life.

The order and development of characterisation affords us another view of the difference between Malory's and Tennyson's treatment of this theme. Among his more significant characters Malory has Arthur, Balin, the Lady of the Lake, Balan, Garlon, Pellam, and an old hoar gentleman. Among his necessarily more selective and more highly developed *dramatis personae* Tennyson includes Arthur, Balin and Balan, a woodman, Garlon, Pellam, and Vivien.

In essence there is little difference between the ordering of both sets of characters. First, for similar reasons, Arthur and Balin are given much the same prominence both in the tale and the poem, but Tennyson gives Balan equal weight, as virtually a complementary half of his more notorious brother. Also, the outstanding dramatic characters of Garlon and Pellam are given the same central prominence in both works, though again with greatly increased symmetry in Tennyson. Malory's Lady of the Lake and an old hoar gentleman become, by a simple inversion, Tennyson's 'hoarhead' woodman (*BB*289) and the furtive Vivien, the Lady of the Lake's evil *alter ego*.[122]

To sum up briefly: while Tennyson completely remodels the outer structure for his own serial presentation, the latent or inner structure remains in many ways uncannily similar to Malory's. However, it is possible to make the following distinction. In the story of Balin and Balan, Malory is not concerned with opposing and complementary forces, either on the psychic or on the cosmic scale, at least not explicitly so. To Tennyson, on the other hand, living with the tensions of the Victorian age, this theme is a constant preoccupation. In the very last of the *Idylls* to evolve, its exploration and dramatisation through split and double personalities are of paramount importance.

[3]

Range of Allusion

A feature of Tennyson's style is that it reflects, often consciously, sometimes unconsciously, imagery and syntax of earlier poets. Some idea of his capacity to echo and reflect Malory has already been demonstrated. He was guided by a superb ear and an incredibly retentive verbal and visual memory. 'His acquaintance with all previous poetry was unlimited, and his memory of it amazing', states J. T. Knowles.[1] Such an unlimited acquaintance and amazing memory is clearly demonstrated in *Idylls of the King*, where the sheer range of allusion – Biblical, classical, Arthurian, medieval, and Renaissance – shows not only the poet's ingenuity but his constant effort to construct a timeless heroic atmosphere in which to set his Arthurian court. The charge of plagiarism often made against such echoings and reflections is well met by Bowra's comment on Camões:

> Learned poetry . . . by awakening echoes of some other poem seeks to add beauty and dignity to its own subject . . . It is wrong to treat passages of such a kind as if they were mere plagiarism. The poet does not wish to pass off the work of others as his own; he aims rather at making us see his theme in the light of some other theme honoured and glorified by classical verse, and find a complex pleasure in the association of the old with the new.[2]

Sometimes Tennyson's academic contemporaries failed to obtain such a complex pleasure. When one of them, John Churton Collins, labelled an important image 'an idea evolved out of a hint from Homer' Tennyson was led to declare:

> People accuse Virgil of plagiarising, but if a man made it his own there was no harm in that (look at the great poets, Shakespeare included). He quoted Goethe's *Du bist ein Narr?* He himself had been 'most absurdly accused of plagiarising', e.g. 'the moanings of the homeless sea,' 'moanings' from Horace, 'homeless' from Shelley. 'As if no one else had heard the sea moan except Horace.'[3]

It is my contention that Tennyson, especially in the poem that he knew was his supreme achievement, 'made . . . his own' every borrowing. Its range and complexity will be sampled in the following pages. My first section considers heroic and chivalric elements in respect to Arthurian weapons and warfare. The following section considers the range and kind of Biblical allusion. Thirdly, I consider Tennyson's echoing of Shakespeare. Finally, I analyse a few passages where 'different' archaisms work together for a combined effect. One function of the apparatus of notes is to supply annotation, and many allusions are traced there as well.

Heroic Allusion

The weapons and accoutrements of Tennyson's warriors have a long heroic history. Arthur's lowered helm 'To which for crest the golden dragon clung / Of Britain' (*G*590) derives from Geoffrey of Monmouth.[4] Excalibur has 'a blade so bright / That men are blinded by it' (*CA*299), recalling Malory's sword which 'was so bright in his enemies' eyes, that it gave light like thirty torches'.[5] When 'elfin Urim' is said to be a feature of Excalibur's hilt (*CA*298), Spenser created the adjective 'elfin' and Milton set the oraculous gems of Aaron's breastplate or 'Urim' into a sword for God's son.[6] Tennyson also draws on Malory for the fact that Excalibur is inscribed.[7] 'Take me' is inscribed on one side of the blade, but in Biblical echo the other side has 'Cast me away' (*CA*302,304) engraved on it.[8] In Balin's sword blade that 'flew / Splintering in six, and clinkt upon the stones' (*BB*389) there may be an echo of Shakespeare: 'the clink and fall of swords'.[9]

In Geoffrey of Monmouth, Arthur 'graced his right hand with a lance, named Ron, which was hard, broad and fit for slaughter'.[10] Tennyson refers to this 'long lance' (*LT*87), presumably in the metaphoric sense that it could reach anywhere to mete out justice. Lancelot's spear is particularly emphasised. In Malory 'he smote down with one spear five knights' and so in Tennyson we have Arthur' sword that Lancelot 'hath overborne / Five knights at once' (*HG*303).[11] In Gareth's encounter with Lancelot:

> Gareth crying prick'd against the cry;
> But when they closed – in a moment – at one touch
> Of that skill'd spear, the wonder of the world –
> Went sliding down so easily, and fell
>   (*GL*1190–3)

Lancelot's spear is like Britomart's: 'for never wight so fast in sell could sit, / But him perforce into the ground it bore'.[12]

Agamemnon rushing against Koön 'grasping his wind-nurtured spear' is in the spear 'of grain / Storm-strengthened on a windy site' (*GL*676) with which the young hero, Gareth, is armed.[13] 'So Gareth ere he parted flash'd in arms' (*GL*674) recalls the Homeric arming of the hero or *Aristeia* when a gleam, promising victory, shines from his arms.[14] Malory and Spenser are also present in the adjective, in that Gareth's spear is 'tipt / With trenchant steel'.[15] In Malory a single spear used by Balin to defend himself in the Grail chapel, becomes a *leitmotif* in Tennyson's *Balin and Balan*.[16] Arthur's lance 'lightly' accomplishes the unhorsing of the two strange brothers. Soon there is a woodman's account of a demon who, with a spear thrown from behind, murders knights in the forest. It is not long before a spear is hurled at Balin. But in his excitement he snaps his own weapon against a branch. Finally, he despatches Garlon, the wood demon, with a sword, only to find himself pursued by twenty spearmen. Fleeing from them into Pellam's chapel, he seizes a spear greater than he has ever seen, and with its help vaults to freedom (*BB*39, 118, 317, 324, 395, 405, 408). However, this spear is as fated as the fatal sword in the original tale, because its point: 'Across the maiden shield of Balan prick'd / The hauberk to the flesh' (*BB*550). The 'maiden shield' recalls the 'maiden sword' in Shakespeare.[17]

Many heroic allusions are cleverly interwoven in Gareth's four combats. Their source in Malory has already been analysed in the previous chapter. Kay's challenge 'Have at thee then' (*GL*739) echoes one made by Bercilak in *Sir Gawain and the Green Knight*: '"Haf at þe þenne" quod þat oþer'.[18] Morning Star's contemptuous dismissal, 'Such fight not I, but answer scorn with scorn' (*GL*930) echoes Milton's 'To whom thus Zephon, answering scorn with scorn'.[19] Gareth's addressing Morning Star as 'Dog' (*GL*936) is typical Homeric taunting.[20] The simile: 'either knight at once, / Hurled as a stone from out a catapult' (*GL*941) originates in Virgil, where Aconteus meets his end in a similar way.[21] Gareth's taunting reply to his third adversary, that he is 'Old, and over-bold in brag!' (*GL*1080) reminds us of Shakespeare.[22] In the ensuing struggle, Evening Star, 'up like fire he started' (*GL*1095), stems from the actions of Virgil's Proteus.[23] Finally, when Gareth is unhorsed by Lancelot, his cry of defeat is Shakespearean: 'Out, sword; we are thrown' (*GL*1205).[24]

Compared to the copious and frequent blood-letting in *Iliad*, *Aeneid*, and other classical literature, little blood is spilled in the *Idylls*. However, when Tennyson does describe what happens in combat, he models himself carefully on Malory. Lancelot pleads with Lavaine:

> O gentle knight, Sir Lavaine, help me that this truncheon were out of my side, for it sticketh so sore that it nigh slayeth me. O mine own lord, said Sir Lavaine, I would fain do that might please you, but I dread me sore an I pull out the truncheon that ye shall be in peril of death. I charge you, said Sir Launcelot, as

ye love me, draw it out. And therewithal he descended from his horse, and right so did Sir Lavaine; and forthwithal Sir Lavaine drew the truncheon out of his side, and he gave a great shriek and a marvellously grisely groan, and the blood brast out nigh a pint at once, that at the last he sank down upon his buttocks, and so swooned pale and deadly.[25]

The poet has compressed the essentials in Malory into little more than half the length:

> Gasping to Sir Lavaine, 'Draw the lance-head:'
> 'Ah my sweet lord Sir Lancelot,' said Lavaine,
> 'I dread me, if I draw it, you will die.'
> But he, 'I die already with it: draw –
> Draw,' – and Lavaine drew, and Sir Lancelot gave
> A marvellous great shriek and ghastly groan,
> And half his blood burst forth, and down he sank
> For the pure pain, and wholly swoon'd away.
>   (*LE*509–16)

A little later in the idyll the words of the disabled Homeric warrior, Diomedes, calling all to hold aloof from battle, 'lest any take wound upon wound', is echoed when Arthur wonders if Lancelot 'Hath added wound to wound' (*LE*565).[26]

However, when Lancelot 'with his heel upon the fall'n, / Rolling his eyes, a moment stood' over the defeated Pelleas (*PE*569–70), the gesture recalls Virgil's Aeneas over Turnus.[27] Here the parallel ends. Turnus begs forgiveness in his dying breath, while Pelleas, whom Lancelot has threatened to kill, begs the great knight to end his life: 'Slay me: I have no sword' (*PE*564).

A sign of Lancelot's prowess is that in the diamond jousts 'King, duke, earl, / Count, baron – whom he smote, he overthrew' (*LE*462–3). With slight modification, this stems from an incidental list in Malory: 'and there was great press of kings, dukes, earls, and barons, and many noble knights'.[28] Tennyson has omitted the last item, and inserted one of his own: 'count', which is the European equivalent of 'earl'. It therefore comes after 'earl' in the list, but because it is specially emphasised by being placed first in the line (and the feeling of intrusion) it comes with the shock of surprise. These jousts may be international, but Lancelot is supreme champion.[29]

Two Homeric sentences: 'All day the men contend in grievous war' and 'But he amid the foremost, I ween, shall lie stricken and many comrades round about their lord at the rising of tomorrow's sun' are fused[30] in the opening words of *Morte d'Arthur*:

> So all day long the noise of battle roll'd
> Among the mountains by the winter sea;

> Until King Arthur's Table, man by man,
> Had fall'n in Lyonnesse about their lord   (*PA*172–5)

This passage describes Arthur's last great battle, but his first great engagement is even richer in literary allusion. *Iliad* vi opens: 'So was the dread fray of Trojans and Achaians left to itself, and the battle swayed oft this way and that across the plain'. At Arthur's battle with the petty British kings 'here and there that war / Went swaying' (*CA*105–6). The entire passage is full of echoes:

> So when the King had set his banner broad,
> At once from either side, with trumpet-blast,
> And shouts, and clarions shrilling unto blood,
> The long-lanced battle let their horses run.
> And now the Barons and the kings prevail'd,
> And now the King, as here and there that war
> Went swaying...   (*CA*100–6)

In the details of battle 'So when the King had set his banner broad' fuses the Biblical 'and in the name of our God we will set up our banners' and Spenser's 'with scutchins gilt and banners broad displayed'.[31] The 'clarions shrilling unto blood' echo Chaucer's 'Clariounes / That in the battle blowen bloody sounds'.[32] When 'The long-lanced battle let their horses run' we recognise Malory's 'then either battle let their horses run as fast as they might'.[33] Often, echoing as dense as this can give too studied a movement to the metre, diction, syntax, but certainly not here, where Biblical, Homeric, Chaucerian, Malorian and Spenserian heroic echoes are blended to simulate the tide of combat.

The catalogue of kings in Malory is selectively modified by Tennyson:

> till Arthur by main might...
> And leading all his knighthood threw the kings
> Carádos, Urien, Cradlemont of Wales,
> Claudias, and Clariance of Northumberland,
> The King Brandagoras of Latangor,
> With Anguisant of Erin, Morganore,
> And Lot of Orkney...   (*CA*108–15)

Clearly Tennyson's list is modelled on Milton, even to the organising principle of having an outstanding title located in the exact centre.[34] There is a phonetic similarity with Milton's chivalric list 'All who since . . . Jousted in Aspramont, or Montalban, / Damasco, or Marocco, or Trebisond'.[35] The irony of the central detail in Tennyson is achieved by adding the definite article to the bombastic name of Brandagoras.[36] The effect is enhanced also in another way. Wales, Northumberland, Erin and Orkney are all names of real places:

Latangor stands out as patently fictitious. But even discounting the
spurious King Brandagoras, the array of rivals whom Arthur has to
overcome to consolidate his power, is formidable. The passage describing his first decisive battle, where he 'threw the kings' ends in
mid-line with 'And Lot of Orkney'. The anti-climax suggests the
total rout of the opposition: the rival kings no longer exist as an
organised unit.

However, the defeat of the indigenous British kings does not
relieve Arthur's realm from attack. Lancelot describes to Elaine and
Lavaine twelve battles against the invading heathen Saxons:

> And Lancelot spoke
> And answer'd him at full, as having been
> With Arthur in the fight which all day long
> Rang by the white mouth of the violent Glem;
> And in the four loud battles by the shore
> Of Duglas; that on Bassa; then the war
> That thunder'd in and out the gloomy skirts
> Of Celidon the forest; and again
> By castle Gurnion, where the glorious King
> Had on his cuirass worn our Lady's Head,
> Carved of one emerald center'd in a sun
> Of silver rays, that lighten'd as he breathed;
> And at Caerleon had he help'd his lord,
> When the strong neighings of the wild white Horse
> Set every gilded parapet shuddering;
> And up in Agned-Cathregonion too,
> And down the waste sand-shores of Trath Treroit,
> Where many a heathen fell; 'and on the mount
> Of Badon I myself beheld the King
> Charge at the head of all his Table Round,
> And all his legions crying Christ and him,
> And break them; and I saw him, after, stand
> High on a heap of slain, from spur to plume
> Red as the rising sun with heathen blood,
> And seeing me, with a great voice he cried,
> "They are broken, they are broken!" for the King,
> However mild he seems at home, nor cares
> For triumph in our mimic wars, the jousts –
> For if his own knight cast him down, he laughs
> Saying, his knights are better men than he –
> Yet in this heathen war the fire of God
> Fills him: I never saw his like: there lives
> No greater leader.' (*LE*284–316)

Lancelot's account is given in a single sentence thirty-three lines long, the longest in the *Idylls*. Such a magnificent set piece has many heroic echoes.[37] It derives from a single paragraph that is part of chapter 56 of Nennius's *Historia Brittonum*, the oldest Arthurian reference that has come down to us. This records that a certain commander named Arthur, by no means the highest-ranking of the leaders then available, enjoyed twelve victories over the Saxons. The sites of these battles are then listed. Tennyson devised his far more elaborate list from the version of Nennius edited and translated by J. A. Giles for a popular compilation.[38] A comparison between Giles's version of Nennius and the form of the twelve battles Tennyson places in the mouth of Lancelot reveals several interesting differences.[39]

For the first of Arthur's battles, Tennyson selects the less probable location Giles supplies in a footnote, the river Glem in Lincolnshire, rather than the more probable river Glen in Northumberland. The choice of Lincolnshire for the first battle has the advantage of spreading the hero's exploits more evenly over the length and breadth of Britain. In the chronicle as it stands, only the battle at Castle Gurnion is conjectured to have taken place near the geographical centre of the kingdom.

In the sixth battle, through a conjunction ('that on Bassa'), Tennyson accepts the correction Giles suggests in another footnote, that the location is an offshore island (the Bass Rock) rather than the river Nennius specified. The change enhances Arthur's fame by showing him as capable a commander on water as on land. In the war that thundered 'in and out the gloomy skirts / Of Celidon the forest' Tennyson echoes Shakespeare's 'skirts of the forest'.[40]

For the penultimate battle mentioned on the list, Tennyson selects the sonorous 'Agned Cathregonion' of Giles's footnote, rather than 'Cat Bregion' of the main text. The chivalric institution of the Round Table introduced into the list at the climactic point,[41] the last battle at Badon, was in fact the invention of the medieval poet, Wace, and unknown both to Nennius and the time the historical Arthur is supposed to have lived. Nennius mentions that in his eighth battle, Arthur bore the image of the Virgin on his shoulders. In Tennyson he bears the same image, but on his cuirass or breastplate.[42] Tennyson echoes the description of Spenser's Prince Arthur whose baldric had

> in the midst thereof one pretious stone
> Of wondrous worth, and eke of wondrous mights,
> Shaped like a Ladies head, exceeding shone[43]

in that his own king

49

> Had on his cuirass worn our Lady's Head,
> Carved of one emerald center'd in a sun
> Of silver rays, that lighten'd as he breathed.

Spenser's Protestant 'a Ladies head' is modified into Tennyson's equally Protestant 'our Lady's Head'. The all-important pronoun significantly remains in lower case.

Nennius concludes his description of Badon and Arthur by saying that the leader had dispatched 940 Saxons, 'no one but the Lord affording him assistance'. Tennyson suggests this when Lancelot says of his king:

> I saw him, after, stand
> High on a heap of slain, from spur to plume
> Red as the rising sun with heathen blood.

Malory may have suggested Arthur red from slaughter: 'And Arthur was so bloody, that by his shield there might no man know him'.[44]

Note how subtly Tennyson brings his battle list to a climax. During the first eleven battles Lancelot becomes more and more elated and at line 301 in mid-line, when speaking of Badon, he passes from indirect to direct speech, reaching the climax with Arthur's repeated cry of triumph: 'They are broken, they are broken'. Longinus in his treatise *On the Sublime* remarks that the sudden interruption in the narrator's account with the direct speech of the combatant is an outburst of passion, and quotes the *Iliad* as an example.[45]

In sharp contrast to Arthur's triumphant cry 'They are broken, they are broken' is the line 'For if his own knight cast him down, he laughs'. Malory portrays Arthur as not outstanding at jousts.[46] It is in battle that he seems to become inspired. Tennyson adds that Arthur laughs, probably to suggest that unlike most great men, Arthur is without a trace of vanity.

The twelve battles just discussed, take place in the first part of Arthur's reign. The last battle destroys the remains of Arthur's kingdom and his knights, leaving himself mortally wounded. The battle fittingly takes place in thick mist:

> For friend and foe were shadows in the mist,
> And friend slew friend not knowing whom he slew;
> And some had visions out of golden youth,
> And some beheld the faces of old ghosts
> Look in upon the battle; and in the mist
> Was many a noble deed, many a base,
> And chance and craft and strength in single fights,
> And ever and anon with host to host
> Shocks, and the splintering spear, the hard mail hewn,
> Shield-breakings, and the clash of brands, the crash

> Of battleaxes on shatter'd helms, and shrieks
> After the Christ, of those who falling down
> Look'd up for heaven, and only saw the mist;
> And shouts of heathen and the traitor knights,
> Oaths, insult, filth, and monstrous blasphemies,
> Sweat, writhings, anguish, labourings of the lungs
> In that close mist, and cryings for the light,
> Moans of the dying, and voices of the dead.
>   (*PA*100–17)

A critic has commented on the passage:

> Perhaps the most striking of the many Homeric echoes in the
> *Idylls* is the final battle in the mist, in which 'friend slew friend
> not knowing whom he slew' and the fallen 'looked up for
> heaven, and only saw the mist.' Though it recalls, like Arnold's
> 'Dover Beach' and Clough's *The Bothie* (ix, 51–4), the night-
> battle in Thucydides vii, the fighting in a mist, the looking up
> to heaven, and the 'cryings for the light' are primarily modelled
> on a passage in the *Iliad* (xvii, 645–7) which Longinus quoted as
> an instance of the sublime. There Ajax prays to Zeus to disperse
> the mist, and 'kill us in the light.' His prayer, unlike those of
> Arthur's knights, is answered.[47]

There are also other heroic effects. The slow and weary alliterations
suggest Anglo-Saxon heroic poetry. 'Ever and anon' is adopted from
Spenser; the fact that it too alliterates helps to sustain the heroic
note.[48] To shriek 'after the Christ' means that Christ has become the
truly divine for them too late.[49] The affirmation of a single God and
order is only made at their last gasp. 'The shouts of heathen and the
traitor knights' is a reminder that Modred, as in Geoffrey of Monmouth, 'leagued him with the heathen' (*G*153) and so deprived
Britain of its sovereignty.[50] The 'monstrous blasphemies' show this
is an Armageddon in which 'men blasphemed God'.[51] The 'cryings
for the light' recollect *In Memoriam*'s 'An infant crying for the light'.[52]
The sun has certainly set on this last great battle.

Biblical Allusion

Malory's language is close to the King James translation of the Bible,
and naturally uses many of its characteristic phrases. Tennyson's
language in the *Idylls* is deliberately archaic, and his allusions to the
Bible help to sustain its archaic flavour.

When Vivien says to Merlin 'ye hardly know me yet' (*MV*353)
she echoes the Old Testament, where Adam 'knew' Eve.[53] Similarly,
Gawain tells Elaine that if she comes to Camelot 'we two shall know
each other' (*LE*696). Lancelot says of the dead Elaine that she 'loved

me with a love beyond all love / In women, whomsoever I have known' (*LE*1284).[54] In exactly the opposite mood, Isolt jealously taunts Tristram about his Breton wife: 'Can I wish her any huger wrong / Than having known thee?' (*LT*591). The taunt may be a deliberate exaggeration, for according to the legend Tristram did not 'know' his Breton wife. In Malory the passage runs that 'other cheer made he none but with clipping and kissing'.[55]

Biblical expression also aids Tennyson in dramatising his characters. When Elaine repeatedly 'lifted her eyes . . . when she lifted up her eyes . . . she lifted up her eyes' (*LE*243, 255, 258) the poet echoes a powerfully expectant Biblical expression, for example 'Lot lifted up his eyes and beheld all the plain of Jordan'.[56] In *Lancelot and Elaine* two others who are framed by having 'lifted' their eyes are Guinevere and Lancelot (*LE*84, 1379). Complementing this action, there is Elaine 'who held her eyes upon the ground' and Lancelot, who 'answer'd with his eyes upon the ground' (*LE*231, 1341). Alliteration greatly intensifies the gesture when Lancelot 'lifted his large eyes' (*BB*272). Such lifting of eyes occurs on six other occasions (*MG*528, *GE*304, *BB*583, *MV*834, *HG*375, *PE*589) and so forms a thread running through the *Idylls*, with its focus in Elaine, Guinevere and Lancelot.

'Mine eye dwells . . .' occurs only once in the Bible, in the Book of *Job*: 'Mine eye dwells on their provocation'.[57] Tennyson, however, studied the book of *Job* in Hebrew, and was apparently struck with the expression.[58] He uses it most effectively at the beginning of a paragraph:

> While thus he spake, his eye, dwelling on mine
> Drew me, with power upon me, till I grew
> One with him, to believe as he believed
> (*HG*485–7)

Here the last expression ('to believe as he believed') is an example of parallelism, which is a feature of poetry in Hebrew.[59]

The Biblical expression 'Pharaoh's wife cast eyes on Joseph' is reflected in Uther, who 'Cast upon (Ygerne) eyes of love' and Gawain 'who cast his eyes on fair Elaine' (*CA*192, *LE*636).[60] Arthur, on first seeing Guinevere, 'felt the light of her eyes into his life / Smite on the sudden' (*CA*56–7). In *Luke* 11.34 'The light of the body is the eye: therefore when thine eye is single, thy whole body is full of light'. In Malory too 'there had Arthur the first sight of Guenever, the king's daughter of Cameliard, and ever after he loved her'.[61]

By examining certain idylls in their narrative order, the function of Tennyson's Biblical echoing can readily be appreciated. In *The Coming of Arthur* Biblical archaism is homely as befits an idyll 'simpler and more severe in style, dealing with the awfulness of Birth'.[62] Thus Arthur's request to Leodogran is to 'give me thy daughter Guinevere to wife'; Leodogran's chamberlain is one 'to whom / He trusted all things'; on seeing Ygerne, Uther 'cast upon her eyes of love'; the Lady of the Lake has 'a voice as of the waters'; on one side of Excalibur's hilt is the command 'Cast me away'; on hearing of Arthur's coronation 'Thereat Leodogran rejoiced, but thought / To sift his doubtings to the last'; Bellicent admits that Arthur 'Spake sweet words, and comforted my heart'; in Leodogran's dream 'A phantom king / Sent out at times a voice' and the seemingly solid earth 'became / As nothing'; and Arthur's knights are 'The fair beginners of a nobler time' (*CA*138, 192, 290, 304, 310, 348, 436, 441, 456).[63] This idyll has a relatively high density of monosyllabic lines, almost one line in seven. Combined with the Biblical simplicity of diction, Tennyson achieves what T. S. Eliot has called the 'auditory imagination': 'The feeling for syllable and rhythm, penetrating far below the conscious levels of thought and feeling ... seeking the beginning and the end ... and fuses the old and obliterated and the trite, the current, and the new and surprising, the most ancient and the most civilised mentality'.[64]

The Biblical allusions in *Merlin and Vivien* serve to show how dangerous an adversary Vivien is; no devil is more adept at perverting scripture for her own ends: 'I better prize / The living dog than the dead lion' (*BB*574).[65] To the scriptural phrase 'Perfect love casteth out fear' she adds 'So Hate, if Hate be perfect, casts out fear' (*MV*41).[66] At the same time, her addition also provides an ironic twist to the voice of the psalmist: 'Do not I hate them, O Lord, that hate thee? Yea, I hate them with perfect hatred'.[67] In her own words, she has been 'sown on the wind' (*MV*45), recalling the passage: 'for they have sown the wind, and they shall reap the whirlwind: it hath no stalk: the bud shall yield no meal'.[68]

Guinevere's question to Vivien also has a Biblical resonance: 'What evil have ye wrought?', and so has Vivien's appeal for shelter 'for mine innocency' (*MV*66, 82).[69] She awakens a sinister scriptural echo when she 'whispered' throughout the court (*MV*137).[70] Her 'sowing one ill hint from ear to ear' recalls 'the sower soweth the word' as well as her own origin in having been 'sown on the wind' (*MV*141).[71]

When Merlin 'walked with dreams and darkness' (*MV*188) he is placed among those 'who leave the paths of uprightness, to walk in the ways of darkness'.[72] The old man who 'went back to his old wild, and lived on grass' (*MV*647) reminds us of Nebuchadnezzar 'and he was driven from men, and did eat grass as oxen'.[73]

Because its theme is spiritual, *The Holy Grail* shows greater density of Biblical allusion than any other poem of the series. Here, indeed, it is fully at home insofar as the narrator, Percivale, and his listener, Ambrosius, are both monks, and the setting is the cloisters of a monastery. Related in the past tense but in the most personal mode of address, the second person singular, the Grail events and quests have an extraordinary vividness. Remote and immediate paradoxically blend. At three points there is an unusually archaic inflection: 'When first thou camest . . . for what is this / Thou thoughtest of thy prowess . . . Nay – but thou errest, Lancelot' (*HG*22,455,877).[74] These strikingly archaic expressions come approximately at the beginning, middle and end of the poem, and form a beautifully proportioned minor arch in the whole.

According to the legend, Joseph of Arimathea brought the Holy Vessel from which Jesus drank at the Last Supper to Britain.[75] Percivale recalls the legend in the words

> After the day of darkness, when the dead
> Went wandering o'er Moriah – the good saint
> Arimathæan Joseph, journeying brought
> To Glastonbury, where the winter thorn
> Blossoms at Christmas, mindful of our Lord.
> (*HG*49–53)

When Arthur returns to find his knights have sworn Grail vows without seeing the Holy Vessel, he asks, ironically echoing Christ's words: 'Have ye seen a cloud? / What go ye into the wilderness to see?' (*HG*286–7).[76] When Percivale reports 'all the heavens / Open'd and blazed with thunder such as seem'd / Shoutings of all the sons of God' (*HG*508–9) he echoes 'When the morning stars sang together, and all the sons of God shouted for joy'.[77] An experience that crowns his own quest is related in the words:

> For now I knew the veil had been withdrawn.
> Then in a moment when they blazed again
> Opening, I saw the least of little stars . . .
> I saw the spiritual city and all her spires
> And gateways in a glory like one pearl. (*HG*522–7)

Percivale has every right to feel exalted. In this heavenly revelation his quest finds fulfilment.[78] Lancelot, however, whom Percivale meets on his quest, is only grimly mindful of duty when he shouts: 'I have been the sluggard, and I ride apace, / For now there is a lion in the way' (*HG*641–2).[79]

Within the general pattern of archaism there are many seemingly incidental Biblical echoes and formulations. First made aware by his sister of the imminence of the Grail, Percivale 'spake of this / To all men' (*HG*130). On a summer night 'it came to pass' that Galahad would sit in the Siege Perilous, and then on hearing of bandits 'so the King arose and went' (*HG*179, 213). 'Then shall the tongue of the dumb sing' is glanced at in Arthur's assertion that 'Taliessin is our fullest throat of song, / And one hath sung and all the dumb will sing' (*HG*300).[80] Then 'Lo' is used twice by Arthur, thrice by Percivale (*HG*219, 286, 396, 416, 438).[81] The crowd call out to the departing knights 'God speed' (*HG*352).[82] At one point Percivale felt 'lifted up in heart' and at another 'lifting up mine eyes . . . I was thirsty unto death' (*HG*361, 375, 378).[83] The hermit to whom Percivale confesses 'made an end' (*HG*457). Finally, there is the coming of 'a sign from heaven' and Arthur's closing reference to 'the high God' (*HG*869, 914).

Tennyson's Biblical echoing becomes more selective in the poems following the Grail. Pelleas, once hailed as a 'pilot star', in the last sparkle of his innocence has a revelation of the fall of Camelot in which he himself is fated to play a part. So Pelleas

> lay,
> Till shaken by a dream, that Gawain fired
> The hall of Merlin, and the morning star
> Reel'd in the smoke, brake into flame, and fell
> (*PE*506-9)

It is not an accident that in approaching the end of the tragedy, the Biblical allusions should mainly refer to the Book of *Revelation*: 'And there fell a great star from heaven' and 'the name of the star is called Wormwood' and to him who beholds it 'was given the key of the bottomless pit'.[84] No wonder in the following idyll Pelleas swears by Hell in his challenge to Arthur (*LT*443). So for the aspiring Pelleas, the star of infinite hope and love knows no fulfilment. He therefore attempts to bring retribution on Arthur's world that he thinks has betrayed him.

Echoes of *Revelation* enhance the doom-laden atmosphere of *The Last Tournament* and the death of Tristram. 'For the hour of his judgment is come' reverberates in the Red Knight's threat to Arthur: 'Say his hour is come' (*LT*86).[85] 'Here is the patience and faith of the saints' is echoed by a sinister, unnamed 'swarthy one' who 'laughed shrilly, crying "Praise the patient saints"' (*LT*217).[86] 'A lake of fire burning with brimstone' is evoked by Dagonet's reproach to Tristram when 'ye play'd at ducks and drakes / With Arthur's vows on the great lake of fire' (*LT*345).[87] 'As the scorpions of the earth have power . . .' becomes part of the Red Knight's oath when he 'sware by the scorpion-worm that twists in hell, / And stings itself to everlasting death' (*LT*450).[88]

A complicated imagery conveys the reversion to savagery of Arthur's young knights:

> Then, echoing yell with yell, they fired the tower,
> Which half that autumn night, like the live North,
> Red-pulsing up thro' Alioth and Alcor,
> Made all above it, and a hundred meres
> About it, as the water Moab saw
> Come round by the East, and out beyond them flush'd
> The long low dune, and lazy-plunging sea.
>
> (*LT*477–83)

Here the remoteness suggested by the alien Arabic names of stars in the Great Bear turns to a remoteness of a different kind: the stone age barbarity in the image of blood-red water seen by the Moabites, who read the sign wrongly and consequently were slaughtered and their territory destroyed by fire.[89] The effect is to universalise and to make primordially immediate what has happened to the Red Knight. The process is continued to the paragraph end.

> Characteristically, Tennyson closes a recital of murder and arson with a phonaesthetically pleasing line, the summer snapshot of some childhood recollection; with 'the long low dune and lazy-plunging sea' we retreat from the yelling and the carnage into the calm rhythm and remote perspective of legend.[90]

Biblical allusion achieves further effects. Tristram, in saying to Dagonet 'I am but a fool to reason with a fool' (*LT*271) is reflecting 'Answer not a fool according to his folly, lest thou also be like him'.[91] In addressing Isolt in the words 'O my soul, be comforted' (*LT*569) Tristram, the composer of songs, speaks in the exalted language of the *Psalms*.[92]

Fearing the approaching doom to his realm, Arthur asks: 'Oft I seem as he / Of whom was written, "A sound is in his ears"?' (*LT*115) where we have to supply the baleful continuation: 'A dreadful sound is in his ears: in prosperity the destroyer shall come upon him'.[93] Here, as elsewhere, Tennyson's Biblical allusion is powerfully compressed. When Tristram speaks of Arthur at the beginning of his reign: 'then, his foot was on a stool / Shaped as a dragon; he seemed to me no man / But Michaël trampling Satan' (*LT*666–8) this fuses together 'I make thine enemies my footstool' and the decree 'Behold, I give unto you power to tread on serpents'.[94] In the same image, Old Testament and New are welded together because 'Michaël trampling Satan' alludes both to 'the dragon shalt thou trample under feet' and to 'Michaël and his angels fought against the dragon'.[95]

Many things testify to Tennyson's love for Shakespeare.[96] Lady Tennyson's diary for 4, 12 and 17 March 1856, records him reading *Hamlet*, *Twelfth Night*, *Much Ado*, and *Measure for Measure* respectively. Then on 19 March: 'A[lfred] said the exquisite song to me from Merlin Vivien [*Merlin and Vivien* 385–402]. He has set to work in earnest on the poem now'.[97] Clearly, reading Shakespeare helped Tennyson to attain a style at once vivid, dramatic and decorous.

Tennyson had more than usual difficulty in composing *Gareth and Lynette*, principally because of the 'snip snap' of the dialogue between the two chief characters.[98] One way of attaining a lively continuity in the repartee of the characters, and of suggesting the liveliness and immediacy of life at Camelot during Arthur's early days, is to interweave into the dialogues many of Shakespeare's colloquialisms. Tennyson does this with unobtrusive skill. 'Heaven yield her for it' (*GL*18) exclaims Gareth of his mother, in echo of 'And the gods yield you for't'.[99] 'An 'twere' but of the goose and golden eggs (*GL*40) is the Shakespearean contraction Bellicent employs in reply.[100] Her 'I charge thee by my love' (*GL*55) echoes 'On thy love, I charge thee'.[101]

Kay, Gareth, and then Lynette twice, use the exclamation 'God wot' (*GL*447, 550, 1038, 1299).[102] Characters who share the same idiom show that they belong to the same world of shared aspirations, ideals and values.

Kay uses the Shakespearean interjection 'Tut' three times, each time in a different combination: 'Tut an . . .', 'Tut, he was . . .', 'Tut, tell me not . . .' (*GL*463, 702, 715).[103] This reveals the character's tetchiness. Arthur's seneschal has another Shakespearean turn of phrase. Malory's Kay declares 'I will ride after my boy in the kitchen' but in his haste and petulance Tennyson's Kay shouts 'I will after my loud knave' (*GL*704).[104]

The fourth fool of the 'allegory' is 'never a whit more wise' than the other three (*GL*620).[105] Lynette adds menace to her tone when she speaks of Gareth being 'met with' and then 'with such a one' (*GL*760).[106] Shakespeare's 'belike' is employed by Kay, Lynette and Gareth (*GL*697, 1043, 1312) showing again how Tennyson covertly links characters and makes them inhabit a shared world.[107]

Adding to Gareth's exuberance at being released from his vow is his cry 'These news be mine' (*GL*529).[108] But Lynette attempts to dispense with him in her repeated cry 'Hence / Avoid . . . Avoid' *GL*733, 935).[109] However, there is a Shakespearean grace in her retraction: 'Sir, – and good faith . . .' (*GL*1133).[110] Lynette's 'Thy much folly . . .' (*GL*897) echoes Shakespeare's use of the adjective.[111] When she says 'Ay, truly of a truth, / And in a sort' (*GL*817)

Tennyson fuses Shakespeare with Malory's character, who declares 'Truly that is a truth'.[112] Shakespeare also provides the source for Gareth, who delares that no knight, not even Lancelot 'his great self', can defeat him (*GL*1153).[113] On his defeat by Lancelot, however, he declares with a fine dramatic gesture: 'Out, sword; we are thrown!' (*GL*1205).[114]

Tennyson's skill in echoing is nowhere more clearly and subtly evidenced than in the three passages from the *Idylls* strongly symbolic of time. Noon is a critical time in *Paradise Lost* and the *Idylls*. At noon Satan decides on his 'dire attempt'.[115] As a condition of her first separation from him, it is also the time when Eve agrees to meet Adam in the bower.[116] Giving way to temptation is easiest when appetite is at its greatest. After the zenith of life's 'day' things must inevitably decline. Thus it is not accidental that the same time enters into Guinevere's recollection of her first meeting with Lancelot. Then they

> Rode under groves that look'd a paradise
> Of blossom, over sheets of hyacinth
> That seem'd the heavens upbreaking thro' the earth,
> And on from hill to hill, and every day
> Beheld at noon in some delicious dale
> The silk pavilions of King Arthur raised
> For brief repast or afternoon repose.
> (*G*386–92)

Hyacinth is associated with Eve's bower before and after the Fall.[117] In Milton's manner, a 'delicious' dale extends the idea of deception to whatever paradise the mind may imagine.[118] Arthur's pavilions raised 'For brief repast or afternoon repose' echoes Eve's promise to return to Adam 'in best order to invite / Noontide repast, or afternoon's repose' with Milton's underlining: 'Thou never from that hour in Paradise / Found'st either sweet repast, or sound repose'.[119] So Arthur's paradise, like Adam's before him, becomes corrupt before it has scarce begun.

If the fall from grace takes place at noon, morning is also symbolic, because a May morning was the occasion for Modred's hatred of Lancelot. Here many literary echoes support Tennyson's invented incident:

> For thus it chanced one morn when all the court,
> Green-suited, but with plumes that mock'd the may,
> Had been, their wont, a-maying and return'd,
> That Modred still in green, all ear and eye,
> Climb'd to the high top of the garden-wall

> To spy some secret scandal if he might,
> And saw the Queen who sat betwixt her best
> Enid, and lissome Vivien, of her court
> The wiliest and the worst; and more than this
> He saw not, for Sir Lancelot passing by
> Spied where he couch'd, and as the gardener's hand
> Picks from the colewort a green caterpillar,
> So from the high wall and the flowering grove
> Of grasses Lancelot pluck'd him by the heel,
> And cast him as a worm upon the way;
>   (*G*21–35)

'One morn' distances the setting, which contrasts in time of day and year with the winter night that sets the main action of the idyll. The formula with which the episode opens ('it chanced') is Spenser, and Modred 'all ear and eye' is modelled on Milton's Adam being 'all ear' at the first words Eve utters.[120] A 'high top' is a feature of Milton's paradise.[121] In making Vivien the 'wiliest and the worst' Tennyson expands the epithet ('wily') he has used twice before for Vivien (*MV* 5, 147) in an exact imitation of Milton's two applications for Satan.[122] He creates the episode to fuse his two chief sources, Malory and *Mabinogion*, because Vivien originates in the former and Enid in the latter. That Modred is 'couched' plays on the fact that previously 'like a subtle beast' he 'lay couchant with his eyes upon the throne, / Ready to spring' (*G*10–12). In this verbal play there are again Satanic overtones.[123] Allusion and echo continue to the paragraph's end:

> But when he knew the Prince tho' marr'd with dust,
> He, reverencing king's blood in a bad man,
> Made such excuses as he might, and these
> Full knightly without scorn; for in those days
> No knight of Arthur's noblest dealt in scorn;
> But, if a man were halt or hunch'd, in him
> By those whom God had made full-limb'd and tall,
> Scorn was allow'd as part of his defect,
> And he was answer'd softly by the King
> And all his Table. So Sir Lancelot holp
> To raise the Prince, who rising twice or thrice
> Full sharply smote his knees, and smiled, and went:
> But, ever after, the small violence done
> Rankled in him and ruffled all his heart,
> As the sharp wind that ruffles all day long
> A little bitter pool about a stone
> On the bare coast. (*G*36–52)

Here 'king's blood', 'full knightly' and Modred's rising 'twice or thrice' are phrases from Malory.[124] 'Full sharply' is Chaucer.[125] The 'sharp wind' that introduces the closing simile, echoes Shakespeare's 'To run upon the sharp wind of the north'.[126] The image itself was suggested by what Tennyson saw at Bonchurch on the exposed southeastern coast of the Isle of Wight.[127] Modred's 'exposure' is all the more dramatic in that Tennyson breaks the paragraph with the image, in the same manner as Wordsworth.[128] Viewed from the perspective of the serial evolution of the *Idylls*, this is only the second such paragraph 'break'.[129]

Tennyson's highly allusive technique comes into play again after the break:

> But when Sir Lancelot told
> This matter to the Queen, at first she laugh'd
> Lightly, to think of Modred's dusty fall,
> Then shudder'd, as the village wife who cries
> 'I shudder, some one steps across my grave;'
> (*G* 52–6)

The last line echoes Francis Grose's observation: 'A person being suddenly taken with a shivering, is a sign that someone has just then walked over the spot of their future grave'.[130] Every echo here has been fully assimilated into Tennyson's verbal texture to present the impression that Modred's hatred for Lancelot is intrinsic to the legend. And this is what the skill behind Tennyson's technique has created.

Time of day is also part of the general allusiveness in another important event in the *Idylls*, Vivien's attempt to seduce Arthur:

> She hated all the knights, and heard in thought
> Their lavish comment when her name was named.
> For once, when Arthur walking all alone,
> Vext at a rumour issued from herself
> Of some corruption crept among his knights,
> Had met her, Vivien, being greeted fair,
> Would fain have wrought upon his cloudy mood
> With reverent eyes mock-loyal, shaken voice,
> And flutter'd adoration, and at last
> With dark sweet hints of some who prized him more
> Than who should prize him most; at which the King
> Had gazed upon her blankly and gone by:
> But one had watch'd and had not held his peace:
> It made the laughter of an afternoon
> That Vivien should attempt the blameless King.
> (*MV* 148–62)

Vivien merely 'heard in thought' what she takes to be 'lavish comment'.[131] She projects her own sense of envy and frustration upon the world. Arthur, like Eve in the garden, is walking all alone when Vivien, like Satan, makes her attempt.[132] He is walking alone in the first place because he is vexed at a rumour that she has originated. Already, in disturbing Arthur and in temporarily isolating him, she has accomplished much. It is the beginning of her hold over Camelot. Eve, when alone, could be corrupted by the serpent. Arthur cannot be, because he has already conquered the serpent dragon and uses it as his footstool (*LT*666). Here, however, he is 'vext' at the 'corruption' that has 'crept', serpent-fashion, among his knights.[133] Then, in echo of Malory, Vivien 'would fain have wrought' on Arthur.[134]

In the 'dark sweet hints of some who prized him more / Than who should prize him most' Vivien has suggested that Guinevere does not value Arthur sufficiently. As Adam 'Astonied stood and blank' when he saw Eve fallen, so Arthur had gazed upon Vivien 'blankly, and gone by'.[135] 'It made the laughter of an afternoon' obliquely places Vivien's attempt to seduce Arthur about midday. A whole afternoon filled with chat about the behaviour of Vivien shows a court already becoming corrupt without knowing it.

Tennyson terminates the incident with a formulation that points up the futility of Vivien's attempt. Just as Aeneas is *pius*, Arthur is 'the blameless King'.[136]

Settings: Natural and Man-made

'Natural description can have but little place in an epic. That of Vergil, when brought in as background to the human figures, is treated with his usual art, but cannot be parted from his story.'[1] In saying that the same observation applies to the *Idylls*, I am well aware of advancing a controversial view. Tennyson, according to the prevalent critical view, is indulging himself in his descriptions purely for their own sake and for his own pleasure. One comment on *The Holy Grail* was that it was 'too forced and artificial . . . this simplicity of conception contrasts strangely with the wealth and almost fantastic variety of the rhythms, and brilliancy of richly-wrought imagery'.[2] I am setting out on a hazardous enterprise in attempting to show that the descriptions in the *Idylls* are an intrinsic part of the story.

To start with descriptions of man-made settings, we shall first consider Enid's ruined castle:

> Then rode Geraint into the castle court,
> His charger trampling many a prickly star
> Of sprouted thistle on the broken stones.
> He look'd and saw that all was ruinous.
> Here stood a shatter'd archway plumed with fern;
> And here had fall'n a great part of a tower,
> Whole, like a crag that tumbles from the cliff,
> And like a crag was gay with wilding flowers:
> And high above a piece of turret stair,
> Worn by the feet that now were silent, wound
> Bare to the sun, and monstrous ivy-stems
> Claspt the gray walls with hairy-fibred arms,
> And suck'd the joining of the stones, and look'd
> A knot, beneath, of snakes, aloft, a grove.   (*MG* 312–25)

Here the feelings of ancient history, intertwined with recent pillage and destruction, are fused with present human action momentous for the future.

In *Mabinogion*, when Geraint follows the haughty knight to his castle:

> . . . the road they took was below the palace of Caerlleon, and across the ford of Usk; and they went along a fair, and even, and lofty ridge of ground, until they came to a town, and at the

extremity of the town they saw a Fortress and a Castle. And they
came to the extremity of the town.[3]

Into the purely descriptive passage of *Mabinogion* Tennyson introduces the human figure, making Geraint more complicated in mood,
and expertly picturing the composition of the town:

> And Prince Geraint, now thinking that he heard
> The noble hart at bay, now the far horn,
> A little vext at losing of the hunt,
> A little at the vile occasion, rode,
> By ups and downs, thro' many a grassy glade
> And valley, with fixt eye following the three.
> At last they issued from the world of wood,
> And climb'd upon a fair and even ridge,
> And show'd themselves against the sky, and sank.
> And thither came Geraint, and underneath
> Beheld the long street of a little town
> In a long valley, on one side whereof,
> White from the mason's hand, a fortress rose;
> And on one side a castle in decay,
> Beyond a bridge that spann'd a dry ravine:
> And out of town and valley came a noise
> As of a broad brook o'er a shingly bed
> Brawling, or like a clamour of the rooks
> At distance, ere they settle for the night.
> (*MG*232-50)

It is notable that anything vivid in the original, here the detail 'and
they went along a fair, and even, and lofty ridge of ground' is used.
Just as Tennyson's verse paragraph opened with an authentication
of Geraint that is also a subtle recapitulation of narrative details, so
it closes with an aural image reinforcing and framing a series of
specific visual images. This is landscape description of a very high
order.

Mabinogion later has a change of scene:

> And early in the day they left the wood, and they came to an
> open country, with meadows on one hand, and mowers mowing
> the meadows. And there was a river before them, and the horses
> bent down and drank the water. And they went up out of the
> river by a lofty steep; and there they met a slender stripling.

A little further on they reach 'a fortified town'.[4] Taking this as his
basis, Tennyson completes the picture of a whole town, and invests
everything with movement, light, colour and clarity:

> So thro' the green gloom of the wood they past,
> And issuing under open heavens beheld

A little town with towers, upon a rock,
And close beneath, a meadow gemlike chased
In the brown wild, and mowers mowing in it:
And down a rocky pathway from the place
There came a fair-hair'd youth, that in his hand
Bare victual for the mowers ... (*GE*195–202)

Again there is a three-dimensional deepening of texture and perspective that shows narrative and dramatic mastery.

We first become inextricably involved with Camelot when we experience it through the eyes and excited sensibilities of Gareth and his two rustic companions:

So, when their feet were planted on the plain
That broaden'd toward the base of Camelot,
Far off they saw the silver-misty morn
Rolling her smoke about the Royal mount,
That rose between the forest and the field.
At times the summit of the high city flash'd;
At times the spires and turrets half-way down
Prick'd thro' the mist; at times the great gate shone
Only, that open'd on the field below:
Anon, the whole fair city had disappear'd.
(*GL*184–93)

Clear outlines rising from a mist confuse a sense of distance and perspective, and this is what makes itself felt in the shifting pattern of alliteration. In the last two lines, amplifying the alliteration, all the emphasis comes down on 'Only', and the long 'o' alternates with the short. The focus is further distorted by the capitalisation of an adjective: 'Royal', echoing Bellicent's earlier description of hearing Arthur 'Kingly speak' (*GL*123).[5]

When Gareth and his companions reach Camelot the main gate comes into focus:

And there was no gate like it under heaven.
For barefoot on the keystone, which was lined
And rippled like an ever-fleeting wave,
The Lady of the Lake stood: all her dress
Wept from her sides as water flowing away;
But like the cross her great and goodly arms
Stretch'd under all the cornice and upheld:
And drops of water fell from either hand;
And down from one a sword was hung, from one
A censer, either worn with wind and storm;
And o'er her breast floated the sacred fish;
And in the space to left of her, and right,

64

Were Arthur's wars in weird devices done,
New things and old co-twisted, as if Time
Were nothing, so inveterately, that men
Were giddy gazing there; and over all
High on the top were those three Queens, the friends
Of Arthur, who should help him at his need.
   (*GL*209–26)

The heroic phrase 'under heaven' suggests the transcendental nature of this gate.[6] Gareth's view of it is dominated by the Lady of the Lake, reflecting Virgil's metaphor for the dress of Venus: 'and her robe flowed right down to her feet'.[7] Tennyson reminds us of 'The great and goodly cities thou buildest not' in his description of her extended arms.[8] The second last line, with its persistent monosyllables, seems to spread its weight evenly, like the three Queens balanced high on the top. Equilibrium is attained, but only just.

    Then those with Gareth for so long a space
Stared at the figures, that at last it seem'd
The dragon-boughts and elvish emblemings
Began to move, seethe, twine and curl: they call'd
To Gareth, 'Lord, the gateway is alive.'
   (*GL*227–31)

Here we can see how Tennyson creates new and bizarre compounds by hyphenation. 'Boughts' is Spenser, but it is attached to its equally outlandish owner by a hyphen. Then Tennyson's novel formation 'emblemings' is set off by an adjective first found in *Sir Gawain and the Green Knight*.[9] New things and old are 'co-twisted' into something equally disorienting and fascinating. When 'the dragon-boughts and elvish emblemings / Began to move, seethe, twine and curl', they disorient us in another way. The second line contains eight different vowels, seven of which are in the six verbs in the line. Four of the verbs are infinitives, and the first three have long vowels. The last, a short vowel, enhances the movement it describes. What is covert becomes overt in the next line as the rustics exclaim: 'Lord, the gateway is alive'.

Tennyson characteristically gives us an idea of Camelot as part of other business. This serves both to dramatise and tantalise. The action and drama is arrested for a moment and then continues. Perspective shifts continually between the speaker and his audience. As an example, I quote Arthur's rejection of Mark's gift:

    Then Arthur cried to rend the cloth, to rend
In pieces, and so cast it on the hearth.
An oak-tree smoulder'd there. 'The goodly knight!
What! shall the shield of Mark stand among these?'

> For, midway down the side of that long hall
> A stately pile, – whereof along the front,
> Some blazon'd, some but carven, and some blank,
> There ran a treble range of stony shields, –
> Rose, and high-arching overbrow'd the hearth.
> And under every shield a knight was named:
> For this was Arthur's custom in his hall;
> When some good knight had done one noble deed,
> His arms were carven only; but if twain
> His arms were blazon'd also; but if none,
> The shield was blank and bare without a sign
> Saving the name beneath; and Gareth saw
> The shield of Gawain blazon'd rich and bright,
> And Modred's blank as death; and Arthur cried
> To rend the cloth and cast it on the hearth.
>   (*GL*392–410)

Note how the paragraph begins and ends with the same detail. The description is framed by Arthur's command. Needless to say, Arthur's custom is Tennyson's invention, and it serves to introduce the very different natures of the two knights with whom Gareth is especially concerned, his brothers. The interior of the hall itself is not presented through detailed description but through the deeds that are enacted or commemorated in it.

As Lynette leaves Camelot in wrath the two great entries of the hall seem to dramatise her passion:

> Now two great entries open'd from the hall,
> At one end one, that gave upon a range
> Of level pavement where the King would pace
> At sunrise, gazing over plain and wood;
> And down from this a lordly stairway sloped
> Till lost in blowing trees and tops of towers;
> And out by this main doorway past the King.
> But one was counter to the hearth, and rose
> High that the highest-crested helm could ride
> Therethro' nor graze: and by this entry fled
> The damsel in her wrath . . .   (*GL*650–60)

The dimension of the entrance into Arthur's hall through which 'the highest-crested helm could ride' may be impressive, but fades into insignificance when compared to the entrance into Milton's hell, where:

> the gates wide open stood,
> That with extended wings a bannered host
> Under spreading ensigns marching might pass through

66

With horse and chariots ranked in loose array,
So wide they stood. (*PL2*, 884-8)

The double entrance into Arthur's hall is similar to that of the Gods upon Olympus.[10] That one entry 'gave upon' a range is the use of an elegant Gallicism.[11] Note how the first six lines of the passage culminate in the soft-contoured and mellifluous 'Till lost in blowing trees and tops of towers', which seems to fade off into unbounded distance.

Camelot is also revealed through the twelve battles Arthur fought against the Saxons. First there is the occasion when Balin is received back into the Order:

Thereafter, when Sir Balin enter'd hall,
The Lost one Found was greeted as in Heaven
With joy that blazed itself in woodland wealth
Of leaf, and gayest garlandage of flowers,
Along the walls and down the board; they sat,
And cup clash'd cup; they drank and some one sang,
Sweet-voiced, a song of welcome, whereupon
Their common shout in chorus, mounting, made
Those banners of twelve battles overhead
Stir, as they stirr'd of old, when Arthur's host
Proclaim'd him Victor, and the day was won.
(*BB*77-87)

Here the battles are celebrated by banners that stir at the shout of welcome accorded Sir Balin. According him the title of 'Sir' already tells us that the prodigal son is welcomed home.[12] As Walter Nash observes:

Stylistically, this is one of the poem's bravura passages, propounded with a studied elevation of manner. One symptom of this is an increase in phonetic density, resolving itself mainly in alliterative patterns. Such patterns are on the whole symmetrical, picking up the outlines of conjoint phrases, as in '*w*oodland *w*ealth of leaf' and '*g*ayest *g*arlandage of flowers', or balancing the pre- and post-caesural halves of a line, as in 'Their *c*ommon shout in *c*horus, *m*ounting, *m*ade . . .' The symmetry is also apparent in the syntactic structure. Thus, there are parallel adverbials governed by a single verb . . . There is also a counterpoise of verb and verb . . . Out of these symmetries, a semantic pattern grows. 'Some one' sings, and his song is taken up in a 'common' chorus. He is 'sweet-voiced', but the choric gesture is a 'shout'. The 'shout' makes the banners 'stir, as they stirr'd of old', when Arthur's host 'proclaim'd him Victor'. The one, the many, singing, shouting, or proclaiming, have their due place in the music of the Order, in a ritual counterpoise which is even reflected in the Biblical allusion to the 'Lost one Found'.[13]

Arthur's military prowess is celebrated not only by banners but also by another feature of his hall:

> Where twelve great windows blazon Arthur's wars,
> And all the light that falls upon the board
> Streams thro' the twelve great battles of our King.
> Nay, one there is, and at the eastern end,
> Wealthy with wandering lines of mount and mere,
> Where Arthur finds the brand Excalibur.
> And also one to the west, and counter to it,
> And blank: and who shall blazon it? when and how? –
> O there, perchance, when all our wars are done,
> The brand Excalibur will be cast away.
>
> (*HG*248–57)

The twelve battles are windows letting in light, because they have been accomplished against the heathen or forces of darkness. The hall also contains a window to the east and the sunrise, celebrating Excalibur. The window to the west and sunset is necessarily blank.

Camelot, which Merlin 'built / To music' (*GL*272) tells of an ample, joyous life. In hard contrast to it is Pellam's forest refuge:

> the castle of a King, the hall
> Of Pellam, lichen-bearded, grayly draped
> With streaming grass . . . low-built but strong;
> The ruinous donjon as a knoll of moss,
> The battlement overtopt with ivytods,
> A home of bats, in every tower an owl.
>
> (*BB*326–31)

The hall of Pellam is a choking and furtive place redolent of death. It cannot be placed in perspective. In Pellam's hall one element shows diminishment, the ruinous donjon (a doublet of 'dungeon') likened to 'a knoll of moss'. The 'lichen-bearded' hall suggests Pellam's age and eccentric relic-worship. 'The battlement overtopt with ivytods' is deliberately unmetrical. Tennyson easily could have written 'O'er-topt with ivytods' but then the uncanny effect would have been lost.[14] Clearly this hall stands in total opposition to Camelot.

As the quoted passages have shown, descriptions of man-made settings are interwoven with natural features, and both provide scenes for human beings to move in. It is only by abstraction that we can separate out compositional elements, among which trees and woodland play an important part, as they do in Malory.

Specifically named trees, for instance, are used most effectively by

Malory. On one occasion Lancelot 'rode into a deep forest, and thereby in a slade, he saw four knights hoving under an oak'.[15] He is involved in other incidents at a high elm, and at some apple trees.[16] Once La Beale Isoud sticks a sword to the hilt in a plum tree.[17] Tennyson also takes every opportunity to be specific. Different from both is *Mabinogion*, which typically restricts itself to generalised description:

> and when they left the forest, they came to a vast plain, in the centre of which was a group of thickly tangled copse-wood; and from out thereof they beheld three horsemen.[18]

Tennyson renders the scene in far more gradation of shading:

> did Enid, keeping watch, behold
> In the first shallow shade of a deep wood,
> Before a gloom of stubborn-shafted oaks,
> Three other horsemen waiting ... (*GE*118–21)

The idyll in which trees and woodland play the most important part is the central, *Balin and Balan*. Alder and poplar help King Arthur, when he comes on the identical twins, to distinguish Balin from Balan:

> So coming to the fountain-side beheld
> Balin and Balan sitting statuelike,
> Brethren, to right and left the spring, that down,
> From underneath a plume of lady-fern,
> Sang, and the sand danced at the bottom of it.
> And on the right of Balin Balin's horse
> Was fast beside an alder, on the left
> Of Balan Balan's near a poplartree. (*BB*21–8)

'The image begins in nature and ends in heraldry; and the effect is both charming and admonitory.'[19] When Arthur challenges they answer in unison, but the king easily defeats them. Neither consoles the other, and they resume their stance beside the carolling fountain, remaining in a kind of magic circle within the forest, the 'fringe of coppice round them' (*BB*44), until an appropriately spangled pursuivant appears with a summons from Camelot.[20]

In heraldic parlance to be savage, salvage or sauvage means a *silvaticus*, a man of the woods. When Balin wishes to substitute Guinevere's simple crest for his elaborate feral one, it is because of his need to replace a forest symbol: 'this rough beast upon my shield, / Langued gules, and tooth'd with grinning savagery' (*BB*193).[21] But when he 'rode the skyless woods' (*BB*287) he has entered again the fabled forest of romance

> Whose loftie trees, yclad with summers pride
> Did spread so broad, that heavens light did hide,

Not perceable with power of any starr[22]

and

> where highest woods, impenetrable
> To star or sun-light, spread their umbrage broad,
> And brown as evening.[23]

As part of such a fallen world, Balin disregards a woodman's warning, calling him a 'churl', the same brutal term he has just applied to himself. The word becomes a distorting and reflecting echo of his own guilt (*BB*281, 290, 297, 302). It is not surprising, therefore, that forest spectres soon beset him. A demon of the woods appears, and in another distorted reflection of himself, a sardonic knight called Garlon.[24] At one point Balin bursts his spear against a forest bough, an action symbolising his loss of knighthood (*BB*324). This is a necessary adjunct to entering Pellam's hall in the heart of the forest. In being 'lichen-bearded', a 'knoll of moss' and 'overtopt with ivy-tods' this appalling place is an example of forest decay (*BB*326–31). During the night Balin is tormented by snake dreams and the forest becomes alive. In a repeated motif, leaves 'Laid their green faces flat against the panes' and 'sprays grated, and the canker'd boughs without / Whined in the wood' (*BB*338–40, 378–80).[25] After destroying Garlon, Balin runs from the castle and to complete his escape dives beneath the boughs (*BB*417). He is so ashamed of his behaviour that he hangs his shield high on a branch, an action that is a chivalric disgrace (*BB*426).[26] When Vivien appears, she is no maid of the greenwood. 'The wholesome music of the wood / Was dumbed' by her singing as she rode along (*BB*430).[27] 'The new leaf ever pushes off the old' she sings with a twisted meaning (*BB*436).

One particular tree, an elm, plays an accidentally important part in the action. Its foliage so attracts Vivien that she notices the shield of Balin hanging on it. Again there is the brief expression of a full picture:

> Then they reach'd a glade
> Where under one long lane of cloudless air
> Before another wood, the royal crown
> Sparkled, and swaying upon a restless elm
> Drew the vague glance of Vivien
>   (*BB*453–7)

Nash comments on this passage as follows:

> This looks like an ordinary piece of verse-reportage, yet the lines have a power, not uncommon in the *Idylls*, to create the sort of image that the reader sees while his attention is distracted; the impression of movement against stillness, precise effect against blurred consciousness. It is phonaesthetic features that

give a contour to this after-image. The l-motif, or consonant-plus-l, informs the whole passage: '*gl*ade', '*l*ong', '*l*ane', '*cl*oud-*l*ess', 'spar*kl*ed', 'rest*l*ess', 'e*l*m', '*gl*ance', and is supported by the casual alliterations of '*r*oyal', and '*r*estless', '*s*parkled' and '*s*waying', '*v*ague' and '*V*ivien', the assonances in '*gl*ade' and '*l*ane', 'sw*a*ying' and 'v*a*gue', and the morphological parallel of 'cloudless' and 'restless'. All this provides a unifying frame for the perspectives and oppositions of the diction. The items 'cloudless', 'restless', 'sparkled', 'swaying', 'vague' are brought into a counter-changing flicker of meaning. 'Cloudless' opposes 'restless', for one suggests stillness, the other movement. 'Sparkled' opposes 'vague', for one is sharp-focused, the other blurred. 'Vague' is concordant with 'swaying', in that both suggest 'undefined', 'not exactly located'. 'Swaying' is obviously concordant with 'restless'. 'Restless' is in concord with 'sparkled', in that both convey a sense of intermittent impulse. 'Sparkled' accords with 'cloudless', in the common association of bright light. 'Cloudless' thus opposes 'restless', which, however, accords with 'sparkled', which is in accord with 'cloudless'. 'Vague' is concordant with 'swaying', which is in accord with 'restless', which accords with 'sparkled', which, however, opposes 'vague'. There is a fascinating chop and change of associations, a semantic play occurring within the definition of a phonaesthetic field.[28]

No wonder the elm Vivien sees, arrests her attention.

Balin admits he is unworthy to bear Guinevere's crest on his shield and in sad identification with his old name and crest he says 'here I dwell / Savage among the savage woods, here die' (*BB*478).

While Balin and Balan lie dying, they express their contempt for Vivien, who has helped to bring about their fatal combat, by saying 'She dwells among the woods' (*BB*603). She, on the other hand, celebrates her triumph over them when she 'leapt her palfrey o'er the fallen oak' (*BB*576). Gone to their deaths like Babes in the Woods, the brothers appropriately die in them. In *Balin and Balan* woodland gives us more than atmosphere. It is an essential unifying and projecting element in Balin's disintegration and fall.

In the enchanted 'wild woods' of Broceliande, the oak is also the means of Vivien's triumph over Merlin in *Merlin and Vivien*.[29] By the exercise of 'charm' Vivien traps him in an oak (*MV*3,404,892,934, 967). From Pliny or Selden, Tennyson would know that the Druids venerated the oak. Thus it is ironic that one of their descendants is trapped in the tree their religion considers most sacred.[30]

Trees are a feature of a hermitage where Lancelot and Lavaine stay overnight on the way to Camelot. Malory describes this place only after the wounded Lancelot has found haven there:

> and so by fortune they came to that hermitage the which was under a wood, and a great cliff on the other side, and a fair water running under it.[31]

In the poem the journey and destination are idyllic, ending in the lines:[32]

> And in the meadows tremulous aspen-trees
> And poplars made a noise of falling showers
>   (*LE*408–9)

It is to this sanctuary that Lancelot flees after being severely wounded:

>   and there, in daily doubt
> Whether to live or die, for many a week
> Hid from the wide world's rumour by the grove
> Of poplars with their noise of falling showers,
> And ever-tremulous aspen-trees, he lay
>   (*LE*518–22)

In these lines the aspen and the poplar change the places they occupied in the previous passage, and so help to express a constant gentle movement that both suggests how ill Lancelot is, and phonaesthetically effects the healing process.

A poplar is also an important tree for Elaine. She is forbidden to go beyond 'the cape / That has the poplar on it' but when she dreams of her own approaching death she asks to be allowed to 'pass at last / Beyond the poplar and far up the flood, / Until I find the palace of the King' (*LE*1033, 1043).

Yews are a feature of Astolat. Inappropriately enough it is among the yews that Gawain attempts to seduce Elaine (*LE*641).[33] Lancelot's last meeting with her on his departure day is also made severely formal by the garden yew setting (*LE*918). The same tree sets the scene for Percivale's narration of the Grail quest:[34]

>   and as they sat
> Beneath a world-old yew-tree, darkening half
> The cloisters, on a gustful April morn
> That puff'd the swaying branches into smoke
> Above them, ere the summer when he died,
> The monk Ambrosius question'd Percivale.
>   (*HG*12–17)

Pelleas is overcome by the noonday sun in the forest of Dean but saw

> Near him a mound of even-sloping side,
> Whereon a hundred stately beeches grew,

And here and there great hollies under them;
But for a mile all round was open space,
And fern and heath: and slowly Pelleas drew
To that dim day, then binding his good horse
To a tree, cast himself down; and as he lay
At random looking over the brown earth
Thro' that green-glooming twilight of the grove,
It seem'd to Pelleas that the fern without
Burnt as a living fire of emeralds,
So that his eyes were dazzled looking at it.
Then o'er it crost the dimness of a cloud
Floating, and once the shadow of a bird
Flying, and then a fawn; and his eyes closed
    (*PE*23–38)

Few forests sound so inviting. The peculiar richness of sound texture in the passage comes out of the interlacing of several kinds of phonological repetition, especially consonants from the 'soft' end of the scale (liquids, nasals, fricatives, aspirates) all of which lengthen the vowels, which are superbly varied. At the close all is so still that the most timid and acute creature of the forest, a fawn, appears. And so Pelleas dreams. At this point Ettarre and her troop ride through the bracken. 'Damsels errant' may initially sound romantic, but the epithet is of dubious worth after Vivien's entry into the poem has been announced in the same way (*BB*432, *PE*61).[35] 'O wild and of the woods' is Ettarre's pointed greeting to him, and such is the effect of her appearance that he 'nor slept that night for pleasure in his blood, / And green wood-ways, and eyes among the leaves' (*PE*95, 131). In abrupt contrast to the relaxed fluidity of the opening is the frenzied movement at the close, after Pelleas discovers Ettarre with Gawain, and feels it to be a betrayal of himself. Then Pelleas rode:

           shouting, 'False,
And false with Gawain!'....
   ... and fled on, and hill and wood
Went ever streaming by him till the gloom,
That follows on the turning of the world,
Darken'd the common path: he twitch'd the reins,
And made his beast that better knew it, swerve
Now off it and now on; but when he saw
High up in heaven the hall that Merlin built,
Blackening against the dead-green stripes of even,
'Black nest of rats,' he groan'd, 'ye build too high.'
    (*PE*529–44)

Tristram is also governed by his association with woodland. To emphasise this, Tennyson changes his name. Malory has Sir Tristram de Liones.[36] Tennyson's knight rides into the tournament as 'Sir Tristram of the Woods' (*LT*177).

> After Tristram has won the ruby carcanet
> thro' the slowly-mellowing avenues
> And solitary passes of the wood
> Rode Tristram toward Lyonnesse and the west.
> Before him fled the face of Queen Isolt
> With ruby-circled neck, but evermore
> Past, as a rustle or twitter in the wood
> Made dull his inner, keen his outer eye
> For all that walk'd, or crept, or perch'd, or flew.
> Anon the face, as, when a gust hath blown,
> Unruffling waters re-collect the shape
> Of one that in them sees himself, return'd;
> But at the slot or fewmets of a deer,
> Or ev'n a fall'n feather, vanish'd again.
>   (*LT*360–72)

According to Walter Nash:

> . . . the opaque word 'fewmets' enables the poet to preserve a romantic eloquence that would hardly survive 'droppings'. . . Tennyson makes occasional use of remote items of vocabulary as a method of fixing the reader's attention. The technical terms 'slot' and 'fewmets' are thus a kind of summary shorthand, stressing Tristram's skill as a hunter; a skill so profound and intuitive that he practises the craft instinctively, noting small signs even while he is apparently engrossed with another matter, his love-relationship with Isolt. The fine simile of still, reflective water periodically disturbed by gusts of wind projects the psychology of the man who is at home in his own domain and whose attention is automatically redirected by shifts in the familiar setting.[37]

What helps us to feel the reflection here, the inner world exactly reflecting the outer, is the symmetry and exact line division of 'Made dull his inner, keen his outer eye' and the cumulative discrimination in 'For all that walk'd, or crept, or perch'd, or flew' which is a mirror of Milton's 'Creatures that lived and moved, and walked or flew'.[38]

There are many distractions in what follows:

> So on for all that day from lawn to lawn
> Thro' many a league-long bower he rode. At length
> A lodge of intertwisted beechen-boughs
> Furze-cramm'd, and bracken-rooft, the which himself

Built for a summer day with Queen Isolt
Against a shower, dark in the golden grove
Appearing, sent his fancy back to where
She lived a moon in that low lodge with him:
  (*LT*373–80)

The protraction and monotony of the journey are phonaesthetically suggested in the first two lines. His guilty desire is projected on the outer world so that it is as if it is through a continuous bower that he rides. There are many distracting elements in the vocabulary and syntax, all reflecting Tristram's inner conflict as he ponders how 'to smoothe / And sleek his marriage over to the Queen' (*LT*390). 'But thou, thro' ever harrying thy wild beasts – . . . art grown wild beast thyself' (*LT*630–2) is Isolt's rejoinder when Tristram reveals only a predator's interest in her. However, just before Mark murders Tristram, the two erstwhile lovers are sentimental about the old days together spent in the forest: 'Now talking of their woodland paradise, / The deer, the dews, the fern, the founts, the lawns' (*LT*719–20). Here the change of vowels evokes the colour of those lost days and the progressive alliterations ('*d*eer', '*d*ews', '*f*ern', '*f*ounts', '*l*awns') a paradisal order their present situation lacks.[39] Only a few moments later, Mark's axe falls.

Thus trees and woodland serve as compositional elements in the same way as the Forest of Arden does for Shakespeare, to convey mood and set scenes for human action. In this respect Victorian poets and painters are alike.[40] What is particularly remarkable in Tennyson is that the natural scene reflects even the human nature of the protagonists in the story. A detailed study of Tennyson's descriptions therefore does not bear out the widespread criticism that they are overdone at the cost of characterisation, and the dramatic movement of the story. They appear, rather, as inseparably bound up with both, and not a mere self-indulgence that violates the artistry of composition.

[5]

Language, Metaphor and Simile

It is a commonplace that the language of a poetic work offers a richer and more varied field for investigation than any other of its elements. Among many possible approaches I am restricting myself to two. First, to examine striking passages in the context in which they occur, and to comment on their use of language and linguistic techniques. Second, to consider Tennyson's language in four aspects: i) his most striking creations, and how these come about; ii) the special vocabulary that Tennyson employs for Arthur's chivalry; iii) Tennyson's creative use of conjunctions; iv) a study of one of his basic images and its fusion with his basic unit of composition, the paragraph. The fusion of language and thought, and its articulation into paragraphs, is a characteristic feature of the *Idylls*. In this respect it differs markedly from many other long poems, notably the contemporaneous *The Ring and the Book*.

Tennyson is fond of recovering useful words that have been discarded or have gone out of use with changes in fashion and culture. These are mainly qualitative words, which were current during the late medieval and Renaissance periods in that 'golden age' when Arthur, as the age's presiding spirit, could be thought to have ruled his kingdom. This recovery of the past serves two purposes. It brings back into use something otherwise lost. It also ensures that the whole language remains healthy. One regards with awe the Victorian confidence with language: Carlyle, Tennyson, Browning, Dickens come immediately to mind. A third aspect of this recovery of language is that it enables the poet not just to renovate what he needs for his special purpose. So radical has his creativity become, that by observing the rules that lie behind language formation, he actually makes or fashions a language of his own. Tennyson shares this radical power with other great poets, for example, Virgil, Spenser, Shakespeare, Milton. What I intend to do is to trace this development in some classes of Tennyson's language. There are, basically, only two ways in which language can be modified or changed (all the roots having already come into existence) and this is by the addition of a prefix or suffix.

Tennyson uses the common prefixes in his creation of vocabulary:

'dis-', 'mis-', 'un-', and occasionally those less common: 'over-', 'ever-', 'all-'.[1]

Malory has several unusual forms in 'dis-'.[2] Tennyson has several words prefixed this way, but four are exceptional. In a fine fanciful flight of aspiration respecting his mother, Gareth hopes to

> Weary her ears with one continuous prayer
> Until she let me fly discaged to sweep
> In ever-highering eagle-circles up
> To the great Sun of Glory. (*GL*19–22)

When Geraint and Edyrn first do battle, 'each, dishorsed and drawing, lash'd at each' and after Balin in his blind panic had burst his lance, he 'dishorsed himself' (*MG*563, *BB*325). Pelleas, in his anguish at finding Ettarre and Gawain asleep together, had exclaimed: 'Ye, that so dishallow the holy sleep, / Your sleep is death' (*PE*437).[3] Not long after, Lancelot tells Pelleas that his request for death because he lacks a sword is not true. He does indeed possess one: 'Yea, between thy lips – and sharp, / But here I will disedge it by thy death' (*PE*566).[4]

On occasion Malory uses the prefix 'mis-'.[5] Gareth tells Lynette that he prefers to fight twenty combats 'Than hear thee so missay me and revile' (*GL*923). Geraint tells Enid she is not 'all mismated to a yawning clown' (*GE*426). Vivien accuses Merlin of 'misfaith' (*MV*530). As accords with myth, Merlin has an alternative fate to being seduced by Vivien. Creating the Siege Perilous does not make the magician immune from it, any more than did wings for Daedalus. According to Percivale 'once by misadvertence Merlin sat / In his own chair, and so was lost' (*HG*175).[6] Isolt, envious of Guinevere for having 'sinn'd against the highest' in preferring Lancelot to Arthur, reflects that she has been 'misyoked with such a want of man' as Mark, that she could 'hardly sin against the lowest' in preferring Tristram (*LT*567).[7]

Malory's frequent use of 'un-' helped to suggest many ingenious forms to Tennyson. 'Unmockingly' Merlin ends his speech to Gareth (*GL*288). In echo of Malory, Gareth tells Kay that he is 'The most ungentle knight in Arthur's hall' (*GL*738). Lynette warns that the last adversary her champion must fight is a 'monster unsubduable' (*GL*837). Balin admits that his name must sound 'unmelodious' to Arthur, and when he escapes from Pellam's hall he is glad to find his charger 'yet unlamed' (*BB*50, 422). With his quest still unaccomplished, it is Balan who hears his brother's yell 'Unearthlier than all shriek of bird and beast' resound in the forest (*BB*538).[8] Merlin tells Vivien she lives 'uncharm'd' because previous practitioners of the spell are now dead: 'The feet unmortised

77

from their ankle-bones' (*MV*548, 550). On visiting the wounded Lancelot, Elaine finds him lying 'unsleek, unshorn' (*LE*810). Guinevere wonders why Ettarre wears such an 'unsunny' face for Pelleas, following his win, and at the close she cannot understand why Pelleas is not able to accept other than 'unfrowardly' a fall from Lancelot (*PE*173, 585). It is 'unruffling' waters that for a moment are smooth enough to reflect Tristram's image in them, and 'Unsay it, unswear' demands Isolt after Tristram has spoken frivolously about their feelings for one another (*LT*369, 636).[9]

Several idylls have special verbal nuances of their own. In *Merlin and Vivien* as part of the process of activating his vocabulary and to create and enhance dramatic tension, Tennyson has several words prefixed with 'over-'.[10] Guinevere declares to Vivien

> Peace, child! of overpraise and overblame
> We choose the last. Our noble Arthur, him
> Ye scarce can overpraise.   (*MV*88–90)

Then Merlin suggests an 'overstrained affection' on Vivien's part might induce her to try out the spell on him (*MV*520). 'Overtrue a tale' is how Vivien dismisses Merlin's defence of Sir Valence (*MV*718). Ironically, she goes on to ask of Valence: 'shall we call him overquick / To crop his own sweet rose before the hour?' (*MV*722). Then Merlin feels that it is only an 'over-fineness' that would see faults in Arthur. Thus it is not surprising that being 'overtalk'd and overworn' is an appropriate description of the magician's fate (*MV*794, 963).[11]

'Ever-' is a prefix Tennyson frequently uses.[12] One small feature of *The Last Tournament* is that it has a greater density of hyphenated and therefore polysyllabic compounds than any other of the series. This loads the lines to suggest phonaesthetically the decay in autumn. Three compounds in 'ever-' are part of this process. Arthur speaks of the heathen as being 'that ever-climbing wave, / Hurl'd back again so often in empty foam' (*LT*92–3). Tristram, when he enters the tournament, appears 'wearing but a holly spray for crest, / With ever-scattering berries' (*LT*172–3). Balefully, however, when he rides towards Lyonnesse and Mark's wife it is under an 'ever-showering leaf' (*LT*491).[13]

Tennyson's suffixing is as important as his prefixing in giving a constant sense of shaping and structuring, and again the main suffixes have a basis in Malory. Here I shall discuss Tennyson's use of '-less' and '-ful'.[14]

Tennyson strikingly frames the first composed of his series with words suffixed by '-less'. Bedivere tells his lord, 'It is not meet, Sir King, to leave thee thus, / Aidless, alone, and smitten thro' the helm' and later he admits, 'I, the last, go forth companionless' (*PA*209,404). 'Aidless' has an unblemished pedigree, being used previously by Shakespeare and Milton, whereas 'companionless' first appears in published literature in Tennyson's poem.[15]

Lynette tells a baron that Gareth is a 'frontless kitchen knave' and Death is said to be 'crowned with fleshless laughter' (*GL*839,1348). A 'blindless' casement helps Geraint to dream, and there is a 'lustreless' fish in the palace pool (*MG*71,649). In his anger Geraint leaves some mowers 'dinnerless'; at one point the measure of the separation between Geraint and Enid is that they remain 'apart by all the chamber's width, and mute / As creatures voiceless thro' the fault of birth'; and one of Doorm's band drives the dust against Enid's 'veilless' eyes (*GE*234,266,529). Balin speaks with pain of the three 'kingless' years he has just spent; Arthur's ambassadors report that Pellam is as 'Christless' a foe as any he has had to deal with; as he rides into them Balin is ominously greeted by 'skyless' woods; and it is 'one long lane of cloudless air' down which Vivien comes riding as she enters the series (*BB*61,94,288,454). Merlin tells Vivien her accusations are 'proofless' (*MV*700). Lancelot 'marvelled at the wordless man' he found at Astolat; to reach it he has crossed many 'bushless downs'; later Arthur 'seeing the homeless trouble' in Lancelot's eyes, feels sorry for his great knight, who is 'wifeless and heirless' (*LE*171,270,398,1354,1360). Percivale's sister sends 'the deathless passion in her eyes' into Galahad, and 'hornless unicorns' are one sign of the devastating effect of the Grail on Camelot (*HG*163,714). Gawain boasts that he will slice any competitor 'handless by the wrist' (*PE*330). Guinevere grows ever more guilty 'Till ev'n the clear face of the guileless King . . . became her bane' and as she recollects her first meeting with Arthur it is to have thought him 'Cold, / High, self-contained, and passionless' (*G*84,403).[16]

As a balance or complement to his suffixing with '-less', Tennyson uses a number of rarities suffixed with '-ful'. It is in a 'showerful' spring that Gareth watches the river in spate; his mother wonders if he is willing to leave his 'easeful biding' at home for Camelot, but when he arrives, it is to see everywhere a 'healthful' people (*GL*2, 126,308). Enid prefers to watch Geraint's 'mightful hand striking great blows' than see him idle at home; later he feels anguish in his 'manful breast' at suspecting his wife, and he is 'a little spleenful yet' as he reaches the enemy's town (*MG*95,121,293). Then a reformed Edyrn believes his nature's 'prideful sparkle in the blood' is now under control (*GE*826). Vivien admits a partial truth to Balin when she tells him she flies a 'lustful' king (*BB*467).[17] Merlin experiences a 'presageful gloom' lasting three days (*MV*318). As a monk Percivale is now far from 'noiseful arms' as 'on a gustful April morn' he tells Ambrosius about the Grail. His fellow monk later recollects only 'mirthful sayings' about the world beyond the monastery (*HG*1, 14, 555). Isolt tells Tristram she is not 'prayerful' like his Breton wife (*LT*602). Finally, Guinevere becomes so guilty that she finds unbearable even the 'trustful courtesies' of domestic life (*G*85).[18]

For his characters Tennyson devises a special vocabulary of chivalric rank. Arthur has 'kinglihood' of which he modestly conceals any outward sign at the beginning, and at the close he commits one last act of 'kinghood' (*CA*50, *PA*163).[19] This variation on 'king' frames the entire narrative action of the poem. 'Kinglihood' symbolises a coming splendour, the assumption of a special power, 'kinghood' the regal office Arthur is now to vacate. Lynette declares Gareth is 'kingliest of all kitchen knaves' in echo of Malory's lively comparatives and superlatives.[20] Balin plaintively speaks of the three 'kingless' years he has spent exiled in woodland (*BB*61).

Tennyson is equally creative with next in rank, prince. Twice there is the rare plural 'princedoms' as a small frame in his opening idyll to show that Arthur's power supersedes all others (*CA*18, 517). Bellicent miscalculates when she thinks her son will be 'too princely proud' to go as a scullion to Camelot (*GL*158). When Geraint goes to fight Edyrn

> Yniol's rusted arms
> Were on his princely person, but thro' these
> Princelike his bearing shone.   (*MG*543–5)

Here Tennyson achieves a special effect by creating a new compound and placing it in the most emphatic position in the line.[21] Finally, Vivien assumes that Balin's abandoned shield is borne by some 'lord-prince of Arthur's hall' and when she meets the knight, she addresses him with flattering clumsiness as 'Sir Prince' (*BB*459, 470).

Naturally, there are several variations on the rank of knight. Tennyson's *Morte d'Arthur* uses the Malory words 'knightly' and 'unknightly'. Never again shall we 'Delight our souls with talk of knightly deeds' laments Arthur to Bedivere. Later he addresses him 'Unknightly, traitor-hearted' and towards the close, in a bold periphrasis, the king's moustache and beard are 'the knightly growth that fring'd his lips' (*PA*187, 288, 388).[22]

Lynette tells Arthur that those keeping Lyonors shut in her castle merely follow 'the fashion of that old knight-errantry'; and in a way that was 'all unknightlike' Evening Star stooped to wrestling in his combat with Gareth (*GL*614, 1122).[23] Balin is 'all glad, /

Knightlike, to find his charger yet unlamed' and the minstrel blown into Tintagel tells that out of 'naked knightlike purity' Lancelot worships no maiden but the great queen herself (*BB*422, *MV*11). Isolt refers to Lancelot as 'this knightliest of all knights' in order to taunt Tristram (*LT*706). When Lancelot apologises 'full knightly' to Modred for his discourtesy, the form again derives from Malory. Tennyson also builds on Malory's compound 'knights-errant' with his own when Arthur asserts to Guinevere that he was 'first of all the kings who drew / The knighthood-errant of this realm' (*G*93, 458).[24]

The knightly title 'Sir' is put to a number of significant uses in the serial poem. As in Malory, there is 'Sir King' for Arthur (*CA*148, *GL*327, 343, 357, 360, 434, 583, 613, 632, *BB*91, *LE*93, *PE*8, *PA*208). The distribution is significant: eight instances in *Gareth and Lynette* are part of the light-heartedness of this idyll. The term's relative scarcity later, and its omission from certain idylls, is a measure, among other things, of the decline in courtesy later in the cycle.

Tennyson's insertion or omission of knightly title is masterly, as can be seen in Gareth, Gawain, Percivale, Tristram, Balin and Lancelot. Only when knighted by the king is Gareth called Sir (*GL*609). Then, to underline his newly created rank and the responsibility that goes with it, his title is used in the next three instances (*GL*630, 661, 666). Title is taken for granted after this, but the rank is used when Tennyson wants to underline chivalric courtesy: '"Damsel," Sir Gareth answer'd gently . . . To whom Sir Gareth answer'd courteously' and it strengthens Lancelot's assertion: 'Blessed be thou, Sir Gareth! Knight art thou / To the King's best wish' (*GL*753, 878, 1226).[25]

Use of title is just as cogent with Gawain. He who is surnamed 'The Courteous' is only three times given his knightly rank.[26] The first is by Gareth, anxious lest he be detected at court by his brothers (*GL*319). On the second occasion Gawain's title is used just after Lancelot has given his account of the Grail quest (*HG*851). Then in the long hall's silence ironically it is as 'Sir Gawain' that the knight blurts out his own parody of a quest in mere dalliance. Thus the third time Gawain is given his title it is only by Ettarre's damsels (*PE*371). Such dishonouring is part of his fading from the design.

Percivale also only becomes 'Sir' when theme requires it. Tennyson is never casual about his knights. On the first two occasions Percivale enters the narrative it is as 'fair Sir Percivale' and 'meek Sir Percivale' (*MV*745, *LE*1256). In using him as narrator of the Grail quests Tennyson does not wish personality to interfere with his witness, and so the knight's title is used only thrice (*HG*2,337, 563). After the Grail there are five references to Percivale, but not once does Tennyson give him his rank. This is because Percivale entered a monastery after the quest, as in Malory.[27]

Tristram's knighthood is early stressed: 'Arthur . . . had made his goodly cousin, Tristram, knight' (*GL*386). In contrast, Mark the Cornish king is denied knighthood by Arthur (*GL*411–27). Malory's title for Tristram is Sir Tristram de Liones, but in Tennyson the knight is announced at tournament as 'Sir Tristram of the Woods' (*LT*177).[28] Such titling is ominous when we consider the respective woodland fates of Balin and Merlin.

Because of his trouble over identity Balin is rarely called Sir Balin. Therefore in the first six occurrences his name is without title. His brother Balan, though knighted during the poem, is never called Sir Balan. Presumably this is because he has no real identity apart from his twin brother.[29] Title is first used as a reinforcement when Balin is accepted back into Camelot as a member of the Round Table brotherhood:

> Thereafter, when Sir Balin enter'd hall,
> The Lost one Found was greeted as in Heaven
> With joy that blazed itself in woodland wealth
> Of leaf, and gayest garlandage of flowers.
>
> (*BB*77–80)

Note the synaesthetic metaphor by which 'joy' is made to 'blaze itself' in 'woodland wealth / Of leaf' and the term poetically created to fit the occasion: 'gayest garlandage of flowers'.[30] Everything underlines this first use of Balin's title.[31]

Poignantly, title appears again when Balin tries especially hard to uphold the ideals of chivalry at court (*BB*194,202,235,245). As long as he stays in Camelot attempting to follow a chivalric model, Balin is termed knight. But after he reverts to the woods 'Sir' only occurs three times, each time with deepening irony: when he makes an unknightly move in striking Garlon, his host, without warning; when he divests himself of his shield in the forest, a knightly disgrace; and in his reaction when his brother rides to attack (*BB*387, 423,544).[32] Part of the same ironic pattern is Vivien's mode of addressing her squire: Sir Chick, Sir Boy (*BB*559,564,573).[33] Naturally at the close, as a reflection of mood and as part of inherent framing, all titles are dropped. The two brothers die anonymously, like Babes in the Woods.

Of course, Tennyson takes the same care with his greatest and mightiest knight, Lancelot. Lancelot is deliberately not given name or title as Arthur and he swear a deathless loyalty when he first enters the poem (*CA*124–33). This is a frame for the knight's named introduction, emphasised through being a paragraph opening:

Then Arthur charged his warrior whom he loved
And honour'd most, Sir Lancelot, to ride forth
And bring the Queen   (*CA*446–8)

Here use of title, superbly balanced in mid-line, accentuates the deep personal bond between Lancelot and his king. It is the epitome of courtesy and trust. Lancelot is never 'Sir Lancelot' during the Grail quest because he fails in it, and the tone in any case is confessional. Arthur uses the rank out of perfect courtesy when he delegates his greatest knight to assume the chair of arbitration over the tournament that, unbeknown to either of them, is to be the Order's last: 'Sir Lancelot, sitting in my place / Enchair'd' (*LT*103). Arthur's reference here to 'my place' suggests this delegation of judicial authority is as much a trial by ordeal as an honour. Arthur makes sure that Lancelot will experience for himself what it is like to have chivalric ideals flouted.

In the next idyll, when 'Sir Lancelot passing by / Spied where he couch'd . . . so Sir Lancelot holp / To raise the prince' the use of Lancelot's title helps to emphasise Modred's unprincely behaviour (*G*30,45). When the novice in the nunnery reports to Guinevere of Arthur: 'gone is he / To wage grim war against Sir Lancelot' (*G*190) use of title helps to show the magnitude of the event.[34] Lancelot's courtesy is emphasised in the last four uses of his title (*G*318,326,349,426).

At one point Arthur himself is addressed by Galahad as 'Sir Arthur' (*HG*290).[35] This is a sign that Galahad has been elevated spiritually to the rank of king, and it is also an indication of the supreme spiritual authority vested in Arthur himself.

Tennyson's naming skill can also be seen in how he deals with the Table Round. There are thirty-two references to Table Round but only four to Round Table. These four references are further restricted in occurring in three of the last five idylls in the narrative series. They thus form a reversal of sign. The four exceptions are all dramatic. 'Have any of our Round Table held their vows?' is the emphatic question of Pelleas to Percivale (*PE*523). 'The glory of our Round Table is no more' declare Lancelot and a byestander at the flickering mockeries and gibes at the last tournament (*LT*189, 212). Bedivere is the last to refer to Round Table in its English order (as *la table Ronde* it was the invention of Wace, a Norman poet) when he laments in echo of Malory: 'But now the whole Round Table is dissolved / Which was an image of the mighty world' (*PA*402–3).[36]

Table without its qualifier occurs eleven times, and in three instances it is written in lower case as an indication of what the Grail coming has done to Arthur's great order (*HG*329,647,*PE*312). Things are at their lowest when the disfigured churl identifies the renegade knight to Arthur as a 'table-knight of thine' (*LT*69). The arrival of the Grail is indeed 'A sign to maim this Order which I made' (*HG*297). Thereafter the Order is literally maimed by having its terms reversed and parodied by the Red Knight who founds another, like Satan, in the north (*LT*78,98).[37] Only its dissolution remains with the ritual disposal of Excalibur.

Conjunctions are among the most general parts of speech. Tennyson's use of certain conjunctions is a deliberate echoing of Malory, who displays amazing flexibility in their use. Beginning with the most essential and commonest, 'and', we can proceed to others that perform more specific functions: 'but', 'for', 'so', and medieval 'an' (which corresponds to modern 'if').

According to one critic 'the majority of Malory's narrative sentences and many of his main clauses begin with "and", "but", "then", "for", and "so". This establishes a continuity in the flow of his prose, each sentence taking up from its predecessor . . . So it is not surprising that the co-ordination within and between Malory's sentences urges the reader steadily on into the story.'[38] 'And' is in such wide use that this conjunction actually opens one of Malory's books, and often chapters open with it.[39] There are twenty three instances of 'and' in one of Malory's shorter chapters, and five sentences in this same chapter open with the word.[40] Perhaps the best example is a single sentence from the return of Excalibur, which employs the conjunction no less than twelve times:

> Then Sir Bedivere departed and went to the sword, and lightly took it up, and went to the water side; and there he bound the girdle about the hilts, and then he threw the sword as far into the water, as he might; and there came an arm and an hand above the water and met it, and caught it, and so shook it thrice and brandished, and then vanished away the hand with the sword in the water.[41]

Tennyson makes extensive and ingenious use of 'and' throughout the *Idylls*. Three of the first seven paragraphs of *The Coming of Arthur* open with it, and three of the first four in *Gareth and Lynette* (*CA*20,46,74,*GL*33,41,61). There are fifty-four paragraphs in *Merlin and Vivien*, and no less than eighteen open with the conjunction, a proportion of one in three. In the first two poems the last paragraphs of each are also introduced by the conjunction (*CA*514,

*GL*1392). In each case this helps to achieve a relaxation from tension as part of the poem's termination or conclusion.

Within his paragraph structure Tennyson makes a very flexible and imaginative use of 'and'. Take, for example, the action between Balin and King Pellam. Although Tennyson transforms Malory's tale so that Garlon takes the place of Pellam, a common element of speed, ease of transition, and the generation of excitement in both lies in the paratactic use of 'and'. Malory's short chapter, eight sentences plus headnote, has no less than twenty-five. From this I quote sentences four and five:

> Then King Pellam caught in his hand a grim weapon and smote eagerly at Balin; but Balin put the sword betwixt his head and the stroke, and therewith his sword burst in sunder. And when Balin was weaponless he ran into a chamber for to seek some weapon, and so from chamber to chamber, and no weapon he could find, and always King Pellam after him.[42]

This is reflected quite clearly in Tennyson's equivalent action:

> Then Garlon, reeling slowly backward, fell,
> And Balin by the banneret of his helm
> Dragg'd him, and struck, but from the castle a cry
> Sounded across the court, and – men-at-arms,
> A score with pointed lances, making at him –
> He dash'd the pummel at the foremost face,
> Beneath a low door dipt, and made his feet
> Wings thro' a glimmering gallery, till he mark'd
> The portal of King Pellam's chapel wide
> And inward to the wall . . .

Once in the chapel he grasps the spear:

> . . . and seizing thereupon
> Push'd thro' an open casement down, lean'd on it,
> Leapt in a semicircle, and lit on earth;
> Then hand at ear, and harkening from what side
> The blindfold rummage buried in the walls
> Might echo, ran the counter path, and found
> His charger, mounted on him and away.
>   (*BB*391–400, 406–12)

Such a virtuoso use of 'and' has a startling effect on the reader. It corresponds to a cinematic process Eisenstein defined as 'partial representation', a technique for achieving spontaneity because

> it includes in the creative process the emotions and mind of the spectator. The spectator is compelled to proceed along that selfsame creative road that the author travelled in creating the image. The spectator not only sees the represented elements of

the finished work, but also experiences the dynamic process of the emergence and assembly of the image just as it was experienced by the author (so) is drawn into a creative act in which his individuality is not subordinated to the author's individuality, but is opened up throughout the process of fusion with the author's intention.[43]

Tennyson's use of 'and' achieves the profoundest of effects by the simplest of means. Examples of 'and' can be observed from any page of the *Idylls*, and so I have selected a further two. There is Arthur's response to Gareth's sudden request for knighthood:

> Here the King's calm eye
> Fell on, and check'd, and made him flush, and bow
> Lowly, to kiss his hand, who answer'd him,
> 'Son, the good mother let me know thee here,
> And sent her wish that I would yield thee thine.
> Make thee my knight? My knights are sworn to vows
> Of utter hardihood, utter gentleness,
> And, loving, utter faithfulness in love,
> And uttermost obedience to the King.   (*GL*536–44)

Here the first three uses of 'and' give the effect of Arthur's regal dignity and near hypnotic control. Following this, the conjunction helps to suggest actual speech, and in the unpunctuated speed of the last line, the authority Arthur as a real king has every right to expect from any knight.

Then there is Percivale's description of the coming of the Grail:

> 'And all at once, as there we sat, we heard
> A cracking and a riving of the roofs,
> And rending, and a blast, and overhead
> Thunder, and in the thunder was a cry.
> And in the blast there smote along the hall
> A beam of light seven times more clear than day:
> And down the long beam stole the Holy Grail
> All over cover'd with a luminous cloud,
> And none might see who bare it, and it past.
> But every knight beheld his fellow's face
> As in a glory, and all the knights arose,
> And staring each at other like dumb men
> Stood, till I found a voice and sware a vow.
> (*HG*182–94)

The Grail fuses everything in the minds of those experiencing it. Percivale can only link the events in this happening in the simplest possible way, though the result is extremely subtle. All cannot be other than spectators.

Note the amazing bonding of different syntactic elements in lines three and four: participle ('rending'), noun ('a blast'), adverb plus noun ('overhead / Thunder') and main clause ('in the thunder was a cry'). 'And' opens line five with a two line image, and the 'and' at the start of line seven parallels this. After ten occurrences of 'and' in nine lines, the 'but' at the start of line ten comes with explosive force. 'And' is also useful for the simplest and most effective of additions. The series is terminated by a one line sentence: 'And the new sun rose bringing the new year'. This use of 'and' helps to suggest that, in the same way as Arthur 'passes from the great deep to the great deep', the process remains open.

'But' is used with as great a freedom and flexibility as 'and'. Tennyson uses the conjunction to open three verse paragraphs in the first poem of his series (*CA*41, 266, 358). Malory seldom opens sentences with the word.[44] No less than eleven paragraphs in *Gareth and Lynette* open with 'but'. Part of a speech in Malory will illustrate something of the flexibility on which Tennyson draws:

> But wayte ye make not many questions with her nor her men, but say ye are diseased, and so hie you to bed, and rise not on the morn till I come to you, for the castle of Tintagil is but ten miles hence.[45]

Tennyson uses the conjunction with as great a flexibility, for example 'but ever', 'But to be won by force', 'but so', 'but wherefore', and 'but say' (*GL*52, 104, 441, 557, 611).[46] The following verse paragraph illustrates the co-ordinated use of both conjunctions so far discussed:

> And Arthur yet had done no deeds of arms,
> But heard the call, and came: and Guinevere
> Stood by the castle walls to watch him pass;
> But since he neither wore on helm or shield
> The golden symbol of his kinglihood,
> But rode a simple knight among his knights,
> And many of these in richer arms than he,
> She saw him not, or mark'd not, if she saw,
> One among many, tho' his face was bare.
> But Arthur, looking downward as he past,
> Felt the light of her eyes into his life
> Smite on the sudden . . .
>   (*CA*46–57)

Tennyson's use of 'then' to open paragraphs and to retain continuity once his story is well on its way also reflects a common Malory practice.[47] There are five instances of this in the opening idyll (*CA*134, 147, 165, 237, 325, 446) and no less than twenty-eight in *Gareth and Lynette*. *Morte d'Arthur* shows the earliest use of this narrative device.[48]

Tennyson's use of 'so' is also based on Malory and the major English poets. Three of Malory's books open with this conjunction, as also many chapters.[49] Perhaps this occasioned Tennyson's most famous example, the 'so' that begins *Morte d'Arthur*: 'So all day long the noise of battle roll'd'.[50] Three of the last paragraphs in *The Coming of Arthur* are introduced by the conjunction to close the poem with a sense of finality (*CA*411,475,502). Arthur is truly established.

There is an amazing variety in the use of 'so' at the beginning of *Gareth and Lynette*. It is a Tennysonian showcase of style, as has already been shown respecting echoing of Shakespeare in chapter 3 (pp.57–8). Notice the range in the conjunction's use: 'So make my manhood mightier day by day . . . Not an hour, / So that ye yield me . . . for so the Queen believed that when her son . . . so should he rest with her . . . so push'd them all unwilling toward the gate' (*GL*91,130,155,159,208) and in one instance, the word opens a paragraph: 'So, when their feet were planted on the plain' (*GL*184).[51] 'So' comes in again at the close of *Gareth and Lynette*. I quote the last two paragraphs because they illustrate once more Tennyson's way of using the conjunctions so far discussed:

> Then sprang the happier day from underground;
> And Lady Lyonors and her house, with dance
> And revel and song, made merry over Death,
> As being after all their foolish fears
> And horrors only proven a blooming boy.
> So large mirth lived and Gareth won the quest.
>
> And he that told the tale in older times
> Says that Sir Gareth wedded Lyonors,
> But he, that told it later, says Lynette.
> (*GL*1386–94)

Two other conjunctions have to be considered, Tennyson's use of 'for' and 'an' (Malory's frequent form for 'if'). Malory never opens with 'for'. The conjunction is always employed within his sentence structure to introduce subordinate clauses. A single example will illustrate this:

> Well, said Merlin, I know whom thou seekest, for thou seekest Merlin; therefore seek no farther, for I am he, and if King Uther will well reward me, and be sworn unto me to fulfil my desire, that shall be his honour and profit more than mine, for I shall cause him to have all his desire.[52]

Tennyson goes much further, and uses the word in the same way as Homer, to introduce a story or theme.[53] Used in this way, the conjunction occurs near the start of most poems in the series (*CA*5,62, *GL*155, *MG*145, *MV*6, *LE*34, *HG*101, *LT*10, *G*9, 21, *PA*6). Elsewhere within his narrative and grammatical structure Tennyson's use is very similar to Malory's.

Malory employs 'an' throughout his prose narrative and for all his characters. In Tennyson, however, this register is confined to fewer characters and only in four poems. Those using the form as a natural part of their speech pattern are Gareth (*GL*37,50,98,1211, 1311), his mother Bellicent (*GL*142), Merlin (*GL*252,271), Lynette (*GL*583,823,1263), Kay (*GL*448,463,695) and Lancelot (*GL*1267).[54] 'An' therefore functions as a small part of the comic and colloquial structure of this idyll. Its use later by Balin during a moment of aspiration adds tenderness to the uncouth character: 'Her likewise would I worship an I might' (*BB*181). 'But an ye will it let me see the shield' (*LE*657) begs Gawain of Elaine. Guinevere uses it to Arthur in speaking of the rubies: 'Make them, an thou wilt, a tourney-prize' (*LT*32) and as part of his informality as a fool Dagonet uses it twice:

'Knight, an ye fling those rubies round my neck
In lieu of hers. . . .

The dirty nurse, Experience, in her kind
Hath foul'd me – an I wallow'd, then I wash'd –
I have had my day and my philosophies –
    (*LT*312–13,317–19)

Clearly the use of conjunctions suggested by Malory's freedom is an important element in Tennyson's narrative technique.[55]

Tennyson's metaphor and simile pattern, the movement of water, especially of the sea, works together with the movement of paragraphs, the basic unit of composition in the serial poem.[56] The unity of this two-fold movement is most strikingly exemplified in Lancelot's combat in the lists for the last diamond (*LE*426–505) that will be examined in detail.

From 1842, Tennyson's basic and recurrent image is of the movement of waters, traditional among great epic and narrative poets, such as Homer, Virgil, Spenser, Shakespeare, to name only a few. In the *Idylls*, Merlin has a premonition of his pending fate:

So dark a forethought roll'd about his brain,
As on a dull day in an Ocean cave
The blind wave feeling round his long sea-hall
In silence: (*MV*228–31)

This image that is metaphor and simile is Homeric in its sweep, but its power and complexity is Tennyson's own. Its internal power is well caught by Christopher Ricks: 'in the cave of the skull, the forethought reaches, its feeling-round beautifully and tentacularly floating through the rhymes and assonances, *cave* exactly into *wave*, and then (as the wave begins to separate and dissolve its unity) *feeling* into *sea-hall*; fear known in the Cyclopean blindness and the silence; and the delicate creativity of sound in the lines themselves strangely played against "In silence"'.[57] And David Shaw notes another feature in the image, that 'the grammar itself leaves its objects drifting. . . . "Blind wave", we expect, will be the subject of a principal verb, but the predicate never comes . . . The point is simply that Tennyson is fusing his sense impressions to make sightless liquidity seem tactile and solid. A principal verb would restore the suspended sea impressions to the temporal world. In its absence the grammatical fragments fluctuate before us like deep-sea film shots'.[58] Here is the Homeric poet, compensating for his lack of sight by relating to the world even more intimately through sound and touch. Indeed in its sound this large image contains the full range and most of the changes in diphthongs in English. The image is a kind of world in itself because it includes Tennyson's favourite devices of capitalisation, the Miltonic colon, hyphenation, prefixing and suffixing, and it opens with that familiar conjunction that opened the *Morte*, in other words nearly all of the devices that give range, power and variety to his blank verse.[59] The image is a resonant one, a great and subtle echo, the inception of whole trains of subterranean echo and reflection.[60] It is also an invocation.[61] Soon Merlin expands upon it:

> O did ye never lie upon the shore,
> And watch the curl'd white of the coming wave
> Glass'd in the slippery sand before it breaks?
> Ev'n such a wave, but not so pleasurable,
> Dark in the glass of some presageful mood,
> Had I for three days seen, ready to fall . . .
> You seem'd that wave about to break upon me
> And sweep me from my hold upon the world,
> My use and name and fame . . .   (*MV* 289–94, 300–2)

As in a glass darkly, Merlin sees reflected, half-fascinated by it, his own wisdom and his own dark fate.[62] Following Vivien's song he tells her:

> when you sang me that sweet rhyme,
> I felt as tho' you knew this cursèd charm,
> Were proving it on me, and that I lay

And felt them slowly ebbing, name and fame.
    (*MV*432–5)

True to his largest image, Merlin 'felt' his name and fame slowly ebbing as he lay within the potent spell of Vivien's beauty.[63] 'O mine have ebb'd away for evermore' (*MV*437) she replies, but this is only deception.

When single-sentence paragraphs occur in tiers or series, like the rising, cresting and breaking of a wave, the effect is elementally moving. Already Tennyson's care in positioning crucial similes has been seen in the case of *Morte d'Arthur* (see pp.10–11). In *Lancelot and Elaine* the splendid simile of the 'wild wave in the wide North-sea' that gives the downfall of Lancelot in the lists, occurs as the last long sentence in such a pattern. Lines 383–96 constitute a single sentence at the end of a long paragraph whose opening contains the longest sentence in the *Idylls* (*LE*284–316) and then the next three paragraphs each consist of a single sentence (*LE*397–410,411–25, 426–42). We can start the movement in complicated stasis as we witness through Lavaine's amazed eyes the jousts for the ninth and final diamond:

> So spake Lavaine, and when they reach'd the lists
> By Camelot in the meadow, let his eyes
> Run thro' the peopled gallery which half round
> Lay like a rainbow fall'n upon the grass,
> Until they found the clear-faced King, who sat
> Robed in red samite, easily to be known,
> Since to his crown the golden dragon clung,
> And down his robe the dragon writhed in gold,
> And from the carven-work behind him crept
> Two dragons gilded, sloping down to make
> Arms for his chair, while all the rest of them
> Thro' knots and loops and folds innumerable
> Fled ever thro' the woodwork, till they found
> The new design wherein they lost themselves,
> Yet with all ease, so tender was the work:
>   (*LE*426–40)

According to R. L. Peters:

> This one very long sentence is intricately built from a series of increasingly subordinate elements which develop like compli-cated interwoven vines about the spare, quiet, tender frame-work of the whole; the run on effect of the central portion with its stress on turning, 'sloping', and dropping, complements the writhing pattern on the robe. The chair's design becomes chaotically involved before the golden dragons tumble down

into a 'new design.' The effect is almost palpably descriptive; the subordinate clauses blend superbly with the visual matter they contain and are totally in its spirit. The appeal is both visual and tactile . . . through the magic of style Tennyson provides his readers with a pleasure like that they might enjoy in moving their hands over elaborate wooden or ivory traceries.[64]

When Lancelot entered the lists

> Lavaine gaped upon him
> As on a thing miraculous, and anon
> The trumpets blew; and then did either side,
> They that assail'd, and they that held the lists,
> Set lance in rest, strike spur, suddenly move,
> Meet in the midst, and there so furiously
> Shock, that a man far-off might well perceive,
> If any man that day were left afield,
> The hard earth shake, and a low thunder of arms.
> And Lancelot bode a little, till he saw
> Which were the weaker; then he hurl'd into it
> Against the stronger: little need to speak
> Of Lancelot in his glory! King, duke, earl,
> Count, baron – whom he smote, he overthrew.
>   (*LE*450–63)

Here the list at the end is so arranged that the end of line break divides it, three items before and two after ('King, duke, earl, / Count, baron') to begin the next line. Thus the crest breaks. Also the list is deliberately anti-climactic, ordered according to rank but therefore regularly descending in importance from item to item. The list functions both as climax (the last item alone having two syllables: 'baron') and anticlimax, and because of this inherent ambivalence we are kept in suspense and seek for a resolution in the next paragraph. There follow three sentences, the third of which contains the famous simile. First we learn of a new factor in the jousts:

> But in the field were Lancelot's kith and kin,
> Ranged with the Table Round that held the lists,
> Strong men, and wrathful that a stranger knight
> Should do and almost overdo the deeds
> Of Lancelot; and one said to the other, 'Lo!
> What is he? I do not mean the force alone –
> The grace and versatility of the man!
> Is it not Lancelot?' 'When has Lancelot worn
> Favour of any lady in the lists?
> Not such his wont, as we, that know him, know.'

> .... a fury seized them all,
> A fiery family passion for the name
> Of Lancelot, and a glory one with theirs.   (*LE*464–76)

There follows the splendid simile:

> They couch'd their spears and prick'd their steeds, and thus,
> Their plumes driv'n backward by the wind they made
> In moving, all together down upon him
> Bare, as a wild wave in the wide North-sea,
> Green-glimmering toward the summit, bears, with all
> Its stormy crests that smoke against the skies,
> Down on a bark, and overbears the bark,
> And him that helms it, so they overbore
> Sir Lancelot and his charger, and a spear
> Down-glancing lamed the charger, and a spear
> Prick'd sharply his own cuirass, and the head
> Pierced thro' his side, and there snapt, and remain'd.
>   (*LE*477–88)

Here the way the lines are managed suggests the movement of the wave, and balance and antithesis with repetition suggests its overpowering sweep. Lines 480–1 are metrically of especial interest. The framed words here: 'Bare ... / ... bears' have following or before them the same number of syllables: 'as a wild wave in the wide North-sea' and 'Green-glimmering toward the summit'. It appears some kind of balance. And yet for the second line to be complete, it has two words added ('with all') that force us to pronounce 'glimmering' as two syllables and 'toward' as one. The line accordingly is crammed with impulses that effect the very instability of the wave as it gathers to a crest, and the cresting is effected phonetically by the long vowel followed by several short in 'Green-glimmering toward the summit'.[65] 'Summit' with its initial sibilant and terminal explosive dental (led up to by '*t*owar*d*') is so placed that the passage fragments like the wave after cresting.

So powerful is this effect that it resonates in other sea imagery Tennyson uses in this idyll, for example 'Sea was her wrath, yet working after storm' to express elemental feeling in *Guinevere* (*LE*1299).[66]

The wave has its fullest breaking with the downfall of the Red Knight. First Arthur characterises the heathen as 'that ever-climbing wave' who 'Hurl'd back again so often in empty foam, / Hath lain for years at rest' (*LT*92–4). When it comes to the Red Knight's downfall he accomplishes this feat himself, for

> ... Arthur deign'd not use of word or sword,
> But let the drunkard, as he stretch'd from horse

> To strike him, overbalancing his bulk,
> Down from the causeway heavily to the swamp
> Fall, as the crest of some slow-arching wave,
> Heard in dead night along that table-shore,
> Drops flat, and after the great waters break
> Whitening for half a league, and thin themselves,
> Far over sands marbled with moon and cloud,
> From less and less to nothing; thus he fell
> Head-heavy. (*LT*457–67)

After first reading this passage, we may be tempted to agree with Bowra respecting Homer:

> Homer's similes are vivid pictures of different corners of life. Each lives on its own and reveals some unsuspected or hidden quality in a situation. But because they are complete, they sometimes tend to pass beyond mere comparison, even of character and atmosphere, and to introduce something which is, strictly speaking, irrelevant. The picture takes command, and the poet so enjoys it that he completes it with some charming touch which makes us almost forget why the simile has been introduced.[67]

But Walter Nash has argued the simile's fitness in Tennyson's larger scheme:

> The Red Knight is not the only presence in these lines; there is also Arthur, silent and motionless. The enormous, slow-straining, forward-leaning, swaying, headlong tumbledown of the knight is not only self-emphasizing, but emphasizes also the grave immobility of the King, who 'deign'd not use of word or sword.' Furthermore the passage constitutes an important alternation in the tempo of the movement. Arthur blows his horn, and the world flares into a panic action, through which the Red Knight comes galloping to scream abuse and defiance at the King. Then the tempo is retarded, the action reduced to the slow motion of the Red Knight's drunken decline from the saddle, so ludicrous, so impotent, after all his violence and loud threatening; whereupon, abruptly, the action erupts again, the tempo accelerating rapidly through the account of the hysterical orgy of violence which follows the Red Knight's fall.[68]

Hence there is no force at the end when

> only the wan wave
> Brake in among dead faces, to and fro
> Swaying the helpless hands, and up and down
> Tumbling the hollow helmets of the fallen,
> And shiver'd brands that once had fought with Rome,
> And rolling far along the gloomy shores

The voice of days of old and days to be.
(*PA*129-35)

Thus, on Milton's model, Tennyson can achieve unity of language and action by composing a paragraph as a single sentence unit. This passage shows clearly that his unit of composition is the paragraph. Saintsbury justly remarks on Tennyson having 'the secret of the paragraph, which he alone of English poets shares with Milton in perfection'.[69] Like Milton he is a master of emphasis.

Songs

Song is one of the subtlest devices in the *Idylls*. Music and song play an intrinsic part in the serial poem, in much the same way as songs do in Shakespeare's plays. Two idylls, *Geraint and Enid* and *The Holy Grail*, lack songs because they would be inappropriate, and *The Passing of Arthur* has only residual elements of music and song. However, in compensation two others, *The Coming of Arthur* and *The Last Tournament*, have two songs apiece.

The first song of the series is one of the subtlest. Bellicent tells Leodogran a riddling song about Arthur that Merlin has composed. The form of the song stems from medieval Welsh poetry. In his book on the Druids, Edward Davies writes:

> Amongst the most curious remains of the old Bards, we may class those metrical sentences, called *tribanau*, or *triplets*. Each of these is divided into three short verses, which are again united by the final rhymes. The most singular feature of these versicles is, that the sense of the first two verses has no *obvious* connection with that of the last. The first line contains some trivial remark, suggested by the state of the air . . . or the like. To this is frequently subjoined, something that savours more of reflection; then the third line comes home to the heart, with a weighty moral precept, or a pertinent remark upon men and manners.[1]

One such triplet was translated as follows: 'It rains without, and here is shelter – What! the yellow furze, or the rotten hedge! Creating God, why hast thou formed the slothful!'[2] Merlin's 'riddling' rhymes in *The Coming of Arthur* are an accurate imitation of this ancient form:

> Rain, rain, and sun! a rainbow in the sky!
> A young man will be wiser by and by;
> An old man's wit may wander ere he die.
> Rain, rain, and sun! a rainbow on the lea!
> And truth is this to me, and that to thee;
> And truth or clothed or naked let it be.
> Rain, sun, and rain! and the free blossom blows:
> Sun, rain, and sun! and where is he who knows?
> From the great deep to the great deep he goes. (*CA*402–10)

The main image in the first triplet is the rainbow, the sign in Hebrew-Christian tradition of reconciliation and a covenant between the everlasting God and mortal man. 'Men perish', said Alkmeon of Crotona, 'because they cannot join the beginning to the end'.[3] The beginning and end of the bow between heaven and earth are open: the sign is itself transitory, like the life of man.

The second and third lines are more specific and refer to events in the *Idylls*. By itself, the assertion 'A young man will be wiser by and by' seems trite. The same can be said of 'An old man's wit may wander ere he die'. Ironically, Merlin will be the one whose wit will wander through the wiles of a *femme fatale*, Vivien. 'A young man will be wiser by and by' may allude to Merlin's warning in Malory: 'But Merlin warned the king covertly that Guenever was not wholesome for him to take for wife, for he warned him that Launcelot should love her, and she him again'.[4]

In the central triplet Merlin speaks most clearly of the limitations in human understanding. Absolute truth eludes him, whether it seem to him 'naked' or 'clothed' in appearance.

The opening words 'Rain, rain, and sun' become a refrain in the second stanza. In the third stanza our expectation is defeated because the order is altered ('rain, sun, and rain') and then reversed ('sun, rain, and sun') as a climax to riddling. The only question the poem contains has no answer, because our beginning and end are mysterious. The 'great deep' of the beginning cannot be joined to the 'great deep' of the end.[5] Both are mysterious to man.

Merlin's song occurs on two other occasions, but only as a fragment. In *The Last Tournament* all that is recollected of it by Guinevere as she works a tapestry is 'Where is he who knows? / From the great deep to the great deep he goes' and at the close, as Bedivere watches Arthur's barge take him to Avalon, he recollects the last line alone (*LT*132, *PA*445).

The second song in *The Coming of Arthur* contrasts markedly with the first. The first is cryptic and a climax to the idyll's inner structure.[6] In their fervour to work for the king, all the new-made knights sing the second song in chorus. The clash and clang of sword and battleaxe sound as if Tennyson had some alliterative model:[7]

'Blow trumpet, for the world is white with May;
Blow trumpet, the long night hath roll'd away!
Blow thro' the living world – "Let the King reign."

'Shall Rome or Heathen rule in Arthur's realm?
Flash brand and lance, fall battleaxe upon helm,
Fall battleaxe, and flash brand! Let the King reign.

'Strike for the King and live! his knights have heard
That God hath told the King a secret word.
Fall battleaxe, and flash brand! Let the King reign.

'Blow trumpet! he will lift us from the dust.
Blow trumpet! live the strength and die the lust!
Clang battleaxe, and clash brand! let the King reign.

'Strike for the King and die! and if thou diest,
The King is King, and ever wills the highest.
Clang battleaxe, and clash brand! Let the King reign.

'Blow, for our Sun is mighty in his May!
Blow, for our Sun is mightier day by day!
Clang battleaxe, and clash brand! Let the King reign.

'The King will follow Christ, and we the King
In whom high God hath breathed a secret thing.
Fall battleaxe, and flash brand! Let the King reign.'
(*CA*481–501)

This song helps to resolve *The Coming of Arthur* by being presented
directly, with no intervening reporter, and by being sung in chorus.
The middle line of the second last verse reflects images seen earlier
(*CA*109,461). The first line of the last verse echoes an affirmation
in the New Testament: 'Be ye followers of me, even as I am also of
Christ'.[8] The effect made by these two poems differs so markedly
that it is hard to believe they both fit into blank verse measure. Their
content also shows the greatest contrast. The first is an unanswered
question, the second is an unquestioning affirmation of Arthur's
kingship.

Lynette sings a song in three parts in *Gareth and Lynette*. The first
stanza starts with an invocation:

O morning star that smilest in the blue,
O star, my morning dream hath proven true,
Smile sweetly, thou! my love hath smiled on me   (*GL*974–6)

At first sight 'O morning star' seems to signify the knight Morning
Star, whom Gareth has just defeated, but Lynette scornfully rejects
such an interpretation. The morning star is Venus, star of love, in
the ascendant.

The second stanza similarly begins with an ambiguous invocation.
Again Lynette, in the derisive running commentary that separates
the stanzas, denies that the opening words 'O Sun' refer to 'this
strong fool' called Noonday Sun, whom Gareth has just defeated:

O Sun, that wakenest all to bliss or pain,
O moon, that layest all to sleep again,

Shine sweetly: twice my love hath smiled on me.
      (*GL*1034–6)
The sun invoked is the source of light and warmth that gives life to
the beautiful natural world of flowers and birds celebrated in the
next two stanzas:

O dewy flowers that open to the sun,
O dewy flowers that close when day is done,
Blow sweetly: twice my love hath smiled on me.

O birds, that warble to the morning sky,
O birds that warble as the day goes by,
Sing sweetly: twice my love hath smiled on me.
      (*GL*1040–2, 1049–51)

After Gareth's victory over the third knight, Evening Star,
Lynette, by way of apology, addresses him as the 'kingliest' of all
kitchen knaves.[9] The third part of her song immediately follows:

O trefoil, sparkling on the rainy plain,
O rainbow with three colours after rain,
Shine sweetly: thrice my love hath smiled on me.

      (*GL*1130–2)
'Thrice my love hath smiled on me' is reflected in the three leaves
of the trefoil and the three colours of the rainbow, both symbolising
fidelity. Helping to resolve the poem at its unexpectedly comic end,
it is 'with dance / And revel and song' that all 'make merry over
Death' (*GL*1388).

Enid sings as she spins, in *The Marriage of Geraint*. Hearing her
song before he has caught sight of her, Geraint declares: 'Here, by
God's grace, is the one voice for me' (*MG*344).[10] Such love at first
hearing may seem romantic, but it is another illustration of 'the
maiden passion for a maid' already exemplified by Arthur's love for
Guinevere (*G*476, *CA*55–7). Geraint's feeling is confirmed when
he does see Enid: 'Here by God's rood is the one maid for me'
(*MG*368).[11] Being monosyllabic, this declaration has the force of a
vow.[12]

Enid's turning wheel is first likened to the wheel of fortune. The
first line of her song refers to her immediate situation. 'Turn, Fortune, turn thy wheel and lower the proud' echoes 'Fortune, good
night; smile once more, turn thy wheel', and the wish to 'lower the
proud' refers to the oppressor, Edyrn, who is frequently stated to
possess an overweening pride (*MG*190, 195, 221, 448, 464, 557).[13]
Geraint has come indeed to break his pride (*MG*221, 416, 424, 476).
A familiar image occurs in the song's second line: 'Turn thy wild
wheel thro' sunshine, storm, and cloud'. Fortune's wheel is 'wild'

because it is ungovernable, even more so than the seasons. But in the last line of the first stanza, Enid declares fortune is not a matter of the emotions: 'Thy wheel and thee we neither love nor hate'.

The second stanza expands upon the last line of the first:

> Turn, Fortune, turn thy wheel with smile or frown;
> With that wild wheel we go not up nor down;
> Our hoard is little, but our hearts are great.

In its repetition the third stanza simulates a movement in spinning:

> Smile and we smile, the lords of many lands;
> Frown and we smile, the lords of our own hands;
> For man is man and master of his fate.

Now Fortune is fading out. It also is subject to the wheel. Man can master blind forces like fate through imagination or spirit or artistic creation, of which spinning something is part. The third line's confidence is assured. Later songs in the *Idylls* offer no such mastery of fate.

The last stanza distinguishes between the 'staring crowd' of mere onlookers, and the individual who participates in the spirit and so is indifferent to blind external forces such as fate:

> Turn, turn thy wheel above the staring crowd;
> Thy wheel and thou are shadows in the cloud;
> Thy wheel and thee we neither love nor hate.

In their last lines the first and fourth stanzas are identical. Fortune is shown to be an illusion. Later, Yniol quotes the central line of his daughter's song: 'Our hoard is little, but our hearts are great' (*MG*374). Tennyson always varies the way he relates each song to the poem of which it is part. Each song seems to grow from its context while enlarging it.

In *Geraint and Enid* the action gives no occasion for a song, and there is none. However, it is 'Half whistling and half singing a coarse song' that marks one of Doorm's followers.[14]

Vivien's entry and her song are subtly connected by phonetic motifs:

> But now the wholesome music of the wood
> Was dumb'd by one from out the hall of Mark,
> A damsel-errant, warbling, as she rode
> The woodland alleys, Vivien, with her Squire.
>   'The fire of Heaven has kill'd the barren cold . . .'
>   (*BB*430–4)

According to Walter Nash:

> The first line of Vivien's lyric reflects, mirror-wise, the major emphases of the last two lines of introduction. Thus 'errant', 'Vivien', 'Squire' are echoed, with a slight distortion but nonetheless recognisably, in 'fire', 'Heaven', 'barren'. No one could

possibly suppose that Tennyson consciously designed this effect, but we may see in it a testimony to the unconscious processes by which he felt his way through the transition to the lyric; the last word of the introduction, 'Squire', seems to be related to 'fire' by direct phonetic association, and the further items 'Heaven' and 'barren' to be the products of a process of phonetic recall.'[15]

Vivien has the voice of a siren when she sings:

> The fire of Heaven has kill'd the barren cold,
> And kindled all the plain and all the wold.
> The new leaf ever pushes off the old.
> The fire of Heaven is not the flame of Hell.
>
> Old priest, who mumble worship in your quire –
> Old monk and nun, ye scorn the world's desire,
> Yet in your frosty cells ye feel the fire!
> The fire of Heaven is not the flame of Hell.
>
> The fire of Heaven is on the dusty ways.
> The wayside blossoms open to the blaze.
> The whole wood-world is one full peal of praise.
> The fire of Heaven is not the flame of Hell.
>
> The fire of Heaven is lord of all things good.
> And starve not thou this fire within thy blood,
> But follow Vivien thro' the fiery flood!
> The fire of Heaven is not the flame of Hell.
>
> (*BB*434–49)

Here fire and dust ominously replace the rain and sunshine of previous songs. Vivien's song consists of a four-line hymn stanza. In it she deliberately confuses heaven and hell. Her refrain gives hell, occupying the key place in the line and repeated four times, all the emphasis. Her equivocation is completed by what she says of heaven following the song: 'This fire of Heaven, / This old sun-worship . . . will rise again / And beat the cross to earth, and break the King / And all his Table' (*BB*450–3). The year-cycle itself makes so pagan an appeal self-fulfilling. The instincts will have their way, as Vivien has always known. When 'the wayside blossoms open to the blaze' her song's imagery suggests violation. This third stanza consists of four separate propositions, each introduced by the definite article. In this way it frames and expands on the first stanza, which consists of three such propositions. Such ruthless logic makes Vivien a formidable adversary, as Merlin is to discover in the following idyll.

Vivien brazenly names herself in the second last line of her song: 'But follow Vivien thro' the fiery flood!'[16] Arthur's knighthood had idealised their king by including both his rank and name in their song (*CA*483-4). By offering to act as guide to hell or 'the fiery flood' Vivien clearly reveals her nature and intentions.

Enhancing her siren image is the fact that Vivien alone is given two songs to sing in consecutive idylls. But in contrast to the war-lock equivocation of her first song, Vivien's second, in *Merlin and Vivien*, is magnificent. She admits it is not her own: 'I heard the great Sir Lancelot sing it once' (*MV*383). So intimate is the song that the only way Vivien could have heard it was by eavesdropping on Lancelot and Guinevere:

> In Love, if Love be Love, if Love be ours,
> Faith and unfaith can ne'er be equal powers:
> Unfaith in aught is want of faith in all.
>
> It is the little rift within the lute,
> That by and by will make the music mute,
> And ever widening slowly silence all.
>
> The little rift within the lover's lute
> Or little pitted speck in garner'd fruit,
> That rotting inward slowly moulders all.
>
> It is not worth the keeping: let it go:
> But shall it? answer, darling, answer, no.
> And trust me not at all or all in all.
> (*MV*385-96)

This song exhibits Tennyson's phonaesthetic power to the full. That 'love' has a capital in the first line is subtle. Lancelot's idealisation shines out in the capitalisation. Only Love could be worthy of Guinevere.

There is a play on nine consecutive short vowels in the first line of the second stanza. This makes the tenth, which is both long and in the key position, most emphatic: 'It is the little rift within the lute'.[17] In the next line there is a regular alternation between short vowels and long, with the emphasis at the end redoubled: 'That by and by will make the music mute'. In 'And ever widening slowly silence all' the lengthening of the words themselves slow down the pace and suggest the slow fading of the tune into silence.

The greatest piece of craftsmanship is displayed in the third stanza, with the first and second lines each having nine short vowels and the tenth long. The long vowel in the first case is intensified by alliteration, in the second by the rhyme word: 'The little rift within the lover's lute / Or little pitted speck in garner'd fruit'. The short vowels occupy the first half of the third line; all the weight falls on the long ones at the close: 'That rotting inward slowly moulders all'. The phonetic pattern is subtly varied as one can see in the last verse. David Shaw points out: 'The blurring of grammatical reference in the first word of the last stanza marks a final wavering. It prepares for the false disjunction of the last line, which hinges on three grammatical uses of the same word – as intensive ("not at all"), as adverb ("trust me . . . all or wholly"), and as pronoun: ("in all")'.[18]

As for the phonetic patterns, short vowels predominate except for the rhyme words in the first two lines, and the song ends emphatically with the last six words alliterating. This emphasis suggests the lover's urgent but delicate pressing of his suit. Lancelot is indeed a poet, and Vivien an expert mimic. The magic of the original song makes itself felt even through the mimicry, as Merlin attests in his reference to it: 'When you sang me that sweet rhyme, / I felt as tho' you knew that cursèd charm, / Were proving it on me' (*MV*433–4).[19] Immediately, Vivien adds a further verse, patently a pastiche on the original song:

"My name, once mine, now thine, is closelier mine,
For fame, could fame be mine, that fame were thine,
And shame, could shame be thine, that shame were mine.
So trust me not at all or all in all."   (*MV*444–7)

Here only the last line is familiar, the flawless refrain from the original song, but now grotesque in its new context. At line end 'mine . . . thine . . . mine' places all the weight on Vivien's possessiveness. The deliberately crude 'chiming' on long 'a' and long 'i' with the second and third lines monotonously identical, drew the wrath of one reviewer: 'There is something ominous when the master of harmonies finds his ears tickled by such a jingle as the following stanza (Vivien's); and the whole song is too much on the same model. Was ever our English chopped into such mincemeat?'[20]

One of the functions of song is to reveal character in a compressed and economic way. This may be seen in many instances. For Vivien the 'cursèd charm' she works in her songs is essential to her evil purposes.

Lancelot attempts to mitigate their offence when he makes the claim to Guinevere that 'many a bard, without offence / Has link'd our names together in his lay' (*LE*112).[21] In reality this does little to exculpate their guilt. Song is an element in Gawain's gaiety. As a boy he 'went, and breaking into song / Sprang out, and follow'd by his flying hair / Ran like a colt' (*CA*319–21).[22] Accordingly, meeting

Elaine at Astolat, 'he set himself to play upon her / With sallying wit, free flashes from a height / Above her, graces of the court, and songs' (*LE*642–4). When he discovers that Lancelot is the knight Elaine loves, Gawain 'leapt on his horse, and carolling as he went / A true-love ballad, lightly rode away' (*LE*699–700).[23]

Elaine's song is plaintive:

> Sweet is true love tho' given in vain, in vain;
> And sweet is death who puts an end to pain:
> I know not which is sweeter, no, not I.
>
> Love, art thou sweet? then bitter death must be:
> Love, thou art bitter; sweet is death to me.
> O Love, if death be sweeter, let me die.
>
> Sweet love, that seems not made to fade away,
> Sweet death, that seems to make us loveless clay,
> I know not which is sweeter, no, not I.
>
> I fain would follow love, if that could be;
> I needs must follow death, who calls for me;
> Call and I follow, I follow! let me die.
> (*LE*1000–11)

There is not a single word of more than two syllables.[24] No line has more than one two-syllabled word in it until the last, which expresses an urgency, a desired haste. Her plaintive song reveals not simply a tormented love but also her tortuous reasonings, which twist and turn in the maze of her torment. The emphasis that falls on the last word of the refrain spells out only one thing: '. . . I . . . die . . . I . . . die'. Accordingly, there is irony in her burial 'not as one unknown, / Nor meanly, but with gorgeous obsequies / And mass, and rolling music, like a queen' (*LE*1323–5).

To the coming of the Grail, no song is appropriate. Arthur accords to the song a limited power to inspire men temporarily: 'Taliessin is our fullest throat of song, / And one hath sung and all the dumb will sing' (*HG*300–1).[25] Galahad is the one singer who has already 'sung' his song. All other knights will at least make the attempt. Lancelot also hears a song during his quest:

> But always in the quiet house I heard,
> Clear as a lark, high o'er me as a lark,
> A sweet voice singing in the topmost tower
> To the eastward . . . (*HG*829–32)

'High up her chamber to the east' it was Elaine who 'Guarded the sacred shield of Lancelot', and 'Sweetly could she make and sing' (*LE*3–4,999). The dread castle of Carbonek ('A castle like a rock upon a rock') for a moment has been transfigured into a 'house' with a maiden singing in it.[26] When Lancelot reaches a door in it

A light was in the crannies, and I heard,
'Glory and joy and honour to our Lord
And to the Holy Vessel of the Grail'
        (*HG*835–7)

A fiery blast 'As from a seventimes-heated furnace' drives him back when he forces the door open.[27] The Grail will not reveal itself to force alone. At the end Arthur reminds his remaining knights that

        every fiery prophet in old times,
And all the sacred madness of the bard,
When God made music thro' them, could but speak
His music by the framework and the chord
        (*HG*872–5)

Pelleas ominously recollects a song of betrayal just before he discovers Gawain with Ettarre. Entitled 'A worm within the rose' this song Pelleas had heard 'sung before the Queen, / And seen her sadden listening' (*PE*388–9):

A rose, but one, none other rose had I,
A rose, one rose, and this was wondrous fair,
One rose, a rose that gladden'd earth and sky,
One rose, my rose, that sweeten'd all mine air –
I cared not for the thorns; the thorns were there.

One rose, a rose to gather by and by,
One rose, a rose, to gather and to wear,
No rose but one – what other rose had I?
One rose, my rose; a rose that will not die, –
He dies who loves it, – if the worm be there.
        (*PE*391–400)

Here the stanza length is significant. Previous song stanzas have been of three lines except those invented by Vivien, deliberately increased to four lines. Now the number of lines to each stanza has increased to five. The year tends to ripeness.

After the stress on the rose in the song Pelleas repeats, it is not surprising that he should see in Ettarre's garden 'roses white and red, and brambles mixt / And overgrowing them' (*PE*413).[28]

On arriving at Ettarre's castle, music helps Gawain to be light-hearted as he had been in his farewell to Elaine. Tennyson's phonaesthesia is at work again when the gay knight blows a bugle 'and that so musically / That all the old echoes hidden in the wall / Rang out like hollow woods at hunting-tide' (*PE*357–9).[29]

In allusion to his skill as a harper, Dagonet tells Tristram he makes but a 'broken music' with his new bride, the Breton Isolt (*LT*258).[30] As a harpist Tristram is also a poet. He prides himself on his first song: 'I made it in the woods, / And heard it ring as true as tested gold' (*LT*283–4).[31] As the woods are now autumnal, their colour is also suggested in Tristram's simile. His song expresses his philosophy of life and love:

> Free love – free field – we love but while we may:
> The woods are hush'd, their music is no more:
> The leaf is dead, the yearning past away:
> New leaf, new life – the days of frost are o'er:
> New life, new love, to suit the newer day:
> New loves are sweet as those that went before:
> Free love – free field – we love but while we may. (*LT*275–81)

The song 'has a blandly seductive form and a trivial content. For what it says, the poem is a fairly poor specimen of the *carpe diem* genre: "stay up-to-date with a new lover every year". But the rhythms and the rhymes and the repetitions convey the air of something momentous and sad and profound . . . The poem is a clever gesture, and it is by virtue of its form that Tristram hopes it may succeed'.[32] Identical first and last lines show sophistication but no development. Punctuation with a colon at every line end, and two sets of dashes at beginning and end and a single one in the exact centre, suggest at best a limp spontaneity. Tristram's complaint to Dagonet that 'Ye might have moved slow-measure to my tune' (*LT*282) suggests how melancholy and spiritless the performance really is.[33]

Form reflects mood, and as the year wears on, the mood drags. Its gravity makes itself felt in the fewer and longer stanzas of the later songs. If the song of Pelleas was two stanzas each of five lines, now the first of Tristram's is a single stanza of seven lines.

His second song, a single stanza of eight lines, heralds the fall of night, and is even more melancholy:

> Ay, ay, O ay – the winds that bend the brier!
> A star in heaven, a star within the mere!
> Ay, ay, O ay – a star was my desire,
> And one was far apart, and one was near:
> Ay, ay, O ay – the winds that bow the grass!
> And one was water and one star was fire,
> And one will ever shine and one will pass.
> Ay, ay, O ay – the winds that move the mere. (*LT*725–32)

To quote Walter Nash:

'The winds that move the mere' are the changes of event that drive from Tristram's instinct-obeying head all but the experience of the moment. He is indeed 'woodman of the woods', an adept in the reading of signs, but a fool in the histories of mind and heart. When the changing wind ruffles the surface of his observation, recollection is cancelled.[34]

What makes the poem 'like an old Gaelic song' is the placing of the refrain at the beginning, and repeating it four times.[35] Tennyson's placing of the dash after the alliterations in the refrain, lengthens this into a wail. By using an exclamation mark at the end of lines one, two and five, Tennyson impels us to expect one in the concluding line. Its absence there, along with the false – in being exploited already – rhyme of 'mere' lets the poem end in an anti-climax. This sad performance is Tristram's swan song, because a few lines later, Mark cuts him down.

The song in *Guinevere* is sung by a little novice to a tune the nuns have taught her. The words express the feelings of the foolish virgins in the famous parable:[36]

> Late, late, so late! and dark the night and chill!
> Late, late, so late! but we can enter still.
> Too late, too late! ye cannot enter now.
>
> No light had we: for that we do repent;
> And learning this, the bridegroom will relent.
> Too late, too late! ye cannot enter now.
>
> No light: so late! and dark and chill the night!
> O let us in, that we may find the light!
> Too late, too late: ye cannot enter now.
>
> Have we not heard the bridegroom is so sweet?
> O let us in, tho' late, to kiss his feet!
> No, no, too late! ye cannot enter now.
>   (G166–77)

In form this exquisite song reverts to the simpler stanza of the four earliest songs, partly, perhaps, because *Guinevere* was among the early idylls to be written. In the narrative order, however, it is placed second last in the serial, and the song itself is last to be sung.[37] But in spite of its lighter, quicker form, it is more tragic than the grave, melancholy autumn songs. To the guilty queen its repeated 'Too late, too late' speaks of the impossibility of making good what has been left undone.

With the lightest touch, the song mourns for the unalterable past, setting the tone for Arthur's visit to the nunnery, and his departure for the last battle.[38] The feeling of impending doom is deepened by the contrast with the fairy music recalled at Arthur's coming by the same young novice. Then

> ... strong man-breasted things stood from the sea,
> And sent a deep sea-voice thro' all the land,
> To which the little elves of chasm and cleft
> Made answer, sounding like a distant horn.
>   (G244–7)

Because they 'made answer' Tennyson gives even the little elves an epic dignity.[39] At the Round Table's foundation there was a bard who

> Sang Arthur's glorious wars, and sang the King
> As wellnigh more than man ...
> But even in the middle of his song
> He falter'd, and his hand fell from the harp,
> And pale he turn'd, and reel'd, and would have fall'n,
> But that they stay'd him up; nor would he tell
> His vision; but what doubt that he foresaw
> This evil work of Lancelot and the Queen?
>   (G284–5, 300–5)

It was exactly in the middle of his song, where expression and insight was at its most profound, that the bard faltered, and would not 'tell his vision'.

Accordingly, it would not be appropriate to have anything more than residual elements of music and song in *The Passing of Arthur*. Arthur, addressing himself to bards of the future, says that he has worn Excalibur 'like a king; / And whensoever I am sung or told / In aftertime, this also shall be known' (*PA*202). His barge, as it departs for Avalon, is likened to

> some full-breasted swan
> That, fluting a wild carol ere her death,
> Ruffles her pure cold plume, and takes the flood
> With swarthy webs ...   (*PA*434–7)

The poem ends with the single remembered line of a song: 'From the great deep to the great deep he goes' (*PA*445).

Thus the songs in the *Idylls* change form and become more elaborate as the year cycle runs on. They are always an apt projection of the characters who sing or create them, not least where they are ironical or deliberately banal (Vivien, Tristram). As the design draws to the close, they once more become simple, till in the final poem there is no song, only allusions and a single line spans the distance between beginning and end.

[7]

Dreams

Dreams give the characters in the *Idylls* an inner life of their own. Guilt as well as the Arthurian ideal betray themselves in dreams. The subtle and ambivalent medium in which dreams express themselves is in symbols. Dreams, therefore, enormously enhance other patterns of symbolism in the poem.

Tennyson understands dreams both in a literal and a metaphorical sense. The very first mention of dreams is metaphorical. Arthur, riding into battle, reflects on his incompleteness unless joined to Guinevere:

> What happiness to reign a lonely king,
> Vext – O ye stars that shudder over me,
> O earth that soundest hollow under me,
> Vext with waste dreams? for saving I be join'd
> To her that is the fairest under heaven,
> I seem as nothing in the mighty world,
> And cannot will my will, nor work my work
>   (*CA*81–7)

In the present passage dreams clearly mean ideals or aspirations. But to realise them a man must stand with both feet firmly planted on the earth, joined to a woman who will make life one and whole. Without such a stable foundation the king's dreams will remain an insubstantial waste.

As against Arthur's dream, that is, aspiration, to lighten 'this dark land', Bedivere dismisses dreams as idle fancies, scorning those who 'dream' that Arthur 'dropt from heaven' (*CA*182).

The first actual dream in the serial poem is dreamt by Leodogran, an otherwise minor character, certainly a near nonentity in Arthurian tradition. The dream comes to him when he has to make the one momentous decision in his life: whether Arthur is fit to marry his daughter. Thus he

> Doubted, and drowsed, nodded and slept, and saw,
> Dreaming, a slope of land that ever grew,
> Field after field, up to a height, the peak
> Haze-hidden, and thereon a phantom king,
> Now looming, and now lost; and on the slope
> The sword rose, the hind fell, the herd was driven,

> Fire glimpsed; and all the land from roof and rick,
> In drifts of smoke before a rolling wind,
> Stream'd to the peak, and mingled with the haze
> And made it thicker; while the phantom king
> Sent out at times a voice; and here or there
> Stood one who pointed toward the voice, the rest
> Slew on and burnt, crying, 'No king of ours,
> No son of Uther, and no king of ours;'
> Till with a wink his dream was changed, the haze
> Descended, and the solid earth became
> As nothing, but the King stood out in heaven,
> Crown'd.
>   (*CA*426–43)

The whole experience is integrated by being a single syntactic unit, a sentence, indeed one of the longest sentences in the *Idylls*. Form, structure, design exert control. 'The dream is a transcendentalist's dream of earthly things as insubstantial shadows and spiritual things as reality. It is a dream that asserts the value and vitality of the ideal, even though it is realized in imperfect ways.'[1] Leodogran has no choice but to accept Arthur as rightful king. His decision, and in a sense the entire story, turns on a dream.

In *Gareth and Lynette*, when the young knight overcomes his adversary, Morning Star, Lynette encourages him 'O star, my morning dream hath proven true' (*GL*975). After the encounter she playfully questions Gareth about birdsong: 'What dream ye when they utter forth / May music?' (*GL*1053). Dreaming expands to its fullest when even the hern, letting down its other leg, 'dreams / Of goodly supper in the distant pool' (*GL*1156).

Gareth's propensity to dream, in the sense of idealising, is well displayed after his defeat by Lancelot. Then

> Silent the silent field
> They traversed. Arthur's harp tho' summer-wan,
> In counter-motion to the clouds, allured
> The glance of Gareth dreaming on his liege.
> A star shot: 'Lo,' said Gareth, 'the foe falls!'
> An owl whoopt: 'Hark the victor pealing there!'
>   (*GL*1280–5)

Arthur's ideals have indeed created powerful dreamers, who hitch their aspirations to stars.[2] Gareth is ready for that last adversary, Death.

Dreaming in widely different senses defines Arthur's kingly aims, and graces the birth of love in *Gareth and Lynette*, but it gives rise to the entire action in *The Marriage of Geraint* and *Geraint and Enid*. On a summer morning the new sun 'heated the strong warrior in his dreams' and so helped to make him feel his wife was unfaithful (*MG*72). Her infidelity is more apparent than real, as he hardly could 'dream she could be guilty of foul act' (*MG*120). The actual dream issues in action insofar as it moves Geraint to submit Enid to a test, which forms the main part of *Geraint and Enid*.

The Marriage of Geraint is notable for Guinevere's first personal appearance in the *Idylls*. (Previously she had been but a symbol at her marriage, and as part of Tennyson's subtle framing she makes no appearance in *Gareth and Lynette*). At the incident of the chase, Guinevere 'lay late into the morn, / Lost in sweet dreams, and dreaming of her love / For Lancelot' (*MG*157–9). Geraint had previously ordered Enid's withdrawal from court because he heard a rumour about the queen 'Touching her guilty love for Lancelot' (*MG*25). This breaks one of Arthur's vows: 'To speak no slander, no, nor listen to it' (*G*469). Rumour seems to be at work before the appearance of Vivien. But in a poetic fiction cause and effect are so interwoven that nothing is certain. From this dreamlike blurring of sharp contours, the poem derives much of its effectiveness.

Enid too has her dreams. Ironically, hers express simply an innocent fear that she may not be able to live up to the queen's ideal. Thus in a long, brilliant and subtle dream sequence of some fifty lines she 'dreamt herself was such a faded form' as the blurred carp in a pool of golden fish (*MG*654). The dream concludes in familiar fashion with someone seizing her. This turns out to be her mother, gently shaking her awake, with the present of a fine wedding dress. She awoke, like Adam in Paradise, and found it true. But in the sequel her dreaming reflects inner disturbance. So, when she is exhausted

evermore

> Seem'd catching at a rootless thorn, and then
> Went slipping down horrible precipices,
> And strongly striking out her limbs awoke
> (*GE*377–80)

Geraint, already confused by a dream, increases the confusion between himself and Enid by the ridiculous assertion that he possesses 'ears to hear you ev'n in his dreams' (*MG*72, *GE*429). Then they enter a way which 'beaten broad' leads from the territory of the false Limours to the waste earldom of Doorm.[3] Such is the unifying power of Tennyson's style that these two bad characters and the landscape in which they operate seem also to be functions of a dream in Geraint's fevered mind.[4]

The meaning of dream is further developed in *Balin and Balan*

Balan chides his brother, Balin, before leaving on his first mission entrusted to him by King Arthur:

Let not thy moods prevail, when I am gone
Who used to lay them! hold them outer fiends,
Who leap at thee to tear thee; shake them aside,
Dreams ruling when wit sleeps! yea, but to dream
That any of these would wrong thee, wrongs thyself.

   (*BB*137–41)

Moods, emanating from dreams that rule 'when wit sleeps', take fiendish form, bedevilling the dreamer, and in metaphoric terms leaping at and tearing him. 'Dreams' and 'to dream' in this passage go far beyond idle dreams and harmless fancies. They now assume the power of deceptive delusions.

In an attempt to obtain privacy, Balin withdraws into a garden bower in Camelot. Here he overhears Guinevere and Lancelot.[5] The queen upbraids her knight: 'Let be: ye stand, fair lord, as in a dream' (*BB*253). The dream or trancelike state she refers to is of course Lancelot's love for her. Lancelot's dreamlike condition complements Guinevere's dream of him while staying abed in the previous idyll sequence (*MG*157–9). Now Lancelot 'with his hand among the flowers' attempts to protect himself by alleging that his dream was of a maiden saint, whose statue happens to stand in a shrine within the garden walk. To dream of any other woman than herself is of course subtly insulting to Guinevere, but even more insulting is his transparent prevarication. Guinevere had been more honest when she overslept, and lay 'dreaming of her love / For Lancelot'.

Balin's disillusionment with the idealised Lancelot and the queen is responsible for his flight back to the forest. There he meets Garlon, who aggravates his disturbed mood by mocking Balin's illusions about Arthur's court, and 'not the less by night, / The scorn of Garlon, poisoning all his rest, / Stung him in dreams' (*BB*377–8). It is Vivien who in the end completes Balin's disintegration by her pretence 'And now full loth am I to break thy dream' (*BB*493). Her talent lies in shaping or breaking dreams. She well understands her power as a magnifying and distorting mirror. Balin is to be her first adult victim.

After the death of Balin and Balan, Vivien transfers her machinations to court. 'As one that labours with an evil dream' she observes Lancelot and Guinevere get to horse, envious of their love:

ride, and dream
The mortal dream that never yet was mine –
Ride, ride and dream until ye wake – to me!

Then, narrow court and lubber King, farewell!
For Lancelot will be gracious to the rat,
And our wise Queen, if knowing that I know,
Will hate, loathe, fear – but honour me the more.
  (*MV*114–20)

In 'the mortal dream that never yet was mine' Vivien admits that the nature of love is foreign to her. The passion she is capable of is perfect hate (*MV*40–1).[6]

According to his ruling passion for knowledge, Merlin's visionary dreams reach out to the stars. In speaking of the stars to Vivien, the astronomer tells her of

          a single misty star,
Which is the second in a line of stars
That seem a sword beneath a belt of three,
I never gazed upon it but I dreamt
Of some vast charm concluded in that star
To make fame nothing.   (*MV*506–11)

Through the premonitory dreams he experiences, Merlin feels the end is near:

He walk'd with dreams and darkness, and he found
A doom that ever poised itself to fall,
An ever-moaning battle in the mist,
World-war of dying flesh against the life,
Death in all life and lying in all love,
The meanest having power upon the highest,
And the high purpose broken by the worm.
  (*MV*188–94)

While Merlin's dream is an example of a prophetic dream, Vivien attempts to minimise 'the jumbled rubbish of a dream' (*MV*345). In one instance, however, she admits the truth of aspiring dreams: 'Man dreams of Fame while woman wakes to love' (*MV*458). Fame is put into capitals to suggest an abstraction that Vivien derides. Love remains in lower case, for even to Vivien, who is incapable of it, love is something real.

Dreams, whether understood concretely or figuratively, are always fragile. 'The tiny-trumpeting gnat can break our dream / When sweetest' says Guinevere to her lover (*LE*137–8).[7] Ominously Guinevere echoes Vivien's words earlier to Balin: 'Full loth am I to break thy dream' (*BB*493). But dreams are not only fragile, they are fanciful when their high aspirations weaken into mere fantasies.

The heroine of *Lancelot and Elaine* is revealingly described at the start: 'so she lived in fantasy' (*LE*27). If 'fantasy' stands for her mode of day-dreaming, so the subtly different 'fancy' characterises the less resilient and ageing Lancelot, who 'full often lost in fancy' wanders to Elaine's castle of Astolat (*LE*163). Her day-dreaming life is also reinforced by real dreams. Lavaine tells Lancelot:

> the maiden dreamt
> That some one put this diamond in her hand,
> And that it was too slippery to be held,
> And slipt and fell into some pool or stream,
> The castle well, belike. (*LE*210–14)

This is a portent of Guinevere's throwing the diamonds into the Thames (*LE*1216–29). At the same time it reflects Elaine's intuitive nature. 'I behold him in my dreams / Gaunt as it were the skeleton of himself' (*LE*758–9) she claims, while he is recovering from his wounds, and her dream turns out to be true. Lancelot dreams 'Of dragging down his enemy' (*LE*808). In one sense the enemy is himself, the struggle in his conscience over loving Guinevere. Towards the close, Elaine relates a dream of 'yesternight' in which 'This night I dream'd / That I was all alone upon the flood', a genuinely premonitory dream of her funeral barge floating down the river (*LE*1039).

In *The Holy Grail* dreams give way to vision, this exalted term occurring no less than sixteen times in the idyll. In the thunderstorm that breaks as the Grail comes to Camelot, Arthur rides back hastily to the city 'In horror lest the work by Merlin wrought / Dreamlike, should on the sudden vanish, wrapt / In unremorseful folds of rolling fire' (*HG*259–61).[8] 'Dreamlike' suggests the fantastic nature of Merlin's creation, a city 'built / To music' (*GL*272), and the fragility of anything spiritual or artistic. Fire is to flare and flicker in the dreams and fantasies of the leading characters after this.

As if to exemplify Vivien's lines: 'Old monk and nun, ye scorn the world's desire, / Yet in your frosty cells ye feel the fire' the monk Ambrosius, cloistered for a lifetime, admits to being, with his brethren, 'plagued with something sweet / Beyond all sweetness in a life so rich' (*BB*439–40, *HG*624–5). A graphic part of Lancelot's quest is his recollection 'And in a dream I seem'd to climb / For ever' (*HG*833).

The balanced perspective of the king closes the idyll:

> Let visions of the night or of the day
> Come, as they will; and many a time they come,
> Until this earth he walks on seems not earth,
> This light that strikes his eyeball is not light,
> This air that smites his forehead is not air
> But vision – yea, his very hand and foot –
> In moments when he feels he cannot die,

And knows himself no vision to himself,
Nor the high God a vision, nor that One
Who rose again . . . (*HG*906–15)

Arthur has his own majestic rhythm and regal diction. In all his
speeches he has a power and sympathy that no other character
remotely approaches.

Dreamlike visions and twilight dreams continue in *Pelleas and
Ettarre*. Seeing Ettarre and her damsels in the forest, they appear to
Pelleas as 'to some old prophet might have seem'd / A vision hover-
ing on a sea of fire' (*PE*49–50). Pelleas dreams in the forest at noon,
the place and time mortals are most susceptible to seduction by
nymphs.[9] He dreams of the ideal:

And since he loved all maidens, but no maid
In special, half-awake he whisper'd, 'Where?
O where? I love thee, tho' I know thee not.
For fair thou art and pure as Guinevere,
And I will make thee with my spear and sword
As famous – O my Queen, my Guinevere,
For I will be thine Arthur when we meet.'
(*PE*39–45)

At first Pelleas, hailed as a 'pilot star', is so innocent that he is pre-
pared to endow with his full affections the first woman he sees. To
his undoing it happens to be Ettarre, anything but the ideal of
purity that Pelleas dreams of.

When he finally discovers her with Gawain, he:

gulf'd his griefs in inmost sleep; so lay,
Till shaken by a dream, that Gawain fired
The hall of Merlin, and the morning star
Reel'd in the smoke, brake into flame, and fell.
(*PE*506–9)

Falling stars symbolise the broken aspirations of the dreamer. How
far the stars in Arthur's heaven have fallen is revealed in *The Last
Tournament*. The call to tournament is no longer stirring: 'the sudden trumpet sounded as in a dream / To ears but half-awaked'
(*LT*151–2).[10] After Tristram has won the prize he departs for Isolt
and Lyonnesse. On the way he lies down and dreams:

He seem'd to pace the strand of Brittany
Between Isolt of Britain and his bride,
And show'd them both the ruby-chain, and both
Began to struggle for it, till his Queen
Graspt it so hard, that all her hand was red.
Then cried the Breton, 'Look, her hand is red!
These be no rubies, this is frozen blood,

> And melts within her hand – her hand is hot
> With ill desires, but this I gave thee, look,
> Is all as cool and white as any flower.'
> Follow'd a rush of eagle's wings, and then
> A whimpering of the spirit of the child,
> Because the twain had spoil'd her carcanet.
>   (*LT*406–18)

According to Walter Nash:

> The dream is for the dreamer a spiritual and prophetic experi-
> ence. Tristram's dream forbodes his death; also, like Lancelot's
> dream in *Balin and Balan*, it projects the anxieties and uncertain-
> ties that underlie the hard assurance of the waking man, and
> shows a mind pronouncing judgment upon itself. Tristram has
> won the trophy of Innocence, but his dream tells him, sym-
> bolically, that he has offended against the innocent spirit.[11]

This dream of Tristram's is introduced by the line: 'then he laid /
His brows upon the drifted leaf and dream'd' and it is terminated
by the introduction of a parallel topic, Arthur's expedition: 'He
dream'd, but Arthur with a hundred spears . . .' (*LT*404,419). This
topic takes up the next sixty-four lines, and when we return to
Tristram unexpectedly, there is still the dream: 'Then, out of
Tristram waking, the red dream / Fled with a shout' (*LT*486–7).
At this point

> the reader will quite certainly refer the phrase (red dream) not
> only to the account of Tristram's dream, but also to events
> freshly related; to the shouts of the unruly knights and the
> lurid reddening of the sky and seascape with reflections of fire.
> Arthur's experiences recede into Tristram's dreaming, and are
> projected from it; fantasy is interpreted in fact, and fact assumes
> the colouring of fantasy.[12]

When he reaches his queen, Tristram's appetite becomes cruder:

> Come, I am hunger'd and half-anger'd – meat,
> Wine, wine – and I will love thee to the death,
> And out beyond into the dream to come.   (*LT*713–5)

This gluttonous lover who jests with dreams also parodies Arthur's
marriage vows: 'Let chance what will, I love thee to the death . . .
King and my lord, I love thee to the death' (*CA*467,469). Seconds
after, Mark makes the vow come true.

In her guilty sleeplessness at Camelot, Guinevere is visited at night
by grim faces. Eventually she has a vast, engulfing dream of epic
proportions:

> or if she slept, she dream'd
> An awful dream; for then she seem'd to stand

On some vast plain before a setting sun,
And from the sun there swiftly made at her
A ghastly something, and its shadow flew
Before it, till it touch'd her, and she turn'd –
When lo! her own, that broadening from her feet,
And blackening, swallow'd all the land, and in it
Far cities burnt, and with a cry she woke.

(*G*74–82)

The association of fire with sunset or night in the three previous idylls is brought to its climax and resolution in Guinevere's dream.[13] Arthur's hold on the ideal is so strong that in his long farewell speech he tells Guinevere he could not 'dream untruth' of her (*G*538). He also stresses that his love for her has in no way diminished:

My love thro' flesh hath wrought into my life
So far, that my doom is, I love thee still.
Let no man dream but that I love thee still.

(*G*555–7)

Arthur is poignantly human. Guinevere echoes her king after his departure:

I must not scorn myself: he loves me still.
Let no one dream but that he loves me still.

(*G*667–8)

In *The Passing of Arthur* a ghostly Gawain visits Arthur in dream.[14] In Virgilian fashion he is blown along a wandering wind:

'Hollow, hollow all delight!
Hail, King! tomorrow thou shalt pass away.
Farewell! there is an isle of rest for thee.
And I am blown along a wandering wind,
And hollow, hollow, hollow all delight.'

(*PA*33–7)

At the start of his reign Arthur could see 'The smallest rock far on the faintest hill, / And even in high day the morning star' (*CA*98–9). It is so at the end. Arthur identifies the voice in his dream: 'Who spake? A dream. O light upon the wind, / Thine, Gawain, was the voice'. The stolid Bedivere takes up the adjective: 'Light was Gawain in life, and light in death / Is Gawain, for the ghost is as the man; / And care not thou for dreams from him' (*PA*46–7, 56–8).[15] But in Arthur's experience dreams have been meaningful, and so it remains with his last dream of foreboding. The following day, after the last battle, Bedivere disposes of Excalibur and the mortally wounded king is received on a barge by three queens who appear 'Black-stoled, black-hooded, like a dream' (*PA*365). Then Arthur speaks his famous words:

> More things are wrought by prayer
> Than this world dreams of.   (*PA*415-6)

From the perspective of the serial evolution there is little to add. Dreams in every sense of the word in which they have appeared in the *Idylls*, but especially in the concrete sense, are inherent in Tennyson's design from the beginning. This is well shown by the lines just quoted, which come from *Morte d'Arthur*, the first idyll to be written. Dreaming is one of Tennyson's most imaginative devices. Through the autonomy of dreams characters are given or denied an inner life. Dreams are the conscience of the soul. That is why Arthur is especially sensitive to them, and his dreams frame, that is to say, help to give unity and coherence to, the entire series. Merlin, an arch-dreamer, built Arthur's 'havens, ships and halls'. In his frivolity Gawain ends as a dream, 'blown along a wandering wind'.[16] Pelleas's loss of sanity manifests itself through dreams. The dreams of Lancelot, Guinevere and Tristram reflect their guilt. Though her own are but 'jumbled rubbish' Vivien knows well their corrupting power. In victory, the dream in action, Gareth is knight to the King's best wish. Dreams and dreaming add a dimension of their own to Tennyson's Arthurian world.

Characterisation

Every part of this book has in some way shown Tennyson's skill in characterisation. This is a contribution of his own to Arthurian legend. Malory and other older writers offer almost no physical description at all. Malory, for instance, has no colour of eyes or hair for his heroes. Deeds or actions alone constitute character, or the occasional vivid gesture or remark: Arthur raising his vizor to reveal a benign face, Bors doffing his helm and smiling, Lancelot with grim humour praising his spear, Percivale having a single episode of temptation during his Grail quest, Gawain's proclivity for fresh fruit.[1] Horses and weapons are often mentioned because they are inseparable from the deeds they help to perform. On the other hand, Tennyson's characters are chivalric types and individuals with subtle differences of voice, appearance, manner. Tennyson secures their individual differences in many ways.

In the first idyll Tennyson introduces a conventional distinction in colouring, dark and fair. Bellicent admits to being dark, and says this too of her predecessors and those from whose lineage Arthur is supposed to descend, Uther or Gorloïs.[2] However, Arthur himself cannot be descended from such dark ancestry, for he is 'fair / Beyond the race of Britons or of men' (CA330). Whatever implications there may be, are at this stage playful. They may not be so when 'under her black brows a swarthy one' comments on the jousts late in the series (LT216–24). 'Black brows' symbolise a temptress in medieval literature, one reason Morgan le Fay is described as having this feature in *Sir Gawain and the Green Knight*.[3] Tennyson's character also 'laugh'd shrilly' (LT217), a characteristic she has in common with Vivien, who 'suddenly laugh'd and shrill' at her first entry into the series (BB486). In this way the poet invites us to speculate about identity, because that expands implications. It is an important part of his poetic technique.

Hair is a feature of some importance. As a boy, Gawain was 'follow'd by his flying hair' as he 'ran like a colt, and leapt at all he saw' (CA320–1).[4] Length of hair is still one of his distinguishing characteristics when he is a grown man. Rebuked by the king, he 'shook his hair, strode off, and buzz'd abroad' (LE717). What Gawain does with his hair is a sign of his vanity. His younger brother, Gareth, has 'a fluent hair and fine' (*GL*455).[5] Already, before reaching Camelot, Vivien is exercising her characteristic power to deceive. In a garbled tale she alleges to have seen Guinevere drawing her 'white hand' from out Lancelot's 'night-black hair', a hand that had 'wander'd from her own king's golden head' (*BB*503, 505). Tristram also speaks of Arthur's hair colour as 'a sun that ray'd from off a brow / Like hillsnow high in heaven' (*LT*661–2).[6] Elaine and Guinevere are blonde as well, like Helen of Troy and Milton's Eve.[7] Lavaine is jokingly told to joust for the last diamond 'And set it in this damsel's golden hair' (*LE*204). Arthur laments of his queen: 'O golden hair, with which I used to play' (*G*544). That their heads are 'crowned' with gold is ironic in king and queen.

Beards are also significant. Gareth notes that Merlin's 'looks as white as utter truth' (*GL*276).[8] 'Broad-faced with under-fringe of russet beard' is part of the barbarity of Earl Doorm, not to speak of the vulgarity of his chewing his beard (*GE*537,712). Vivien tells Mark she seeks 'one curl of Arthur's golden beard' but she quickly adds: 'To me this narrow grizzled fork of thine / Is cleaner-fashion'd' (*MV*58–60).[9] Also Tristram notes Arthur's 'golden beard that clothed his lips with light' (*LT*663). As 'the knightly growth that fring'd his lips' the symbol of Arthur's masculinity is emphasised at the poem's end (*PA*388).

Lips are also expressive. Elaine observes about Lancelot that 'the living smile / Died from his lips' for a cause she would never understand (*LE*321). Guinevere 'sat / With lips severely placid' when the knights forgot to pledge her health with Lancelot and instead drank to him and the lily maid (*LE*735). In a silence that is to extend throughout the whole series, 'Modred, biting his thin lips, was mute' (*GL*31).[10] The long vowel after several short vowels accentuates this feature. Right through, Modred doesn't say a word, which is all the more striking because it is Modred who brings about the final destruction of Arthur's kingdom and his death. Tennyson's skill in characterising the true nature of a person through outward appearance is nowhere more evident than in the case of Modred: 'He chill'd the popular praises of the King / With silent smiles of slow disparagement' (*G*13–14). His 'heart-hiding smile, and gray persistent eye' haunt Guinevere (*G*63). Modred is almost the perfect embodiment of the ambiguity of appearance. It can both hide and reveal reality.

The eye is usually regarded as most expressive of the soul. 'For large her violet eyes look'd' to hapless Pelleas, struck dumb by Ettarre's beauty, and deceived by it 'as tho' it were the beauty of her soul' (*PE*67,75). Lancelot has 'large black eyes' (*LE*829).[11] Enid's 'meek blue eyes' are a feature of sufficient importance to be repeated (*GE*771,840). Isolt's 'blue-black Irish hair, and Irish eyes' draw Tristram back home (*LT*403).[12] He also speaks of Arthur's 'steel-blue' eyes which go with his golden beard and unearthly fairness (*LT*662). Significantly, Guinevere's eye-colour is not revealed.[13]

'Kindling' and 'listening' eyes show how alert Camelot is in its early days, but the 'king's calm eye' nonetheless oversees everything (*GL*61,320,536).[14] Vivien, of course, uses hers to great effect, except for Arthur, on whom she had gazed 'with reverent eyes mock-loyal . . . at which the King / Had gazed upon her blankly and gone by' (*MV*155,159). When he 'dragg'd his eyebrow bushes down, and made / A snowy penthouse for his hollow eyes' (*MV*805–6) Merlin is grotesque.[15]

In a poet so conscious of sound it is only to be expected that voice is an integral part of characterisation. Both at Arthur's coronation and his marriage the Lady of the Lake is present, she who has 'a voice as of the waters' (*CA*290,464).[16] Then the ninth wave of the sea, 'gathering half the deep / And full of voices' bears the infant Arthur to land (*CA*379–80). It is to the summons of a 'wind which with full voice / Swept bellowing thro' the darkness on to dawn' that Gareth responds (*GL*173–4). On reaching Camelot he responds to another:

> Then into hall Gareth ascending heard
> A voice, the voice of Arthur, and beheld
> Far over heads in that long-vaulted hall
> The splendour of the presence of the King
> Throned, and delivering doom
> (*GL*310–14)

Here the long vowels are part of a phonaesthetic pattern suggesting a regal sonority in the king. In an idyll where full articulation of voice is exceptionally important, the absence of it is ominous: 'nor have I heard the voice' (*GL*1302) of the last antagonist to be defeated.

Geraint and Enid complement one another through their voices. Enid is struck by Geraint's 'noble' voice, and even before he has seen her, he declares: 'Here, by God's grace, is the one voice for me' (*MG*98,344). Vivien's voice is also an important part of her physical make-up. It is with 'shaken voice' that she attempts to seduce Arthur (*MV*155).[17] When she sings to Merlin 'so tender was her voice' that he is easily seduced. Towards the end of the idyll 'her false voice made way, broken by sobs' (*MV*155,399,855).

Just as Geraint declares his love for Enid from the moment he hears her sing: 'Here, by God's grace, is the one voice for me', so

Elaine is 'won by the mellow voice' of Lancelot before she closely looks at him (*MG*344, *LE*242).

Arthur's voice of authority which Gareth 'ascending heard . . . delivering doom' (*GL*310, 314) is complemented by his voice of compassion:

> But, if a man were halt or hunch'd, in him
> By those whom God had made full-limbed and tall,
> Scorn was allow'd as part of his defect,
> And he was answer'd softly by the King
> And all his Table . . . (*G*41–5)

Arthur's knights take their cue from the king. Ambrosius knows Percivale has been a member of the Round Table purely from his courteous tone (*HG*22–4).[18] Galahad's voice 'shrilling along the hall to Arthur' announces he has seen the Grail (*HG*289). Only on the wilfully corrupt has Arthur's voice an unpleasing sound. 'I never heard his voice / But long'd to break away' complains Ettarre (*PE*247–8). Late in the cycle there is an ominous sound from the crowd at the last tournament, when Lancelot

> heard
> The voice that billow'd round the barriers roar
> An ocean-sounding welcome to one knight.
> (*LT*167–8)

Such an elemental reworking of Tristram's welcome in Malory is full of foreboding.[19] It is the last gathering of the wave before it breaks in the figure of the Red Knight. At the end of the idyll Arthur only hears the fool sobbing in the darkness:

> about his feet
> A voice clung sobbing till he question'd it,
> 'What art thou?' and the voice about his feet
> Sent up an answer, sobbing, 'I am thy fool,
> And I shall never make thee smile again.'
> (*LT*752–6)

Guinevere is keenly aware of 'vermin voices' spreading scandal but at the end she passes 'to where beyond these voices there is peace' (*LE*138, *G*692). At Arthur's coronation the Lady of the Lake was present as 'a voice as of the waters' and at the close the three Queens greet him with 'one voice, an agony / Of lamentation' (*CA*290, *PA*369). However, there is concord at the close. When Arthur's barge sinks below the horizon, Bedivere hears faintly 'as if some fair city were one voice / Around a king returning from his wars' (*PA*460–1).

Tennyson's Arthurian world is peopled with highly individualised men and women, not with mere stock figures. Even the minor

actors who put in only one appearance are individuals, and the
heroes and heroines express their human feelings by laughter, sighs
or frowns. The great king whom the bard sang 'as wellnigh more
than man' (*G*285) displays the humour of a well-balanced nature,
when he 'laugh'd upon his warrior whom he loved' (*CA*124).[20]
On being asked Arthur's origins, Merlin merely 'laugh'd as is his
wont' (*CA*400). Humour is a traditional trait of the magician.[21]
However, Vivien's expression of humour is all unnatural. She 'suddenly laugh'd and shrill' at her first appearance (*BB*486). With her,
smiling is always qualified. She smiles 'sunnily', 'scornfully',
'saucily', 'mournfully', and 'as in wrath' (*BB*520, *MV*37, 266, 309,
436, 524, 649). Everything she does is a pretence. In contrast
Arthur's humour is genuine. In Camelot at the height of his reign
he beams out well-being: 'With a kindly hand on Gareth's arm /
Smiled the great King' (*GL*564–5).[22] When his baron wished to
fight single-handed against two strange knights 'Arthur laugh'd
upon him' (*BB*14). In jousting with his own knights, if one 'cast
him down, he laughs / Saying, his knights are better men than he'
(*LE*312–13).

Lancelot shares this exemplary humour with the king. 'When he
mark'd his high sweet smile / In passing' Balin envies Lancelot's
power to make others 'from being smiled at happier in themselves'
(*BB*157–60). So bountiful a smile has, ironically, a most devastating
effect on Elaine. '"So ye will grace me" answer'd Lancelot /
Smiling a moment' when he agreed to wear her favour at the jousts. Later,
however, she notes how quickly 'the living smile / Died from his
lips'. Nonetheless when the time comes for him to leave for the
diamond jousts 'he bound / Her token on his helmet with a smile'
(*LE*222, 321, 372). Then in the attempt to soften his final departure
he tells her 'You yourself will smile at your own self'. As if carrying
out this wish she does indeed, as viewed by the observers of her
funeral barge: 'But fast asleep, and lay as tho' she smiled' (*LE*946,
1154).[23] After this, Lancelot smiles no more.

Misinterpreting the smile on the face of a churl leads to Balin's
banishment (*BB*217). After this there is a steady deterioration. When
Gawain is introduced, it is 'with smiling face and frowning heart'
(*LE*551). When Arthur hears of Gawain's failure to carry out his
quest 'the seldom-frowning King frown'd' (*LE*710). A shadow has
fallen on Camelot. Laughter gradually becomes sardonic (*BB*486,
*MV*161, *PE*125). When Pelleas is so abashed by Ettarre's beauty
that he cannot reply to her question

> Then with a slow smile turn'd the lady round
> And look'd upon her people; and as when

> A stone is flung into some sleeping tarn,
> The circle widens till it lip the marge,
> Spread the slow smile thro' all her company.
> Three knights were thereamong; and they too smiled,
> Scorning him; for the lady was Ettarre,
> And she was a great lady in her land.
>   (*PE*87–94)

Considering the effect Arthur's appearance makes on others, there is a staggering lack of perception in Guinevere on the first occasion she sees him: 'one among many, tho' his face was bare' (*CA*54). Had she already been blinded by love for Lancelot, her insensitiveness to Arthur's stature would be natural, but in fact she meets Arthur before she meets Lancelot.

In contrast to Guinevere's baffling indifference are the three fair queens at Arthur's coronation, 'tall, with bright / Sweet faces, who will help him at his need' (*CA*277). Lancelot's face 'seam'd with an ancient sword-cut on the cheek' is a contrast to the 'clear-faced King' (*LE*257,430). The mean narrowness of a face is set off against Lancelot's 'broad clear brow' ('The Lady of Shalott' iii 28) and the ample imaginative brow of Arthur:

> And once the laces of a helmet crack'd
> And show'd him, like a vermin in its hole,
>   Modred, a narrow face.   (*LT*164–6)

This brief account has shown how composite is Tennyson's characterisation. It is achieved not only through complement and contrast, but also through varying perspectives in which characters are always seen through the eyes and personalities of one another. What is already implicit in our first strong impression of them grows palpable as they interact with one another. Owing to the nature of a serial and the widely spaced entries and exits of the actors, the reader is constantly called upon to take an active part in the drama. We have already seen many examples of how various characters interact. We shall now consider briefly the most ambiguous of these relationships, that between Lancelot and Guinevere. Of course, these two cannot be isolated; directly or indirectly Arthur is constantly present, and the whole court is more than a shadowy background.

Tennyson himself considered Lancelot an outstanding type of the hero in man.[24] This may be thought to contradict what we have said before, that Tennyson's characters are highly individualised. But this is only one side of the coin. One of Tennyson's most subtle achievements is to present his heroes as types embodied in individuals.

Tennyson's own estimation of Lancelot is reflected in literary criticism, which has always paid much attention to this central figure of the *Idylls*: 'Lancelot is the favourite of the old romances; Mr Tennyson makes him a more noble-minded man than they do'.[25] Curiously enough, Guinevere has received little attention. It may have a purely technical reason: her appearances are fewer and in less dramatic situations than her lover. Yet there are telling passages from which her character stands out round and whole. Her lack of discernment as far as Arthur is concerned already characterises her in a negative way. His noble figure, which strikes everyone else, fails to impress her: he is just one among many. Her indifference continues when she first comes face to face with him as the king and her husband. She

> glanced at him, thought him cold,
> High, self-contain'd, and passionless, not like him,
> 'Not like my Lancelot' (*G*402–4)

Her ruling characteristic is only hinted at in this passage. Feeling no earthy passion for him herself, she judges him to be passionless and unearthly, except for his 'passionate perfection' (*LE*122). She scorns his aspiration to ideals, betraying the common human weakness of despising what is too good for her. In Lancelot, she knowingly chooses the lesser man:

> I for you
> This many a year have done despite and wrong
> To one whom ever in my heart of hearts
> I did acknowledge nobler ...
> I am yours,
> Not Arthur's ... (*LE*1201–4, 134–5)

Resentment of Arthur's nobility colours all her judgments of him. She despises him because

> He never had a glimpse of mine untruth ...
> Rapt in this fancy of his Table Round,
> And swearing men to vows impossible,
> To make them like himself ...
> A moral child without the craft to rule,
> Else had he not lost me.
>   (*LE*125, 129–31, 145–6)

Inevitably her untruth towards Arthur must lead her into self-deception, betrayed in the line 'Else had he not lost me'. From the first, it is patently evident that Arthur could never have lost her, having never had her love.

Her relationship to Lancelot, who starts out as the perfect knight, the embodiment of chivalric ideals, is bound to corrupt him too:

> The great and guilty love he bare the Queen,
> In battle with the love he bare his lord,
> Had marr'd his face and mark'd it ere his time.
> (*LE*244–6)

His premature ageing goes hand in hand with the degeneration of his soul.[26] His tendency to prevaricate creeps into his relation with Guinevere, as well as with others: 'vext with having lied in vain' to the king (*LE*102). He goes on to say to Guinevere: 'many a bard, without offence, / Has link'd our names together in his lay', evading the truth behind the rumours that are now disturbing the once peaceful court. When Guinevere reproves him for dreaming, he defends himself with transparent prevarication, that he was dreaming of a 'maiden saint' (*BB*256).

In their relationship, Guinevere is the dominant partner. Her physical charm is unmatched by any charm of character, and that is why the love she inspires is slavish. Her jealousy may arise from her love for Lancelot: her *hauteur* and peremptoriness do not. Nor are they merely the manners expected from a queen, as is shown by her furious outburst against the novice in the nunnery after she had renounced her queenly rank (*G*354–65).

Guinevere's contempt for the pure ideal of chivalric love and her preference for a 'touch of earth' (*LE*133) find a much readier acceptance in our permissive times than in Tennyson's own Victorian age. The earthiness of love seems to us natural and normal, and pure love abnormal, almost sickly. In its own time, however, the chivalric ideal of courtly love, the adoration of the Lady, had a real justification in the grossness and licentiousness of the Dark Ages, which reached well into the Middle Ages, just as cloistered life offered a much needed refuge to the sensitive and retiring natures who could not survive the brutal savagery of their times.

From the beginning critics have seized on Arthur as the chief weakness of the *Idylls*: 'It has been a mistake to suggest King Arthur, alive or dead, mythical or actual, as a subject for a poem of magnitude or seeming aim', 'the blameless king is personally a shadow', 'the real, tangible presence of the king is too little with us', 'Arthur is too dim, too undefined to serve as centre to the movement of the various poems', 'the reality of his manhood convinces us as little as it did Guinevere', 'a characterless king (who) represents the soul'.[27] These comments suggest that Tennyson has failed to dramatise the traditional Arthur. In Malory the young king Arthur commits a great crime, of which Merlin warns him: 'Ye have done a thing late that God is displeased with you, for ye have lain by your sister, and on her ye have gotten a child that shall destroy you and all the knights of your realm'.[28] Then, Herod-like, King Arthur 'let send for all the children born on May-day . . . For Merlin told King Arthur that he that should destroy him should be born on May-day'.[29] The children perish except for the one, Modred, who in the last battle 'smote his father, Arthur'.[30]

There is no doubt that Malory's incestuous mass murderer is a much more 'swinging' figure than Tennyson's noble king, who aspires to 'Have power on this dark land to lighten it' (*CA*92). It is true that Malory's king also reforms. In fact he comes fairly close to Tennyson's noble Arthur: 'for there was never yet man could prove King Arthur untrue to his promise'.[31] The code each prescribes to his knights is similar. Malory's king:

> stablished all his knights, and gave them that were of lands not rich, he gave them lands, and charged them never to do outrageousity nor murder, and always to flee treason; also, by no means to be cruel, but to give mercy unto him that asketh mercy, upon pain of forfeiture of their worship and lordship of King Arthur for evermore; and always to do ladies, damosels, and gentlewomen succour, upon pain of death. Also, that no man take no battles in a wrongful quarrel for no law, nor for no world's goods.[32]

Tennyson's Arthur makes his knights:

> lay their hands in mine and swear
> To reverence the King, as if he were
> Their conscience, and their conscience as their King,
> To break the heathen and uphold the Christ,
> To ride abroad redressing human wrongs,
> To speak no slander, no, nor listen to it,
> To honour his own word as if his God's,
> To lead sweet lives in purest chastity,
> To love one maiden only, cleave to her,
> And worship her by years of noble deeds,
> Until they won her. (*G*464–74)

Whatever the similarities and differences between the two Arthurs, the cardinal point is how Tennyson himself succeeds or fails in creating the central character of his own Arthurian world.

The first point to be noted is that Arthur is developed with great consistency, and to an unusual degree he practises what he preaches. He has no relationship outside his marriage, in observance of the code of monogamy he prescribed to civilise men. He is found in a position of central authority and initiates action in every idyll. He always speaks in character. Tennyson's development of his key character is a triumph of style and tone. This general assertion I shall now attempt to support with a detailed examination. When he

> pitch'd
> His tents beside the forest. Then he drave
> The heathen; after, slew the beast, and fell'd
> The forest, letting in the sun . . .   (*CA*57–60)

Arthur establishes himself with the minimum of fuss. Having proved himself so efficiently, he may demand efficiency from others.

Arthur's own speeches in *Gareth and Lynette* show the wise and decisive ruler (*GL*336–41, 363–75, 411–27). The last of these shows Arthur every inch a king, as he dismisses with contempt Mark's request to be made a Round Table knight:

> 'More like are we to reave him of his crown
> Than make him knight because men call him king.
> The kings we found, ye know we stay'd their hands
> From war among themselves, but left them kings;
> Of whom were any bounteous, merciful,
> Truth-speaking, brave, good livers, them we enroll'd
> Among us, and they sit within our hall.
> But Mark hath tarnish'd the great name of king,
> As Mark would sully the low state of churl:
> And, seeing he hath sent us cloth of gold,
> Return, and meet, and hold him from our eyes,
> Lest we should lap him up in cloth of lead,
> Silenced for ever – craven – a man of plots,
> Craft, poisonous counsels, wayside ambushings –
> No fault of thine: let Kay the seneschal
> Look to thy wants, and send thee satisfied –
> Accursed, who strikes nor lets the hand be seen!'
>   (*GL*411–27)

Every item of the list dismissing Mark is drawn from Malory. In the whole sweep of Arthur's contempt, the line that marks its climax contains ten different vowels: 'Craft, poisonous counsels, wayside ambushings'.[33] Tennyson's phonetic underpointing is always effective.

In a significant change from Malory's narrative, Arthur's compassion is shown when he details Lancelot to shadow the young knight:

> So with a kindly hand on Gareth's arm
> Smiled the great King, and half-unwillingly
> Loving his lusty youthhood yielded to him.
> Then, after summoning Lancelot privily,
> 'I have given him the first quest: he is not proven.

128

Look therefore when he calls for this in hall,
Thou get to horse and follow him far away.
Cover the lions on thy shield, and see
Far as thou mayest, he be nor ta'en nor slain.'
  (*GL*564–72)

Arthur's special rhythm and diction, his total command of language, is evident again when he tells Geraint that he has come on a tour of inspection to the outlying districts of his realm:[31]

'Prince, when of late ye pray'd me for my leave
To move to your own land, and there defend
Your marches, I was prick'd with some reproof,
As one that let foul wrong stagnate and be,
By having look'd too much thro' alien eyes,
And wrought too long with delegated hands,
Not used mine own: but now behold me come
To cleanse this common sewer of all my realm,
With Edyrn and with others: have ye look'd
At Edyrn? have ye seen how nobly changed?
This work of his is great and wonderful.
His very face with change of heart is changed.
The world will not believe a man repents:
And this wise world of ours is mainly right.
Full seldom doth a man repent, or use
Both grace and will to pick the vicious quitch
Of blood and custom wholly out of him,
And make all clean, and plant himself afresh.
Edyrn has done it, weeding all his heart
As I will weed this land before I go.
I, therefore, made him of our Table Round,
Not rashly, but have proved him everyway
One of our noblest, our most valorous,
Sanest and most obedient: and indeed
This work of Edyrn wrought upon himself
After a life of violence, seems to me
A thousand-fold more great and wonderful
Than if some knight of mine, risking his life,
My subject with my subjects under him,
Should make an onslaught single on a realm
Of robbers, tho' he slew them one by one,
And were himself nigh wounded to the death.'
  (*GE*887–918)

In diction and syntax this long speech accords with Coventry Patmore's observation: 'Since the definite formation of the English language no poetry has been written with so small an admixture of Latin . . . and what will sound still stranger in the ears of those who have been in the habit of regarding the Latin element as essential to the dignity of poetry, no language has surpassed in epic dignity the English of these poems'.[35] Only when Arthur admits to having been too aloof does he use Latin diction to make the point ('alien eyes', 'delegated hands') and even this fits his role as legislator and judge, and legal diction and metaphor are important in these two idylls.[36] 'Full' as an intensifier is used in the *Idylls*, and the most exalted and rarest form in the pattern is employed for Arthur now: 'Full seldom'. Repentance happens very rarely, so rarely that it requires a special emphasis.[37]

The figure of quitch that Arthur uses to illustrate how insidious is habit and custom, derives from immediate experience. During the composition of the poem Tennyson had been much exercised by the removal of quitch from his Farringford lawn.[38]

The speech in its calmly controlled rhythm and flexibility exhibits the man accustomed to supreme authority, and wise in the ways of human nature. He is no otherworldly idealist: 'The world will not believe a man repents: / And this wise world of ours is mainly right'. Throughout the serial poem Arthur never departs from this stance.

The same discernment is shown in Balin's readmission to the Round Table:

> Said Arthur 'Thou hast ever spoken truth;
> Thy too fierce manhood would not let thee lie.
> Rise, my true knight. As children learn, be thou
> Wiser for falling! walk with me, and move
> To music with thine Order and the King.
> Thy chair, a grief to all the brethren, stands
> Vacant, but thou retake it, mine again.   (BB70–6)

Here is the word of kindly authority and command. In seven lines Arthur has made seven assertions. His speech displays a deep understanding of Balin's nature and the forlorn knight's need for reassurance. Balin's outspokenness in word and deed strikes a chord in the king. Arthur is forgiving. 'As children learn, be thou / Wiser for falling' is not condescension on Arthur's part. Balin has the mind of a child. The invitation to 'move / To music' is realised phonaesthetically in the sound and rhythm of Arthur's invitation. Ensuing developments are all the more pathetic when Balin leaves the 'kindly warmth of Arthur's hall' for the depths of the forest (BB231).

Arthur says nothing in *Merlin and Vivien*. He 'had gazed upon her blankly and gone by' (MV159) when Vivien attempted to seduce him. In this case his silence is more eloquent than speech.

Integral to Arthur's 'ideal manhood closed in real man' ('To the Queen' 38) is that he will neither speak any 'slander, no, nor listen to it' (*G*469). He, therefore, harbours no suspicion of how totally he has been deceived until the kingdom falls. Guinevere and Lancelot, mainly at Guinevere's instigation, exploit Arthur's trust and confidence. The queen feels safe because her husband is 'Rapt in this fancy of his Table Round' (*LE*129), underestimating as usual both Arthur's motives and his love for her. Where the real weakness of Arthur's relationship to Guinevere lies is indirectly brought out in Lancelot's and Arthur's speech at Elaine's burial:

> Then answer'd Lancelot, 'Fair she was, my King,
> Pure, as you ever wish your knights to be . . .
> Yea, to be loved, if what is worthy love
> Could bind him, but free love will not be bound.'
>
> 'Free love, so bound, were freëst,' said the King.
> 'Let love be free; free love is for the best.'
>   (*LE*1363-4, 1367-70)

By free love, of course, Arthur means the freely bestowed love that Lancelot, obsessed with 'the bright image of one face' (*LE*877), was unable to confer on Elaine. For once, Arthur fails to apply his tenet to himself. Even he is not far enough ahead of his time or mindful of the prerogative of a king in love, ever to have asked whether Guinevere freely returned his love.

Arthur's Achilles heel lies in his relationship to the woman who matters most both to him and to the harmony of the realm, for Vivien's machinations could not have been so successful without some foundation in fact.

As far as the duties of government are concerned, Arthur is most conscientious. As soon as he realises he has neglected the supervision of the outlying 'marches' he immediately sets himself on the road to remedy the situation (*GE*887 ff.). But it is not only his own concern to protect and improve the realm. It is the first duty also of the Round Table knights. The vow by which he binds them to himself is designed to ensure the welfare of the kingdom. Even the vow 'to love one maiden only, cleave to her' serves to raise the standard and stability of family life.[39] Arthur's insistence on purity for men has been much derided, but it has a very practical purpose. It is to raise the status and dignity of women in a necessarily male-dominated society. And if we disregard modern prejudices against purity, it may be considered an early attempt to abolish the double standard of morality that has in most societies and under the most varying conditions demanded purity from women and accorded licence to men. It is a modern prejudice, rare though not unknown in history, usually in periods of decay, to grant women the same licence as men. Since there could be no question of this in Arthur's time, the only way to overcome the double standard was to approximate men's conduct to women's.

There is not one word in the original vows about the Holy Grail and the scattering of the knights in a quest after it. 'Had I been there, ye had not sworn the vow' (*HG*276) Arthur says when he finds that the Grail has come to Camelot in his absence. As he himself has just been on an expedition to ensure the safety of the realm, his words are given added weight. Only when he has fully carried out his normal responsibilities can Arthur

> Let visions of the night or of the day
> Come, as they will; and many a time they come,
> Until this earth he walks on seems not earth,
> This light that strikes his eyeball is not light,
> This air that smites his forehead is not air
> But vision – yea, his very hand and foot –
> In moments when he feels he cannot die,
> And knows himself no vision to himself,
> Nor the high God a vision, nor that One
> Who rose again: (*HG*906–15)

Through Arthur's reflections Tennyson states clearly his belief that intimations of the divine are not given simply to romantic questers. True spiritual experience occurs in all walks of life, and in the sphere of common duties, as Arthur's previously quoted metaphor ('the King . . . is but as the hind / To whom a space of land is given to plow') shows. In the present instance he deprecates the romantic quest as an illusion: 'Have ye seen a cloud? / What go ye in the wilderness to see? . . . ye follow wandering fires' (*HG*286–7,319). For him genuine spiritual experience comes direct and immediate and is often repeated.

The coming of the Grail puts Camelot to the trial from which Arthur's spirit emerges as eminently practical, and puts the Grail quest into perspective.

The last tournament degenerates into an orgy in Arthur's absence. Before departing, Arthur senses what is happening as he remarks to Lancelot:

> 'Is it then so well?
> Or mine the blame that oft I seem as he
> Of whom was written, "A sound is in his ears"?
> The foot that loiters, bidden go, – the glance
> That only seems half-loyal to command, –

A manner somewhat fall'n from reverence –
Or have I dream'd the bearing of our knights
Tells of a manhood ever less and lower?
Or whence the fear lest this my realm, uprear'd,
By noble deeds at one with noble vows,
From flat confusion and brute violences,
Reel back into the beast, and be no more?'
   (*LT*114–25)

There is in fact a double dissolution of the kingdom, both at court
and in the field. The tournament degenerates to the point that
Guinevere has to break it up. But at the same time Arthur's own
expedition against the Red Knight ends in his loss of control over
his younger knights. They run amok:

Nor heard the King for their own cries, but sprang
Thro' open doors, and swording right and left . . .
Till all the rafters rang with woman-yells,
And all the pavement stream'd with massacre . . .
So all the ways were safe from shore to shore,
But in the heart of Arthur pain was lord.
   (*LT*471–2, 475–6, 484–5)

Almost all criticism of the figure of Arthur is centred on the king's
speech to his fallen queen in *Guinevere*. The king says:

'Yet I must leave thee, woman, to thy shame.
I hold that man the worst of public foes
Who either for his own or children's sake,
To save his blood from scandal, lets the wife
Whom he knows false, abide and rule the house:
For being thro' his cowardice allow'd
Her station, taken everywhere for pure,
She like a new disease, unknown to men,
Creeps, no precaution used, among the crowd,
Makes wicked lightnings of her eyes, and saps
The fealty of our friends, and stirs the pulse
With devil's leaps, and poisons half the young.
Worst of the worst were that man he that reigns!
Better the King's waste hearth and aching heart
Than thou reseated in thy place of light,
The mockery of my people, and their bane.'
   (*G*508–23)

One class of criticism condemns the cold, passionless Arthur, ab-
sorbed in the affairs of the kingdom, suddenly turning on his now
repentant queen: 'if you really did this, you were the Pecksniff of the
period'.[40] But what evidence do we have in the *Idylls* that Arthur is

cold, passionless and unloving to Guinevere? Only Guinevere's own testimony, and she is a forsworn witness. Guinevere herself admits the baseness of her motives, when she says of Arthur:

> To whom my false voluptuous pride, that took
> Full easily all impressions from below,
> Would not look up, or half-despised the height
> To which I would not or I could not climb –
> I thought I could not breathe in that fine air
> That pure severity of perfect light . . .
> . . . now I see thee what thou art,
> Thou are the highest and most human too.
>   (G636–41, 643–4)

Unlike the repentant Guinevere, however, literary critics fail to see the human feeling in Arthur, and condemn him for his far too harsh treatment of his queen: he is an 'impeccable prig'.[41] The answer to these critics is that they live in a historical vacuum. They ignore what Arthur would have been perfectly within his rights to do, and in fact what he may have been expected to do.[42] In a much more sophisticated age than Arthur's, King Henry VIII beheaded his adulterous wives, and he was by no means an exception. A century and a half later, the first Hanoverian king by due process of law had his wife imprisoned for life and her lover executed. The penalty for adultery has often been death until comparatively recent times. Mohammedan law prescribes death by stoning, and it is still in force in Saudi Arabia.

Everything considered, Guinevere is let off lightly by her husband. Yet his strictures on her are the favourite target for ridicule by literary critics. Henry James dismisses Arthur as 'a prig', Swinburne as a 'wittol' and as 'the Prince Consort'.[43] Are these witticisms to pass for an impartial critical appraisal? They are a historical provincialism, which sets up the standards or lack of standards of its own little time as the absolute measure to which all ages must conform. The proper critical question to ask is whether Arthur's conduct at this point is consistent with his character and with the spirit of Tennyson's Arthurian world. There is not a single passage to suggest that Arthur's condemnation of Guinevere is out of character. The severity of the condemnation, moreover, is not a prerogative of Victorian Englishmen but is common to many different cultures and ages.

Before his departure for the last battle, the allegedly passionless 'prig' speaks the lines that are surely amongst the most moving in the whole poem:[44]

> How sad it were for Arthur, should he live,

To sit once more within his lonely hall,
And miss the wonted number of my knights,
And miss to hear high talk of noble deeds
As in the golden days before thy sin.
For which of us, who might be left, could speak
Of the pure heart, nor seem to glance at thee?
And in thy bowers of Camelot or of Usk
Thy shadow still would glide from room to room,
And I should evermore be vext with thee
In hanging robe or vacant ornament,
Or ghostly footfall echoing on the stair.
For think not, tho' thou wouldst not love thy lord,
Thy lord has wholly lost his love for thee.
I am not made of so slight elements.
   (*G*493–507)

Before the last battle, Arthur goes through an agony of doubt and betrayal: 'My God, thou hast forgotten me in my death', followed by a recovery: 'Nay – God my Christ – I pass but shall not die' (*PA*27–8). At the end of the battle, when he lies mortally wounded on the barge, Sir Bedivere cries:

'Ah! my lord Arthur, whither shall I go?
Where shall I hide my forehead and my eyes?

   And slowly answer'd Arthur from the barge:
'The old order changeth, yielding place to new,
And God fulfils himself in many ways,
Lest one good custom should corrupt the world.
Comfort thyself: what comfort is in me?
I have lived my life, and that which I have done
May He within himself make pure! but thou,
If thou shouldst never see my face again,
Pray for my soul. More things are wrought by prayer
Than this world dreams of. Wherefore, let thy voice
Rise like a fountain for me night and day.
For what are men better than sheep or goats
That nourish a blind life within the brain,
If, knowing God, they lift not hands of prayer
Both for themselves and those who call them friend?
For so the whole round earth is every way
Bound by gold chains about the feet of God.
But now farewell. I am going a long way
With these thou seëst – if indeed I go
(For all my mind is clouded with a doubt) –

K   135

> To the island-valley of Avilion;
> Where falls not hail, or rain, or any snow,
> Nor ever wind blows loudly; but it lies
> Deep-meadow'd, happy, fair with orchard lawns
> And bowery hollows crown'd with summer sea,
> Where I will heal me of my grievous wound.
>   (*PA*407–32)

From first to last, therefore, Arthur speaks and acts as a king.[45] His words are always measured.[46] A man of infinite humanity and a model of courtesy, he is Tennyson's subtlest and most poetic character, the unifying figure of the whole poem, as 'From the great deep to the great deep he goes'.

One criticism levelled against Tennyson is that he 'could not tell a story at all'.[47] His work is therefore poor, undramatic, as for example the story of Guinevere in the nunnery. How she got there in the first place is only told later, necessitating the use of flashbacks. The assumption in this criticism is that the straightforward unfolding of a story from beginning to end is dramatically preferable. This assumption can be reasonably supported. But, on the other hand, we cannot reject the flashback method as necessarily undramatic (the tragedy of King Oedipus, for instance, unfolds through this method). There is much to be said for presenting a person in an unusual, tense or decisive situation, which arouses our attention and interest in how he or she got into this situation as well as the *outcome* of the situation. Attention as it were, branches off into both directions, past and future. It can be very effective to present a person in a dramatic situation to begin with, then to follow it up with precedents and antecedents (for example, Elaine). Besides, Tennyson has an excellent precedent for the flashback technique: Dante's *Inferno*. Dante, going through the Inferno meets tormented souls in their last, irretrievable extremity, and the actions and circumstances that have led them into this situation are necessarily told in a flashback.

The criticism that the poem was too decorative was begun by John Ruskin: 'I am not sure but I feel the art and finish in these poems a little more than I like to feel it'.[48] Ruskin was not the only one to consider the descriptions too elaborate: 'Our main criticism is this: that, whereas the great drift of the poem is moral, the energy of the poet has been in too great a degree expended on the descriptions'.[49] Such highly finished description distracts from the drama, and from the attention Tennyson pays to the actors in the drama, that is, that these descriptions are worked out at the cost of character. Further, they slow up the movement of the story greatly. This certainly seems to me applicable on occasion, particularly to the early poems, for instance, the long and detailed attention paid to dress in the Geraint idylls. Malory's terse style in many passages is certainly not improved by Tennyson, and it is also true that too elaborate descriptions do slow up the action. On the other hand similar criticisms can be levelled against every other long poem. Even Homer's masterpiece has its *longueurs* if we are honest; so has Dante's *Commedia*, not to speak of *The Faerie Queene*, which Macaulay, with unusual candour, admitted he was incapable of finishing.[50]

It seems that these valleys are almost inevitable in long poems, and it is hard to see how the peaks could stand out without the valleys.

As to the criticism that the poem is neither historical nor Victorian, one may raise similar doubts about Homer.[51] Does Homer give an historical account of the Trojan war as it really took place, or does he let his account reflect his own time? The answer, of course, is that he does neither and both. He constructs a Homeric world in which mythical, historical and contemporaneous elements are fused into a poetical whole.

As every chapter has shown, Tennyson's scheme is unified and mediated by a great number of devices. He has achieved what he set out to create, a 'compacted and vertebrate poem'.[52]

Past criticism of the *Idylls* has often been prejudiced and frequently irrelevant, however much it gave voice to genuine feelings. With a fuller understanding of Tennyson's style, narrative methods, and his use of sources it now appears that the *Idylls* joins *Troilus and Criseyde*, *The Faerie Queene*, *Paradise Lost*, *The Prelude*, and *The Ring and the Book* as one of the successfully sustained long poems in English.

Notes and References

Introduction
1. Baum (1948) p. 205.
2. Boas, *The Nineteenth Century* 90 (1921) 830.
3. *Memoir*, ii, 423.
4. *Memoir*, i, 453: 'Perfection in art is perhaps more sudden sometimes than we think: but then the long preparation for it, that unseen germination, *that* is what we ignore and forget.'
5. Chew (1948) p. 1389.
6. *Memoir*, ii, 506.

CHAPTER ONE
Serial Evolution
1. Crump (1920) pp. 112–13, has the following conjectured order of composition: III, I, IV, II, VI, VII–XII (order uncertain), V.
2. *The Last Tournament* appeared first in *Contemporary Review* for December 1871, and then with *Gareth and Lynette* as a separate volume, published by Strahan in 1872. For a clear view of how T.'s serial poem appeared to its readership and how the poet integrated the work externally and from within see Kathleen Tillotson (1962) who stresses the fact that T.'s form and subject matter was new, and that 'form and procedure were interdependent'.
3. In the narrative order of 12 poems, Tennyson's first phase opens with poem 6 and closes with 7; the second phase opens with poem 8 and closes with 9; and the final phase opens with poem 10.

CHAPTER TWO
Arthurian Legend
1. *Memoir*, ii, 13.

2. Malory xxi 4. T. had two pocket editions of Malory, named after the printers 'Walker and Edwards' and 'Wilks', both 1816. He also possessed Thomas Wright's somewhat better edited 1858 version. Because there are no substantival differences, I have used the most convenient Malory available, the Everyman edition. Many of the major passages of Malory echoed or recalled by T. are to be found in the standard edition of T. by Christopher Ricks (1969, hereafter Ricks), below the text of the *Idylls*. Usefully supplementing Ricks is *A Variorum Edition of Tennyson's 'Idylls'* by John Pfordresher (hereafter Pfordresher), 1973.
3. Malory Books xviii and xix open with 'so'.
4. Malory xxi 4.
5. See Frye, *Anatomy*, p. 223: 'the cross under the sunset being the antithesis of the tower under the moon'. For full cycle T. has this latter symbol also, see $HG810-15$, $PE384,415,447-51$.
6. Malory xxi 5.
7. Cp. $PL 2,688,746$ 'To whom the goblin full of wrath replied . . . To whom thus the portress of Hell gate replied'. T. has several interesting variations on the epical 'so spake' formula ($GL824,938,GE557$, $LE714,1328,HG203,916$). 'Ceased' is used to end speeches until the Grail ($MG732,BB529$, $MV17,612,932,LE241,1123,1194$, $HG748$) and then 'ended' in the next idyll ($LT51,454,699$). For finality of effect this parallels the fact that there are eight instances of the

formula in the first eight books, and
eight in the last four books, of
Paradise Lost.

8. 'Unknightly' occurs Malory x 70,
72. See *PL* 1, 738, 2, 185 'unheard
or unadored', 'unrespited, unpitied,
unreprieved'.

9. e.g. 2 *Sam.* 17.1 'I will arise and
pursue after David'.

10. Malory xxi 5.

11. *Aen.* 2, 487: *at domus interior
gemitu miseroque tumultu | miscetur
penitusque cavae plangoribus aedes |
femineis ululant: ferit aurea sidera
clamor*. Bedivere's 'this way and that
dividing the swift mind' (*PA*228)
is also Virgilian, *Aen.* 4, 285: *atque
animum nunc huc celerem, nunc dividit
illuc*.

12. Malory xxi 6.

13. Malory xxi 5.

14. For the Homeric allusions, see
Ricks, p. 596. Excalibur originating
'from out the bosom of the lake'
(*PA*198) echoes Eidothea, daughter
of Proteus, *Od.* 4, 435 'she had
plunged into the broad bosom of
the sea'. 'Nine years she wrought it'
(*PA*273) is redolent of the work of
another smith, Hephaistos, *Il.* 18,
400.

15. Malory iv 1. Matthew Arnold
ends *Tristram and Iseult* with
Merlin's seduction by Vivien, and
the last line 'for she was passing
weary of his love' echoes Malory
'And always Merlin lay about the
lady to have her maidenhood, and
she was ever passing weary of him'.
In T. it is Merlin who says 'I am
weary of her' (*MV*836).

16. Here Malory's 'so by her subtle
working' is echoed in the fact that
Vivien 'ever sought to work the
charm' (*MV*213). J. P. Eggers
(1971) 83–5 provides a thorough
and amusing survey of
contemporary critical attitudes to
Vivien, ranging from embarrassed
silence to outspoken protest that a
harlot was worth serious or any
treatment in poetry. Kaplan's

chapter on Merlin (1972) and
Adler's and Slinn's articles (1970,
1973) are useful for understanding
the idyll.

17. In Malory both are the same
person, Nimue. In dividing her into
two contrasting characters, T. keeps
them well apart. The Lady of the
Lake, an otherwise insignificant
character, occurs briefly in *The
Coming of Arthur, Gareth and Lynette,
Lancelot and Elaine*, and *The Passing
of Arthur*. Vivien occurs in *Balin and
Balan, Merlin and Vivien*, and
Guinevere. It would have been a
contradiction to include both in the
same idyll.

18. Echoing work' divinely
wrought' *PL* 6, 761. Ricks, p. 590
compares Pope's *Iliad* xviii 468–72.

19. Malory ix 15.

20. 'Valence þe Erl of sylchestre',
l. 162 of *Arthur, A Short Sketch of
his Life and History in English Verse
of the First Half of the Fifteenth
Century*, ed. F. J. Furnivall, EETS,
1864.

21. e.g. Malory iv 4 speaks of 'a
good knight and full desirous in
arms'.

22. Turner (1976) p. 160.

23. Malory xiv 9.

24. Malory iii 1.

25. As the original edition of Lady
Charlotte Guest's translation of the
Mabinogion is rare, I have used the
commonly available edition of her
work in the Everyman series (1919),
where this item occurs, p. 390.

26. *Mabinogion*, p. 222.

27. ibid., p. 223.

28. ibid., p. 224.

29. ibid., p. 225.

30. ibid., p. 230.

31. 'Branched' *OED* 2b 'adorned
with a figured pattern in
embroidery', *TN* 2.5.54; 'flowered'
OED 3 'embellished with figures of
flowers, or with flower-like
patterns', *ROM* 2.4.64.

32. *Mabinogion*, p. 241.

33. *Blackwood's* 86 (Nov. 1859) 611.

34. *Mabinogion*, p. 221.
35. See, for example, Nicoll and Wise (1896) 269–71.
36. 'Dissolutely' *OED* 3 'in a profligate manner; licentiously; in dissipation and debauchery', records only three instances before T.
37. *Mabinogion*, p. 406.
38. Emily, Lady Tennyson's letter diary (Tennyson Research Centre, Lincoln) records for 9th July 1857 'He brings me the first lines which may be the nucleus of the parting of Arthur and Guinevere'.
39. Geoffrey's *Historia* xi 1.
40. Malory xx 3–4.
41. 'Creatures' *OED* 3c 'expressing reprobation or contempt', *JC* 1.1.1. T.'s use of 'thing' *OED* 10b 'without qualification, in contempt or reproach, implying unworthiness to be called a person', ironically by the monster, Caliban, of Trinculo, *TMP* 3.2.54, so T. of a dwarf, and the boorishness of Limours and Doorm is shown in a similar use (*MG*412, *GE*325, 614).
42. Towers are a small motif in Malory. Percivale's sister, Malory xvii 11, states 'as soon as ye three come to the city of Sarras, there to achieve the Holy Grail, ye shall find me under a tower arrived, and there bury me in the spiritual place'. In Malory ix 19 when Isoud, hearing of Tristram's death, tries to kill herself, Mark 'bare her away with him into a tower; and there he made her to be kept, and watched her surely, and after that she lay long sick, nigh at the point of death'. In Malory xi 1 'here is within this tower a dolorous lady that hath been there in pains many winters and days' and in Malory xx 5 there is a character called 'Sir Selises of the Dolorous Tower'.
43. Malory xxi 10.
44. Malory xxi 7.
45. Malory xviii 9. The precise location of T.'s poetic Camelot and Astolat excited many Victorians. See Edward Conybeare's comments in his abridgement of Malory (1868) 319 n 3, 320 n 1, 335 n 2, and contributors to *Notes and Queries* 3rd. ser. 11 (1867) 215, 336, 464.
46. Malory xviii 9. 'From spur to plume / Red as the rising sun' (*LE*306) redolent of *H5* 4.6.6 'from helmet to the spur all blood was he'.
47. The Lady of Shalott has a spell or 'curse' upon her as a condition of the poem. The equivalent in Elaine is her propensity to dream, and so to see the future (*LE*210–14).
48. Malory xviii 8.
49. Malory xviii 9.
50. Malory xviii 13, xxi 13.
51. e.g *Gen.* 13.10 'Lot lifted up his eyes and beheld all the plain of Jordan.'
52. Malory xviii 15.
53. Malory v 9. Lavaine's 'making a roan horse caper and curvet' (*LE*787) echoes 'caper', 'to prance as a horse' *LLL* 5.2.113 and 'curvet', 'a leap of a horse in which the fore-legs are raised together and equally advanced, and the hind-legs raised with a spring, before the fore-legs reach the ground' *AWW* 2.3.299.
54. Malory xii 4.
55. Malory xviii 20.
56. Gurteen (1895) p. 415, protested at T.'s alteration to Malory: 'So again, according to Tennyson, "Arthur spied the letter in her hand" whereas the old romancer tells us, "then the queen espied the letter in the right hand and told the king thereof", a far more natural situation than that which the poet's imagination suggested. The king would naturally be too much occupied with the "faire corpse" to see so trifling a thing as a letter in the hand. It would take a woman's keen perception in such matters (as the old romancer well knew) to detect this.'
57. Malory xviii 21.

58. Malory xvi 5.

59. Malory xiv 7.

60. Malory xiii 7.

61. 'And' opens Malory xii, and often chapters open with it, e.g. Malory i 7, 11, 12, 17; ii 5, 17; iii 8. See ch. 5 pp.84–7 for a fuller discussion.

62. Note the amazing bonding of different syntactic elements in lines three and four: participle ('rending'), noun ('a blast'), adverb plus noun ('overhead / Thunder') and main clause ('in the thunder was a cry').

63. Malory xiv 7.

64. *Rev.* 21.21 'And the twelve gates were twelve pearls; every several gate was of one pearl'.

65. Malory xvi 2.

66. Malory xiv 6.

67. Malory xvii 20.

68. Malory xvi 11. When Bors 'heard the hollow-ringing heavens sweep / Over him' (*HG*675–6) this echoes *FQ* I xi 7 'That with their horrour heaven and earth did ring' and *PL* 7, 562 'The heavens and all the constellations rung'.

69. It may also have suggested an opposite image, when 'once the laces of a helmet crack'd, / And show'd him, like a vermin in its hole, / Modred, a narrow face' (*LT*164–6).

70. Malory xiii 16, xvi 1.

71. 'The Jeaste of Sir Gawain', (relating Gawain's adventures with a girl in a pavilion) in *Sir Gawayne*, ed. Madden, Bannatyne Club, 1839.

72. Malory xiii 17, 18–19.

73. Malory xv 2.

74. Malory xvii 16 (set out below the text in Ricks, pp. 1684–5).

75. 'Great angels, awful shapes, and wings and eyes' echoing *Ezek.* 10.12 'And their whole body, and their backs, and their hands, and their wings, and the wheels, were full of eyes round about'. 'And in the great sea wash away my sin' (*HG*803) echoing *Acts* 22.16 'Arise,

and be baptized, and wash away thy sins'.

76. *Matt.* 10.39 'He that findeth his life shall lose it: and he that loseth his life for my sake shall find it'.

77. In 'Sir Galahad' (1834, pub. 1842) T. did make him the speaker.

78. Malory xvii 23. The moral character of Bors is drawn from Malory xvi 6, 11: 'All is welcome ... that God sendeth me', 'for wit ye well there is nothing in the world but I had lever do it than to see my lord Sir Launcelot du Lake to die in my default', reflected in T.'s character admitting of the Grail 'he well had been content / Not to have seen, so Lancelot might have seen' and who said it was 'beyond all hopes of mine, / Who scarce had prayed or asked it for myself' (*HG*650–1, 687–8). Malory xvi 6 has the bird feeding its own young from its blood, which T. transfers to the crest of Bors, as dramatically observed by Percivale: 'One night my pathway swerving east, I saw / The pelican on the casque of our Sir Bors / All in the middle of the rising moon' (*HG*632–4). T. makes Bors' crest a pelican on the legendary basis that it pierces its breast to feed its offspring with its own blood (like the bird in Malory), a symbol of Christlike self-sacrifice appropriate to Bors.

79. Malory xvii 23.

80. Malory xiii 7.

81. Malory xiii 8.

82. Malory i 1–2.

83. Uther dies fifteen years after Arthur's birth in Geoffrey's *Historia* ix 1, and in Malory i 4 only two years after. In T. for complete ambiguity he expires at the time Arthur is born: 'that same night' (*CA*208). In name alone another character, Bellicent, derives from a footnote in Wright's edition of Malory, vol. 1 p. 5 (Belicent). In making her the mother of two children initially (Gawain and

Modred) T. follows Geoffrey's *Historia* ix 9 rather than Malory i 19 where the equivalent queen has four children at the outset. Tennyson's Bleys who 'wrote / All things and whatsoever Merlin did / In one great annal-book' (*CA*156–7) follows the character in Malory i 17 'All the battles that were done in King Arthur's days, Merlin did his master Bleise do write'. T. also links Ulfius, Brastias and Bedivere (*CA*135,444). In Malory i 7 the first two are linked, but Bedivere is only introduced in Malory v 5. However there is a Bedwer early associated with Arthur in Geoffrey's *Historia* ix 12 and a Bedwyr and Kai head the list of Arthur's supporters in the oldest tale in *Mabinogion*.

84. Malory xxi 6.

85. Malory xxi 2–3.

86. Malory i 19.

87. Malory xxi 4.

88. *FQ* iii i 19, iii i 24. Malory xviii 21 has a huntress 'and no men went never with her, but always women, and they were shooters, and could well kill a deer'.

89. Malory iv 21. The 'broken utterances' (*PE*106) which express the embarrassment of Pelleas, spring from the *infringi linguam* of Catullus 5, and 'with promise of large light on woods and ways' (*PE*385) the *large . . . lumine* of Lucretius, *De Rerum Natura* iii 22 (see also T.'s *Lucretius* 99 'light is large'). Ettarre's 'rich beauty' (*PE*230) echoes Chaucer's identical phrase for Criseyde, *TC* 5, 818.

90. Malory vii 6,7,8,9. 'Heaven's azure' for sky (*GL*914) echoes the identical phrase, *PL* 1, 297.

91. Malory vii 5. Gareth's claim to Arthur: 'I have stagger'd thy strong Gawain in a tilt / For pastime' (*GL*532–3) echoes *FQ* iii i 6 'Nathelesse it bore his foe not from his sell, / But made him stagger, as he were not well'. T.'s incident was suggested by a tournament in

Malory vii 29 where Gareth 'by fortune . . . met with his brother Sir Gawaine, and there he put Sir Gawaine to the worse, for he put off his helm'. When Gareth 'so shook him in the saddle' (*GL*29) being shaken in the saddle is listed as a knightly disgrace in T.'s copy of Clark and Wormull's *Introduction to Heraldry* (1779) p.54.

92. Malory vii 4.

93. 'His great self' echoes *H8* 3.2.336.

94. *Memoir*, i, 194.

95. For example the characters Mark, Tristram, and Kay.

96. Malory vii 10.

97. Malory vii 15.

98. Suggested by the idea of *semé* (sown) 'an irregular strewing without number all over the field' in Clark and Wormull's *Heraldry*, p.48. Other heraldic ideas are to be found *GL*519, 1273, *GE*265–9, *BB*193, *MV*469–79, *LE*193, *HG*633 *LT*174, *G*11. J.C. Dunlop (1888) p.226 states 'Lancelot du Lac had six bends of or and azure – *haut en naissance en vaillance en amour*'. T. adds to this by having blue lions crowned with gold (*GL*571, 1186, 1273, *LE*659). J.G. Brault in *Early Blazon* (1972) pp.44,47 has Lancelot's crest 'argent, three bands gules', Arthur's 'three crowns or' and Guinevere's pennant of a blue field with golden crowns (loc. *Lancelot propre*, iii, 402). T. simplifies her crest to a single crown (*BB*196, 532). In Malory xii 6 the arms of Lancelot when in exile from Guinevere consisted of 'a shield all of sable, and a queen crowned in the midst, all of silver, and a knight clean armed kneeling afore her', which may have suggested Lancelot's crest in 'The Lady of Shalott' 78–80: 'A red-cross knight for ever kneeled / To a lady in his shield, / That sparkled on the yellow field' as well as the red cross badge and identical shield of the knight of the Red

Cross, *FQ* 1 i 12. Sir Torre's 'yet-unblazon'd shield' (*LE*377) stems from the 'still unblazoned' shield of Helenor, *Aen.* 9, 546.

99. Malory x 40.

100. Malory vii 17.

101. Malory x 6.

102. Sea metaphor and simile work throughout the *Idylls*, as they do in *Iliad, Odyssey*, and *Aeneid*. The metaphor here is part of the same function as Arthur's characterising the heathen as 'that ever-climbing wave, / Hurl'd back again so often in empty foam' and the cresting and falling flat of the wave which suggests the drunken fall of the Red Knight (*LT*92–3, 460–83). Cp. Dido, *Aen.* 4, 531–2: *ingeminant curae rursusque resurgens / saevit amor, magnoque irarum fluctuat aestu* ('her torment redoubled; her love came back again and again, and heaved in ocean-tides of wrath') and 'Sea was her wrath, yet working after storm' (*LE*1299) for Guinevere. When Guinevere 'flung herself / Down on the great King's couch, and writhed upon it' (*LE*605–6) this reflects the action of Malory xi 8 when on hearing Lancelot had been in bed with Dame Elaine, Guinevere 'writhed and weltered as a mad woman'.

103. Malory viii 26.

104. Malory x 67–8. In 'a spear, a harp, a bugle' (*LT*174) T. draws on Malory x 52 'for as books report, of Sir Tristram came all the good terms of venery and hunting, and all the sizes and measures of blowing of an horn' and Malory viii 3 'and so Tristram learned to be an harper passing all other'.

105. Malory x 26–7 has Mark's 'poisonous counsels'; viii 13 his 'wayside ambushings'; x 7, 26–7 'a man of plots, / Craft'; ix 37 'who strikes nor lets the hand be seen'. Mark actually destroys Camelot in one of the late medieval romances, *Guiron le Courtois*. Pfordresher,

p. 890 gives the deleted line 'Whom no man loved, not even his own dogs'.

106. Malory xix 11.

107. The shock is all the more sudden for being confined to a single short clause: 'and clove him thro' the brain' (*LT*748).

108. *Psyche and Symbol* (1958) p. 123.

109. Malory ii 2.

110. Malory ii 13.

111. Malory ii 5, 17.

112. Malory ii 6.

113. Malory ii 13, 16.

114. Geoffrey's *Historia* iii 1.

115. Malory ii 6.

116. Malory ii 12, 13, 14.

117. See the first story in *Mabinogion*, entitled 'Pwyll Prince of Dyved' who changes places with another underworld king.

118. *BB*599–604.

119. Named from the Vulgate *Merlin*, see Ricks, p. 1594.

120. Malory ii 18.

121. Bearing a blank or 'maiden' shield shows an unproved knight, see Malory xix 1, *Aen.* 9, 548.

122. See note 17.

CHAPTER THREE
Range of Allusion

1. *The Nineteenth Century* 33 (Jan. 1893) 165.

2. *From Virgil to Milton* (1963) p. 104.

3. *Memoir*, ii, 385. Collins's remarks are in *Illustrations of Tennyson*, p. 139.

4. *Historia* ix 4.

5. Malory i 9.

6. *FQ* 1 v 22; *Num.* 27.21; *PL* 6,761.

7. Malory ii 19, xvii 4.

8. *Eccles.* 3.6 'A time to get, and a time to lose; a time to keep, and a time to cast away'. For 'the dew of their great labour' (*MG*568), a periphrasis for battle sweat, *OED* gives Southey, *Joan of Arc*, Scott, *Lord of the Isles*, and then T.

9. *OTH* 2.3.234. Cp. Ovid, *Met.* 5, 204 *sonuit tinnitibus ensis acutis*. 'A lance that splinter'd like an icicle'

(*GE*89) recalls *Aen.* 12, 738 'the mortal blade as it struck flew in splinters like brittle ice'.

10. *Historia* ix 4.

11. Malory vi 7. T. modifies the heroic identification of Lancelot and his horse in Malory xviii 17: 'That courser leapt mightily when he felt the spurs; and he that was upon him the which was the noblest horse of the world, strained him mightily' so that it is 'Not to be spurr'd, loving the battle as well / As he that rides him' (*GL*1269–70). 'The sound of many a heavily-galloping hoof' (*GE*447) imitates in metre Virgil's famous effect in *Aen.* 8, 596: *quadrupedante putrem sonitu quatit ungula campum.*

12. *FQ* III iii 60.

13. *Il.* 11, 256.

14. As with Diomedes, Agamemnon and Hector, *Il.* 5, 1–7; 11, 44, 62. When Vivien 'rather seem'd a lovely baleful star / Veil'd in gray vapour' (*MV*260–1) she is modelled on an image describing Hector, *Il.* 11, 60: 'Like a baleful star that at one moment shines out in all its splendour from behind a cloud and at the next is hidden by the mist'.

15. Spenser invariably, and Malory iii 2 speak of swords being 'trenchant'. T. is more specific in application to steel.

16. Malory ii 13–15.

17. *1H4* 5.4.133 'Full bravely hast thou fleshed / Thy maiden sword'.

18. 1. 2288.

19. *PL* 4, 834.

20. e.g. Achilles to Agamemnon at the opening of *Iliad*: 'You drunken sot . . . with the eyes of a dog and the courage of a doe!'; *FQ* II iii 7, *TC* 2.1.8 etc.

21. *Aen.* 11, 617.

22. 'Brag' as a noun, *AYL* 5.2.34, *TRO* 4.5.257; 'over-bold' *MAC* 3.5.3.

23. *Georg.* 4, 442. The 'hardened skin' of the third knight (*GL*1067, 1115) was suggested by the title

'Sir Ironside' in Malory vii 23, and the wrestling from *FQ* II xi 20–46. The Star of Even's shield glittering over the 'saddle-bow' (*GL*1091) is a heroic term for the arched front part of a saddle, Malory ix 15, *Venus and Adonis* 14. During the action 'grovelling on his knees' echoes Malory vii 12 'that they fell grovelling on the ground'.

24. *MND* 5.1.301, *CYM* 4.1.24. Gareth's fourth adversary, who 'wears a helmet mounted with a skull, / And bears a skeleton figured on his arms' (*GL*624–5) is redolent of Spenser's Maleger, *FQ* II xi 22 'Upon his head he wore an Helmet light, / Made of a dead mans skull, that seemd a ghastly sight'. When Gareth 'split the skull. / Half fell to right and half to left and lay' (*GL*1370) this recalls the way Turnus slays Pandarus, *Aen.* 9, 750 'with the blade he dealt a ghastly wound, splitting his brow midway between his temples . . . and his head divided, lolled on his right shoulder and on his left'. When Gareth 'clove the helm / As throughly as the skull' (*GL*1372) the manner ('throughly') is Spenser, *FQ* v ii 17 and when 'out from this / Issued the bright face of a blooming boy / Fresh as a flower new-born' (*GL*1372–4) the revelation is redolent of *FQ* IV vi 19 where a fierce knight has his helmet shorn away to reveal a pert girl's face beneath. Other aspects of the description stem from Malory vii 6, 13, 15.

25. Malory xviii 12.

26. *Il.* 14, 130. Lancelot's 'hindering wound' (*LE*580) is redolent of *Aen.* 2, 431 'Pelias who was hampered by a wound from Ulysses'.

27. *Aen.* 12, 919–20. The same gesture of rage occurs thrice, *Sir Gawain and the Green Knight* 229, 304, 2246. Doorm first appears 'rolling eyes of prey' (*GE*538). Lancelot 'with his heel upon the fall'n' (*PE*568) is redolent of tramping on

an enemy's chest after killing him, *Il.* 5, 620; 6, 65. In 'The Lady of Shalott' l. 76 Lancelot's 'brazen greaves' echo Goliath, 1 *Sam.* 17.6 who 'had greaves of brass upon his legs'. Lancelot 'chief of knights' (*LE*140, 187) from Malory vii 13 'for of all knights he may be called chief of knighthood'. When Gawain 'smote his thigh' (*LE*660) the gesture stems from *Jer.* 31.19, *Ezek.* 21.12.

28. Malory xviii 10.

29. The inclusion of 'count' occasioned the query that it was a tautology, *Notes and Queries* 6th ser. 10 (16 Aug. 1884) 130. If nothing else, this demonstrates how Victorians pored over the text of the *Idylls.*

30. *Il.* 6, 1; 8, 537.

31. *Ps.* 20.5, *FQ* iv iii 5.

32. *Knight's Tale* l. 1653. See also *House of Fame* 3, 150 'Blody soun / In trumpe, beme and clarioun'.

33. Malory i 15. 'Long-lanced battle' (*CA*103) constructed on Homeric lines; 'The Powers who walk the world / Made lightnings and great thunders over him' (*CA*106–7) is also Homeric.

34. See Alastair Fowler's edn. *Paradise Lost* (1974) pp. 20–1.

35. *PL* 1, 583–4.

36. Malory i 10 does so also, with 'the King Claudas'. Arthur's call of 'Ho' (*CA*120) echoes Merlin's in Malory i 17, and 'foughten field' (*CA*134, *HG*857) echoes *PL* 6, 410. Enemies who 'made head against' Arthur (*CA*67) echo *FQ* 11 x 38, *PL* 2, 992. 'And none or few' to scare or chase the beast (*CA*22) echoes Shakespeare, *Son.* 73.2 'and none, or few do hang / Upon those boughs'.

37. e.g. answered him 'at full' (*LE*285, *PA*211) a heroic feature of the histories, see *2H4* 1.1.135, *H5* 2.4.140, *2H6* 2.2.6, also *PL* 1, 641. 'Helped his lord' (*LE*296)

litotes or heroic understatement to convey Lancelot's modesty.

38. *Six Old English Chronicles* (1848).

39. In Malory vi 1 Lancelot is introduced long after these wars.

40. *AYL* 3.2.354. See also *PL* 11, 882 'the fluid skirts of that same watrie cloud' and 'Brightening the skirts of a long cloud' (*PA*222).

41. See Howie (1979) p. 323: 'Sappho is in addition exploiting another special property of the catalogue form in the first part of her catalogue, namely its power to build up excitement which climaxes in its final item'.

42. Arthur bears an image of the Virgin on his shoulders, Geoffrey's *Historia* ix 4.

43. *FQ* i vii 30.

44. Malory i 16.

45. sec. viii: 'I would affirm with confidence that there is no tone so lofty as that of genuine passion, in its right place, when it bursts out in a wild gust of mad enthusiasm and as it were fills the speaker's words with frenzy' and sec. xxvii: 'There is further the case in which a writer, when relating something about a person, suddenly breaks off and converts himself into that selfsame person'.

46. Malory x 73, xviii 23.

47. Turner, *Tennyson* (1976) p. 164. Note also the last battle in Layamon's *Brut* 28558–63 where 'might no man in the fight know any warrior, nor who did worse, nor who did better, so was the conflict mingled! for each slew downright, were he swain, were he knight'.

48. At least five times in Spenser (*Col.* 168, *FQ* 11 ix 41, 111 ii 5, 111 ix 28, 111 x 58). *OED* wrongly gives first *LLL* 5.2.101. Also occurs *1H4* 1.3.38.

49. 'The Christ' 18 times New Testament.

50. *Historia* xi 1.

51. *Rev.* 16.21.

52. *In Mem.* liv 19. See also the phrase used by Lucretius and Virgil to signify death: *lumen ademptum* ('the light was taken from them').

53. *Gen.* 4.1. See also *MWW* 1.1.257, *PL* 4, 827–32.

54. Echoing 2 *Sam.* 1.26 'love was wonderful, passing the love of women'. Rosenberg treats Tennyson's use of Biblical allusion thoroughly, see particularly pp. 158 n 5, 162 n 16.

55. Malory viii 36.

56. *Gen.* 13.10.

57. Only in R S V, *Job* 17.2. A V has 'and doth not mine eyes continue in their provocation'. See also *R3* 4.2.66 'Tear-falling pity dwells not in this eye.'

58. At one time he planned a poem on the theme, *Memoir*, ii, 23, and with that in view read *Job* in Hebrew.

59. See Peake's *Commentary*, p. 23, for a brief account.

60. *Gen.* 39.7.

61. Malory i 18.

62. *Memoir*, i, 483.

63. 1 *Kings* 2.17; *Gen.* 39.7; 'thing' or 'things' common; *Rev.* 14.2; *Eccles.* 3.6; 'sift' as metaphor, *Isa.* 30.28; *Ps.* 119. 103 'how sweet are thy words' and *Gen.* 18.5 'comfort your hearts'; *Ps.* 68.33; *Isa.* 40.17 'All nations before him are as nothing'; *Heb.* 12.2 (and Malory ix 4).

64. *The Use of Poetry and the Use of Criticism* (1933) 118–19.

65. *Eccles.* 9.4. See also Rosenberg, pp. 86, 112–15, 162 n 16.

66. 1 *John* 4.18.

67. *Ps.* 139.21–2.

68. *Hos.* 8.7.

69. *Hos.* 8.5.

70. e.g. *Ps.* 41.7, *Isa.* 29.4.

71. *Matt.* 13.3–9. See also Edyrn who 'sowed a slander in the common ear' (*MG*450).

72. *Prov.* 2.13.

73. *Dan.* 4.33.

74. 'Camest' and 'spakest' (*HG*22,

881) are common Biblical terms, but 'thoughtest' (*HG*455) only occurs once, *Ps.* 50.21. T. uses both registers of 'thou', intimate or scornful, to great effect. Arthur customarily uses 'thou' ('thee', 'thy', 'thine') to express the bond of affection between himself and Lancelot (*CA*128–33, *LE*1345–62, *HG*276–9, *LT*103–7) as with ironic overtones do Lancelot and Guinevere (*BB*245–71) and it is part of Vivien's duplicity (*BB*463–564). The contempt in Malory ii 14 is reflected in Balin and Garlon (*BB*352–6, 388). 'Thou' is one means by which Ettarre and Gawain deceive Pelleas (*PE*121–5, 335–49). As in his model in Malory vii 16, T. has the Red Knight achieve a paroxysm of invective (*LT*443–53). T. poignantly ends four idylls with the intimate mood (*BB*607–14, *LE*1345–62, *PE*585–8, *LT*754–6). It is an important framing word tempering Arthur's speech to Guinevere with dignity and humanity (*G*419, 522). Regulation of tone and modulation are attained by this means (*G*445–52, 481–4, 497–508). Apart from the change in metre and tempo, a sign of forgiveness is the repeated and consistent use of second person singular at the end of Arthur's speech (*G*529–77). Guinevere is made to feel fully forgiven, and responds in kind (*G*643–5).

75. Malory xi 5 has Bors see an old man who 'sat him down in a fair chair, and there seemed to be two adders about his neck; and then the old man had an harp, and there he sang an old song how Joseph of Arimathie came into this land'. T.'s ref. to Arviragus (*HG*61), who gave Joseph 'an isle of marsh whereon to build' Glastonbury, stems from Geoffrey's *Historia* iv 13–16.

76. *Matt.* 11.7.

77. *Job* 38.7.

78. *Rev.* 21.21.
79. *Prov.* 26.13.
80. *Isa.* 35.6.
81. 'Lo' frequent. Kay's 'Lo ye now' (*GL*445) from *WT* 1.2.106 'Why, lo you now'; Vivien's and Arthur's 'Lo now' (*MV*440, *HG*286) from *FQ* II ii 19, *ANT* 1.2.76; 'Lo there' (*BB*458, *HG*219, *LT*428) from *1H6* 4.2.31; 'for lo!' (*CA*69) *2H4* 4.1.149, *ROM* 2.3.53; 'when lo' (*G*80) *LLL* 5.2.91, *Venus and Adonis* 320; Balin's fiery 'Ha!' (*BB*387) modelled on *TGV* 2.1.3, and Lancelot's 'Tirra lirra' ('The Lady of Shalott' l. 107) from *WT* 4.3.9.
82. *2 John* 10–11.
83. All expressions with a Biblical resonance.
84. *Rev.* 22.16, 9.1, 6.13. Pfordresher p. 857 shows the painstaking prose drafts that preceded these complex effects.
85. *Rev.* 14.7.
86. *Rev.* 13.10.
87. *Rev.* 19.20.
88. *Rev.* 9.3, *Mark* 9.44 'where their worm dieth not, and the fire is not quenched'.
89. *2 Kings* 3.22.
90. Nash (1972) p. 162.
91. *Prov.* 26.4. T. recaptures the Hebrew parallelism in his own form. When Arthur reminds Guinevere of 'the sin which thou hast sinn'd' (*G*452) he echoes *Exod.* 32.30 'ye have sinned a great sin'; Arthur's 'yet needs must work my work' (*CA*88) echoes *Hab.* 1.5 'I will work a work in your days which you will not believe, though it be told you'; when Balin and Balan 'slept the sleep' (*BB*619) this echoes *Ps.* 76.5 'spoiled, they have slept their sleep'; when Arthur's knights 'Stood round him, and rejoicing in his joy' and he had hoped Guinevere would have been 'one to feel / My purpose, and rejoicing in my joy' (*CA*458, *G*483) they echo *1 Kings* 1.40 'pipes, and rejoicing with great joy'.

92. *Ps.* 16.2.
93. *Job* 15.20–1.
94. *Ps.* 110.1, *Matt.* 5.35, *Luke* 10.19.
95. *Ps.* 91.13, *Rev.* 12.7. T. uses the Bible formula 'went his way' with great care. Enid 'went her way' and Arthur towards Lancelot and Guinevere 'glanced first at him, then her, and went his way' (*MG*383, *LE*95). In the Grail each knight 'thence departed every one his way' (*HG*360). After Ettarre brazenly accuses Guinevere of withholding Lancelot from the lists so that Pelleas can win, the queen 'As one whose foot is bitten by an ant, / Glanced down upon her, turned and went her way' (*PE*177–8). With both Arthur and Guinevere the formula comes at the paragraph end, which gives it the force of dismissal, modelled on *Gen.* 18.33, the last verse of the chapter.
96. See, for example, the articles by Lawrence Poston (1966) and J. O. Hoge (1976).
97. Emily Tennyson's letter diary, Tennyson Research Centre, Lincoln.
98. *Memoir*, ii, 113–14.
99. *ANT* 4.2.33. Note Dyboski's comment (1907) p. 436 'ein Shakspersches Antithesenspiel' for Gareth's 'Good mother is bad mother unto me! / A worse were better, yet no worse would I' (*GL*16–17). The idyll has several similar puns: 'brake his neck . . . brake his heart'; 'follow the deer? follow the Christ, the King'; 'Quick! the proof to prove me to the quick!'; 'let be my name until I make my name'; 'Earth has earth enough to hide him'; 'for an your fire be low (kitchen fire) ye kindle mine (fire of wrath)'; 'They have bound my lord (fettered) . . . Bound am I (obliged) to right the wrong'd' (*GL*57, 116, 147, 562, 695, 784, *GE*554).

100. *MND* 1.2.72.
101. *OTH* 2.3.178.
102. *R3* 2.3.18 etc. See also the Lord of Astolat (*LE*196).
103. Frequent in Shakespeare.
104. Malory vii 4, *TGV* 3.1.384 etc. 'I'll after . . .'; Yniol's request to Geraint: 'But in, go in' (*MG*310) echoing *ERR* 5.1.37.
105. *SHR* 1.1.240 'ne'er a whit'.
106. Malory vii 5, *WIV* 3.3.122.
107. Frequent in Shakespeare.
108. Frequent in Shakespeare.
109. *CYM* 1.1.125, *ANT* 5.2.242.
110. *WIV* 1.4.159. Shakespearean also are 'good lack' (*GL*105), 'good cheer' (*GL*294), 'good cause' (*GL*800, *MV*603), 'good now' (*GL*807, *LT*261), 'good truth' (*MG*290), 'good faith' (*MG*405), the phrasing 'Good my brother' (*BB*136), 'good morrow' (*BB*247), 'ill news . . . good news' (*LE*595, 598), 'Give me good fortune' (*ANT* 1.2.13, *LE*1064).
111. 'Thy much goodness', 'thy much misgovernment' *MM* 5.1.534, *ADO* 4.1.99. See also Malory vii 1 'This much young man' (of Gareth).
112. Malory vii 4, *TMP* 2.1.104.
113. *H8* 3.2.336.
114. *MND* 5.1.301. Note also *H5* 3.3.38 'your naked Infants spitted upon Pykes' and 'And on the spike . . . Spitting the child' (*CA*39); Cavall, Arthur's hound 'of deepest mouth' (*MG*186) is an echo of *1H6* 2.4.12 'Between two dogs, which hath the deeper mouth' rather than T.'s own comparison to *MND* 4.1.128 'matched in mouth like bells'; 'My nature's prideful sparkle in the blood' (*GE*826) and *3H6* 1.1.184 'In whose cold blood no spark of honour bides'; *SHR* 4.1.211 'This is a way to kill a wife with kindness' is reflected in Vivien's 'killed with inutterable unkindliness' (*MV*884); *ADO* 3.3.157 'Bids me a thousand times good night' lies behind Gawain's

exaggerated leavetaking of Elaine: 'Fare you well / A thousand times! – a thousand times farewell!' (*LE*692); *ROM* 2.2.148 Juliet's 'And follow thee my lord throughout the world' is recalled in Elaine's 'To serve you, and to follow you thro' the world' (*LE*934); *R2* 2.3.85 'Grace me no grace nor uncle me no uncle' is imitated in 'Diamond me / No diamonds' (*LE*502). T.'s diction frequently shows a Shakespearean origin, e.g. 'heat' (*CA*168), flowers which 'blow' (*CA*408, *GL*1003, 1042, *HG*668), 'presently' in the sense of 'immediately' (*CA*390), 'frequent' in the sense 'often in company with a person' (*GL*122), 'fair-spoken' (*GL*279), 'co-mates' (*GL*985), 'hubbub' (*MG*264), 'scantly' (*MG*287, *BB*372), 'state' (*MG*430), 'flaws' (*MG*764), 'home' for destined place, vital point (*GE*159), 'stomach' for 'appetite' (*GE*213), to 'mouth' (*BB*374), 'rummage' (*BB*410), 'vantage ground' (*BB*526), 'brokenly' (*BB*592), 'betimes' for 'in a short time, speedily' (*MV*46), 'gives him the lie' (*MV*51), 'full-fed' (*MV*690), 'instance' for 'proof' (*MV*799), 'soilure' (*LE*7), 'tarriance' (*LE*567), 'blossom' for Elaine (*LE*965) from *1H6* 4.7.16; 'take' in the sense of 'enchant, charm' (*HG*383), Gawain 'in his mood' (*LT*1), 'belike' (*LT*200, 245, 247, 529), 'pettish' (*LT*214), 'but 'tis eating dry' (*AWW* 1.1.175, *LT*249), 'broken music' (*ADO* 1.2.150, *LT*258), 'Good now' (*LT*261), 'Pish' (*LT*298), 'Tuwhoo' (*LT*346), 'plash' (*LT*421), 'darkling' (*LT*456), 'sweet' 'a beloved person, darling, sweetheart' (*ROM* 3.3.162, *LT*622), 'him' for 'himself' (*G*153), 'gadding' (*G*311). See also 'breathed upon' (*GE*950) *OED* 9 'to infect or contaminate' *TGV* 5.4.131.

115. *PL* 4, 30.
116. *PL* 9, 401, 739.
117. *PL* 4, 701, 9, 1041.
118. *PL* 2, 400, 4, 132 'the soft delicious air', 'delicious Paradise'.
119. *PL* 9, 403, 407. T.'s time effects are subtle. 'And at the closing of the day' ('The Lady of Shalott' l. 132) echoes *1H4* 3.2.133 'The closing of some glorious day'; and 'high peep of dawn' (*MV*558) echoes Gray's *Elegy* 98 'Oft have we seen him at the peep of dawn'.
120. *PL* 4, 410. The echoing begins before this: 'cause of flight', 'popular praises', pejorative use of 'brood', 'strong hate' (*G*9, 13, 16, 20) echoing *PL* 4, 922, *PR* 2, 227, *PL* 2, 863, *PL* 9, 491 'stronger hate'.
121. *PL* 8, 303, *PR* 2, 286.
122. *PL* 9, 91, 184, 625; Satan as 'wily snake', full of 'subtle wiles' and 'wily Adder'.
123. *PL* 4, 405–6 when Satan 'Straight couches close, then rising changes oft / His couchant watch'. Miltonic diction includes 'dusk' for 'dark coloured' (*GL*672), 'agape' (*GL*1274), sight being 'allured' (*GL*1282), 'mantling' flowers (*GL*1357), 'gemm'd' (*MG*339), 'turkis' (*MG*661), 'beeves' (*GE*601), 'tendance' (*GE*925) associates Enid with Eve, *PL* 8, 47; 'wealth of leaf' (*BB*79); *PR* 2, 167–8 'lead / At will the manliest, resolutest brest, / As the Magnetic hardest Iron draws' is recalled when 'magnet-like she drew / The rustiest iron of old fighters' hearts' (*MV*571), and when Vivien looks on Merlin as 'her own, the first of men' (*MV*615) this recalls Adam, *PL* 4, 408; 'wandering fires' (*HG*319); *PL* 4, 237, 252 Eden's 'crisped brooks' and 'lawns' recur when Percivale 'saw deep lawns, and then a brook, / With one sharp rapid, where the crisping white / Played ever back upon the sloping wave' (*HG*380–2), 'mid-heaven'

(*LT*27), 'brood' in a pejorative sense (*G*16).
124. Malory xi 3 or xviii 12; Malory vii 20 or xi 3; 'twice or thrice' Malory x 64, *TGV* 1.2.117, *H5* 5.1.79. T. uses other number formulae from Malory and Shakespeare: 'once or twice' (*LT*610) from *WIV* 3.5.103, *2H4* 5.1.53; 'an hour or maybe twain' (*G*235) recalling *MAC* 3.1.28. 'for a dark hour or twain'; 'a day or twain before' (*PE*19). 'Within three days or four', 'three or four days', and Dinadan 'rode over Agravaine five or six times' in Malory ii 14, x 25, xviii 16; Pfordresher, p. 503 shows 'By five or six' a first thought in *Merlin and Vivien*; the Grail is 'A legend handed down thro' five or six' (*HG*87); Mark came 'with six or seven' men to force Isolt to return to Tintagil (*LT*382), another Shakespearean formula. T.'s 'thrice beaten' (*PE*283) from *AWW* 2.5.33. See also 'With some surprise and thrice as much disdain' and 'thrice your own' (*MG*557, *GE*736).
125. *RR* 1723; also Chaucerian are T.'s 'full merry' (*GL*1259) from *B.NP* 4449 (Pfordresher, p. 263 shows T. first had 'right merry'), 'full tenderly' (*TC* 4, 353, *FQ* II xi 49, *MG*508), 'full courtly' (*D.Sum.* 1802, *LE*235), 'full lowly' (*TC* 2, 1072, *LE*821), 'full easily' (*E.Cl.* 423, *FQ* III i 54, *G*637). From Malory are 'full loth', 'full simple', 'full well', 'full ill', 'full meekly', 'full fain', 'full knightly' (*BB*493, *LE*667, 685, 939, 971, *PE*12, *G*39). When there rode 'Full slowly by a knight, lady, and dwarf; / Whereof the dwarf lagged latest' (*MG*187–8) T.'s dwarf echoes *FQ* I i 6 'Behind her farre away a Dwarfe did lag' and 'full slowly' reflects *FQ* I x 5 'gate full slow'. 'Full quickly' (*HG*258) cp. Malory ii 6, 16, *FQ* I iii 12 'full fast'; 'full wonderingly' (*PE*577) reflects *PER* 3.3.7. Common forms are 'full many' (*MV*544, *LE*874,

G_{276}) and 'full often' ($LE_{163}, 877$, G_{312}). Seemingly T.'s own are when Lynette declares that it is 'by some device / Full cowardly' that Gareth has defeated his master, Kay; when 'full willingly' the little novice sings to Guinevere, and when 'full passionately' the queen responds (GL_{749}, G_{165}, 178).

126. *TMP* 1.2.254. Pyre (1921) p. 205 notes what he terms 'counter caesural inversion', citing as examples 'Climb'd to the high top of the garden wall' and 'So from the high wall and the flowering grove' ($G_{25}, 33$). The metrical irregularity is of course to simulate the main features of the incident, Modred's climbing and being dislodged.

127. *Memoir*, i, 466.

128. *Prelude* 1, 269, 300, 325, 339, 400, 424, 463 end verse paragraphs with images.

129. Judged from the evolution of the series, the first 'break' in paragraphing occurs at GE_{556}. See ch. 5, n 56.

130 *A Provincial Glossary* (1790) p. 43. In the Tennyson Research Centre, Lincoln.

131. 'Lavish' *OED* 1 'loose, wild, licentious' *2H4* 4.4.64 etc. 'comment' *OED* 4 'the action of commenting, animadversion, criticism, remark' first in *Prin.* iii 35, stemming from 'comment' *OED* 1 vb. 'to devise, contrive, invent (espec. something false or bad)' in *FQ* VII vii 53.

132. *PL* 9, 385–8, 422.

133. Serpent motion echoing *Gen.* 1.24, *PL* 7, 476.

134. Malory iv 1 'Fain would have been delivered of him ... wrought by enchantment ... wrought so there'.

135. *PL* 9, 890. 'Blankly' *OED* first gives Froude, 1863, but T.'s poem dates from 1856 (composition) and 1859 (publication).

136. 'The blameless King' repeated ($GE_{811}, 931, 969, MV_{777}, HG_{865}$) and as 'Arthur the blameless' perversely by Vivien (BB_{472}). Pfordresher, pp. 282, 290, 626 shows T. attempting to work in the epithet on three other occasions. It was parodied in 'The Very Last Idyll', *Pall Mall Gazette* 16 (1872) p. 5, where it occurs four times in 160 lines. In *St James Magazine* 8 (1863) R. W. Buchanan's 'Mordred' echoes T. when a dark demon urges his character 'to join / Against the blameless king'. T.'s Arthur is also the 'good King' ($GL_{1044}, 1143$, $MG_{152}, BB_{525}, MV_{781}, LE_{278}$, $G_{95}, 207, 219$) and he has the companion epithets 'clear-faced', 'faultless' and 'guileless' (LE_{121}, 430, G_{84}). Malory ix 31, x 69 etc. has 'the noble king Arthur', and T. has 'noble King' (BB_{270}, LE_{648}) and 'noble Arthur' (MV_{89}).

CHAPTER FOUR
Settings: Natural and Man-made

1. F. T. Palgrave, *Landscape Poetry from Homer to Tennyson* (1897) p. 51.

2. *British Quarterly Review* 51 (1870) 205. See also *Quarterly Review* 128 (1870) 7 'whereas the great drift of the poem is moral, the energy of the poet has been in too great a degree expended on the descriptions'. J. P. Eggers, pp. 68–77 discusses the whole question.

3. *Mabinogion*, p. 224.

4. *Mabinogion*, pp. 245–6, 251.

5. Suggested by Milton's capitalisation of epithets for God: Deity, Godhead, Son of God, Grace, Father etc. and suggesting in turn that Arthur is divine, and God's supreme representative on earth, which accords with T.'s view that 'individuality is divine' and that Arthur is the soul (Knowles, 1893, pp. 169, 182).

6. Biblical, Homeric, also Malory i 16, ii 10 etc.

7. *Aen.* 1, 404: *pedes vestis defluxit ad*

imos. T.'s 'slipt like water to the floor' (*LE*825) echoes *Aen*. 11, 501: *ad terram defluxit*.

8. *Deut*. 6.10.

9. *FQ* I xi 11 (which contains the form 'bras-scaly'); *Sir Gawain and the Green Knight* l. 681.

10. *Aen*. 10, 5: *bipatentibus*.

11. *OED* 43 'afford a view or passage' (a Gallicism, cf. Fr. *donner sur*).

12. T.'s use of knightly title is discussed in ch. 5, pp. 81–3. *Sir Gawain and the Green Knight* shows a similar skill in its use of knightly title. 'Gawain' occurs 69 times, and 22 times as 'Sir Gawain' (e.g. 1207, 1225, 1247 by the lady, 1872, after resisting temptation a third time, and 1926 when the lord returns).

13. Nash (1972) pp. 24–5. T. later speaks of this 'flowery' welcome (*BB*142) *OED* 6 'abounding in flowers of speech; full of fine words and showy expressions', an echo of *MM* 3.1.83.

14. 'Ivytod' exclusively literary; as 'Yuie tod', 'Ivy tod' and 'ivy-tod' it occurs before T. only in Spenser, Drayton, Coleridge. Note T.'s form is all one word, unhyphenated and plural. Pellam's castle 'low-built' (*BB*328) from *Samson Agonistes* 1069 'His pile high-built and proud'.

15. Malory vi 13.

16. Malory vi 1, 16, xv 5.

17. Malory ix 19.

18. *Mabinogion*, p. 243.

19. Nash (1972) p. 11. T.'s fountain which 'Sang, and the sand danced at the bottom of it' (*BB*25) echoes *TRO* 3.3.312. 'My mind is troubled, like a fountain stirr'd; / And I myself see not the bottom of it'.

20. Pursuivants occur in Malory ix 24.

21. 'Langued gules' means red-tongued in heraldry.

22. *FQ* I i 7.

23. *PL* 9, 1086–8.

24. See my monograph (1971) pp. 10, 15–18, 39–43, 55.

25. See Nash (1972) pp. 51–4, 345.

26. A note on *FQ* II v 26 in H. J. Todd's edn. of Spenser (1805) states it was the custom in ages of romance to suspend the shields of conquered knights on trees. In Malory vii 15 Gareth 'espied upon great trees, as he rode, how there hung full goodly armed knights by the neck, and their shields about their necks with their swords'. *FQ* I x 60 gives the opposite of this: 'And high emongst all knights hast hong thy shield' which is reflected in T.'s Camelot: 'For, midway down the side of that long hall . . . There ran a treble range of stony shields' (*GL*396, 399).

27. 'Dumb' *OED* 2 'to render dumb, silent, or unheard' *PER* 5 *Pro*. 5.

28. Nash (1972) pp. 337–8.

29. 'Wild woods' *FQ* III vi 1, *AYL* 5.4.165, *PL* 9, 910.

30. In *Mabinogion*, p. 390 Villemarqué calls Merlin 'le vieux druide'.

31. Malory xviii 12.

32. 'The long backs of the bushless downs' (*LE*398) cp. *PL* 7, 285 'Immediately the mountains huge appear / Emergent, and their broad bare backs upheaven / Into the clouds' and *Prel*. 14, 43 'A hundred hills their dusky backs upheaved'. Ultimately modelled on a Homeric trope, *Il*. 8, 511 etc. 'over the broad back of the sea'.

33. No seduction attempt in Malory, but see *Lancilotto Panciatichiano*: 'In the garden Gareth draws the father aside that Gawain may speak with her. When he makes love to her, she rebukes him, declaring first that she is beneath him . . .' Gardner, *The Arthurian Legend in Italian Literature*, p. 125).

34. *Memoir*, ii, 53 records from Emily Tennyson's journal, April 1868: 'There has been a great deal of smoke in the yew trees this year. One day there was such a cloud that it seemed to be a fire in the shrubbery'.

35. *FQ* II i 19 'Errant damozell'.
Terms which derive from Spenser
include 'breathed' (*CA*176), 'ruth'
(*GL*873, *GE*101, 203, 250),
'throughly' (*GL*1372), 'doubling'
(*MG*195), 'stranger knight'
(*MG*286), 'guerdon' (*MV*552),
'rathe', 'joyance' (*LE*338, 1313),
'communed' (*HG*739, *G*148), 'hest'
(*PE*196, *PA*211), 'prowest'
(*PE*342), 'ensample' (*G*487).
Geraint being 'molten down in mere
uxoriousness' (*MG*60) recalls *FQ*
II xii 73 'quite molten into lust and
pleasure lewd'. Note also *FQ* I ix 30
'halfe dead' and 'half-dead' (*GL*670,
780), also *FQ* I x 48 'The mossy
braunches of an Oke halfe dead' and
'A stump of oak half-dead' (*LT*12);
FQ I iii 38 'halfe ashamed' and
'half-ashamed' (*GL*847); *FQ* III iv
61 'as halfe in great disdaine' or *FQ*
II ix 38 'halfe in disdaineful wise'
and 'half disdain' (*LE*1230); *FQ* I
vi 1 'halfe amazed', *PL* 4, 820 'half
amaz'd' and 'half-amazed' (*LT*236);
FQ I i 43 'halfe angrie' and
'half-anger'd' (*LT*713); *SC May*
233 'halfe aghast', *FQ* v xi 28 'halfe
agast' and 'half-aghast' (*Aylmer's
Field* 330); *T. M.* 363 'Thoughts
halfe devine' and *In Memoriam* xiv
20 'The man I held as half-divine'.
FQ II i 11, III vi 19 'halfe wroth'
and 'half-wroth' (*BB*421).
36. Malory viii 5.
37. Nash (1972) p. 151.
38. *PL* 8, 264.
39. 'Lawns', a paradisal feature, *PL*
4, 252 (*OED* 1 'an open space
between woods; a glade').
40. Nash, p. 429 observes that 'in
Victorian painting of the narrative
genre, trees and foliage likewise
appear in the double function of
compositional elements and
symbolic agents. See, for instance,
the chestnut-tree in Henry Arthur
Bowler's *The Doubt: Can These Dry
Bones Live?* (Tate Gallery), or the
oppressively luxuriant foliage
round the hapless lovers in Arthur

Hughes' *The Long Engagement*
(Birmingham Art Gallery)'. 'When
both our mouths went wandering
in one way, / And aching sorely,
met among the leaves' is how the
queen in Morris's *The Defence of
Guenevere* 136–7, describes her first
embrace with Lancelot.

CHAPTER FIVE
Language, Metaphor and Simile
1. Among less common prefixes
there is an intensifier, 'a-': 'afresh'
(*GE*904) from *R3* 1.2.56; 'abeat'
(*BB*102) *OED* gives two instances
only, the first pre-Conquest, the
second c. 1400 (T. probably devised
it to achieve a rustic effect: 'a-' as an
intensifier is common in
Lincolnshire dialect, see *Northern
Farmer, Owd Roä* etc.); 'afield'
(*LE*457) from *TRO* 5.3.67;
'awearied' (*HG*741) *OED* gives
1604, 1848, but prob. from 'a-weary'
MAC 5.5.49, which T. also uses in
'Mariana'. 'Be-' is found in
'bemoan'd', 'beknaved' (*GL*72,
766), the latter occurring in Skelton,
Pope; 'bethought' (*MG*134, 602,
647) from Malory iv 11, *PER*
5.1.44; 'befool'd and idioted'
(*Aylmer's Field* 590), the first prob.
Carlyle, the second a coinage (T. is
fond of such creations, see 'cairn'd'
and 'lichen'd', *MV*636, *LE*44).
'Co-' in 'co-twisted' (*GL*222) *OED*
gives 'co-twisting' Lamb, 1833;
'co-mate' (*GL*985) from *AYL*
2.1.1; 'counter-' as 'counter-
changed' (*MV*464), heraldic for
one thing changed for another;
'de-' in 'decrescent' (*GL*519),
heraldic, the waning moon; 'en-' in
'enchair'd' (*LT*104), T.'s coinage,
another of Arthur's special
vocabulary; 'mid-' as in mid-thigh-
deep' (*GL*790), 'midmost' (*GE*85,
*PE*250) in heroic contexts in
Cowley, Dryden, Pope;
'mid-warmth' (*GE*280), 'mid
might', 'mid-sickness' (*LE*552,
873), 'mid-banquet' (*PE*143), 'mid

forest' (*LT*488), 'mid-heaven'
(*LT*739) from *PL* 12, 263, and
there is 'under-' as in 'undershapen'
(*MG*412), T.'s coinage. Suffixes
also create many unusual words.
Among those in '-able' there is
'unburiable' (*GL*80), prev. 1853;
'marriageable' (*GL*102), prev. 1555,
1625, 1712, 1841; 'pardonable'
(*GL*639), prev. 1548, 1712, 1800;
'unsubduable' (*GL*837), 1611, 1622,
1810, 1840; 'serviceable' (*MG*393,
*LE*762) from *LR* 4.6.257;
'laughable' (*GE*326) from *MV*
1.1.56; 'learnable' (*BB*171), prev.
1629, 1818, 1840, 1857; 'unloveable'
(*MV*174), prev. 1570 (T.'s use not
in *OED*); 'pleasureable' (*MV*294),
1548, 1712, 1800; 'believable'
(*MV*760), 1382, 1548, 1611;
'consolable' (*MV*856), 1721,
Johnson 1755, then T.; 'inutterable'
(*MV*886) from *PL* 2, 626; the fact
that there are none in the last half of
the series suggests no enabling from
mid-point on. Note also 'achievable'
(*Prin.* iii 283) prev. only c. 1630.
Constructions in '-er' and '-ster'
include 'beginners' (*CA*457) from
Malory ix 4; 'railer', 'reviler'
(*GL*361, 774); 'roisterer' (*GE*274)
Scott 1820, 1827, Macaulay 1849;
'lander' (*MG*330) T.'s coinage;
'judger' (*GE*433) prev. 1449, 1556,
1630; 'fabler' (*BB*302), 1548, 1579,
1607; 'backbiter' (*MV*824);
'tonguester' (*LT*393) T.'s coinage;
'rover' (*LT*543) *OED* 3a 'one who
roves or wanders' from *WT* 1.2.176,
with *OED* 3b 'an inconstant lover,
a male flirt'; 'succeeder' (*Aylmer's
Field* 294) from *R3* 4.4.128;
'benchers' (*Aylmer's Field* 473)
COR 2.1.92. Note the use of plural
to make present participles clearly
nouns: 'elvish emblemings'
(*GL*229), 'wayside ambushings'
(*GL*424), 'burrowings' (*MV*55),
'neighings' (*LE*298), 'chafferings
and chatterings' (*HG*558). Finally,
there is the use of '-ling' as a
diminutive: 'changeling' (*CA*363,

*GL*200), 'reckling' (*MV*709) *OED*
'the smallest and weakest animal of
a litter; the youngest or smallest
child in a family' in the first sense,
1782, in the second T. only; and the
coinage 'cageling' (*MV*901).
2. e.g. 'discomfit', 'disherit',
'disport', 'disworship'.
3. Also when Geraint's victory over
bandits 'served a little to disedge /
The sharpness of that pain' Enid
felt at his previous treatment of her
(*GE*189).
4. 'Discaged' prev. Daniel, 1649;
'dishorsed' T.'s coinage; 'dishallow'
Lamb, 1833; 'disedge' prob. *CYM*
3.4.96. Note also 'half-disfame'
(*MV*463), 'disfame' prev. 1460,
1620; 'dislink'd' (*MV*907) 1610,
1621, *Prin. pro.* 70 (Pfordresher,
p. 592 shows T. first had even rarer
'dislockt').
5. e.g. 'misadvised', 'miscomfort',
'miscreature', 'misdid'.
6. Suggested by Malory ii 19 where
Merlin 'let make there a bed, that
there should never man lie therein
but he went out of his wit'.
7. 'Missay . . . missaid' (*GL*923,
1136) is Malory vii 11 'All the
missaying that ye missayed
furthered me in battle'; 'mismated'
prev. 1825, 1858; 'misfaith' Wyclif,
then T.; 'misadvertence' T.'s
coinage; the first three examples of
'misyoked' are from Milton's
divorce pamphlets, which adds
poignancy to the word's use by
Isolt (*LT*567). See also 'mischance'
(*MG*112) from *1H6* 1.1.89 (T.'s
first use 'The Lady of Shalott' l. 129
'Like some bold seer in a trance, /
Seeing all his own mischance'
perhaps echoing Merlin in Malory
i 20 who predicts 'I shall die a
shameful death to be put in the
earth quick'); 'misadventure'
(*BB*469) from Malory iv 1, ix 17.
8. 'Unearthlier' the culmination of a
train of comparatives. These,
because open as process, are
frequently more compelling than

superlatives. Note use of comparatives of what are normally absolute states in the positive: 'truer', 'lustier', 'mightier', 'my brother and my better', 'gladlier', 'ten-times worthier', 'wealthier', 'purer', 'strictlier', 'happier', 'gentler', 'fierier and stormier', 'sweeter ... sweeter still' 'season-earlier', 'viler', passing into superlatives (*BB*329 ff.) until 'unearthlier' (*BB*7, 17, 31, 52, 65, 66, 89, 101, 154, 160, 204, 224–5, 269, 295, 534). Comparison of adjectives and adverbs in the *Idylls* can be said to be a structuring device, one way T. attains 'a compacted and vertebrate poem' (*Memoir* ii 506). *Gareth and Lynette* exploits the positive, even to a play on 'good' (*GL*12, 15, 16, 42, 105, 305, 415, 440, 516, 539, 726, 1028, 1044, 1143, 1200, 1255, 1276). As we have seen above, *Balin and Balan* occupies a median position and exploits the most emphatic register, comparatives which are open as process. As part of a high heroic style *Lancelot and Elaine* has many superlatives (*LE*5, 63, 74, 76, 138, 220, 221, 253, 255, 261, 334–5, 359, 524, 589, 614, 663, 665, 707, 768, 864–5, 1070–3, 1087, 1135, 1176, 1403, 1408). In emphasis on the positive, comparative and superlative the second, fifth, and seventh poems of the series help to create 'a compacted and vertebrate poem'.

9. 'Unmockingly' T.'s coinage; 'ungentle' echoing Malory vii 4 'I know you for an ungentle knight of the court'; 'unsubduable' 1611, 1622, 1810, 1840 (Carlyle's 'unsubduable granite') then T.; 'unmelodious' 1665, 1748, 1777, 1808; 'unlamed' not in *OED*; 'unearthlier' (*BB*534 only); 'uncharmed' *ROM* 1.1.217; 'unmortised' Richardson, *Clarissa*, then T.; 'unsleek' T.'s coinage, rel. to 'sleek' (*MV*897, *LT*390) as in *MAC* 3.2.27; 'unsunny' T.'s

coinage; 'unfrowardly' T.'s coinage (these two new forms 'frame' this idyll, *PE*173, 585); 'unruffling' in the sense of becoming unruffled is T.'s own; 'unsay' and 'unswear' are used thrice and twice by Shakespeare. Note also 'unhooded' (*MV*128), a falconer's term; 'unfaith' (*MV*386).

10. e.g. 'overgoverned', 'overmatched', 'overstrong', 'overhasty'.

11. 'Overblame' T. made from 'overpraise', prob. deriving from *PL* 9, 615 'Serpent, thy overpraising leaves in doubt / The vertue of that fruit'; 'overstrained' only Thynne, 1599; 'overtrue' only Hooker, 1597; 'overquick' 1560, 1663, then T.; 'over-fineness' (*MV*794) T.'s coinage; 'overtalk'd' 1635 then T.; 'overworn' *OED* 4 'spent in time, passed away' *Venus and Adonis* l. 866, then *In Mem.* i 15–16 'Behold the man that loved and lost, / But all he was is overworn'. Note also 'overbore' and 'overborne' (*MV*594, 798).

12. There are 30 examples in A. E. Baker's *Concordance*.

13. 'Ever-' very much the property of the poets, espec. Spenser. T. also has compounds in 'all-' (frequent in Shakespeare: Leigh Hunt makes the point when he speaks of 'the all-including genius of Shakspeare'): 'all-accomplished' ('Dedication' 18), 'all-amorous' (*GE*360), 'all-shamed' (*GE*852), 'all-puissant' (*MG*86), 'all-silent' (*MV*180).

14. e.g. Malory has 'wifeless', 'speechless', 'swordless', 'beardless'.

15. 'Aidless' *COR* 2.2.116, *Comus* 574. 'Companionless' *OED* gives *Prel*. 4, 82 (1851) really 4, 399; and *Jane Eyre* xvii (1847). As T. heard Wordsworth read in 1835 it is just possible he adopted it by way of compliment, through two rarities with the same suffix following in

traditional descent from the three greatest blank verse exponents. **16.** 'Frontless', 'unblushing, shameless, audacious, daring' prev. Jonson 1605, Chapman's *Od.* 1633, Cibber 1739, Boswell 1791, 1823, Leigh Hunt 1850; 'fleshless' first Marlowe; 'blindless' Bronte, *Villette* xx, 1853; 'lustreless' 1810, 1851; 'dinnerless' 1661, 1708, 1720; 'voiceless' prev. Coverdale 1535, Shelley 1817, De Quincey 1849; 'veilless' Milman 1822; 'kingless' 1297, 1300, *Merlin* c. 1450, 1683, Byron 1812; 'Christless' 1652, 1683, 1816; 'skyless' 1848, 1871; 'cloudless' Peele 1598, Sylvester 1605, Milton 1671, Cowper 1791; 'proofless' 1610, 1795; 'wordless' 1648, 1836; 'bushless' T.'s coinage, first *Ode to Memory*, 1830; 'wifeless' echoing Malory vi 10 'But one thing, sir knight, methink ye lack, ye that are a knight wifeless'; 'heirless' 1425, 1845; 'deathless' *fig. PL* 10, 775; 'hornless' 1398, 1611, 1766, 1812; 'handless' *TIT* 3.1.67; 'guileless' Thomson, Shenstone, Scott; 'passionless' 1612, 1659, 1844, Macaulay 1855. See also 'selfless' (*MV*441, 790) first Coleridge 1825, then T. Pfordresher, pp. 143, 146, 198, 403, 925 shows the discarded forms 'dreamless', 'tongueless', 'dateless' (from *R2* 1.3.151), 'masterless' (from *FQ* i vii 19), 'starless'. **17.** Of course it is Mark who is the 'lustful' king. **18.** 'Showerful' T.'s coinage; 'easeful' *3H6* 5.3.6, Milton, Keats; 'healthful' *JC* 2.1.319, *HAM* 3.4.141; 'mightful' *TIT* 4.4.5; 'manful' in medieval uses, T. not noted (but see Malory xvi 15 'right manfully'); 'spleenful' *TIT* 2.3.191, Heywood, Dryden, Keats; 'prideful' 1450, 1533, 1572, 1740, Coleridge, Carlyle; 'lustful' 1579, *SHR in.* 2.40, Walton, Savage, Coleridge; 'noiseful' Dryden, Pope; 'gustful' 1825; 'mirthful' *OED* 2 of

things; 'affording mirth, amusing' *3H6* 5.7.43; 'prayerful' 1626, 1702; 'trustful' *OED* 2 'trusting, confiding' only in *In Mem.* cix. Pfordresher, pp. 501, 511, 744 shows the forms 'wileful' (presumably T.'s own, not in *OED*); 'tideful' (prob. from Drayton, *Polyolb.*); 'brimful' (prob. *2H4* 3.1.67). Note also 'feastful' ('The Palace of Art' 177) from Milton, *Sonnet* ix 12; 'deedful' (*Aylmer's Field* 196), first in Blackwood's, 1834; 'faultful' (*Prin.* vii 248) from *Lucr.* 715; 'rageful' (*Aylmer's Field* 336) from Sidney, *Arcadia*; 'songful' (*Demeter and Persephone* 45). Note 'So grateful is the noise of noble deeds' (*MG*437) where 'grateful' means 'pleasing', as in *SHR* 2.1.76. **19.** 'Kinglihood' T.'s coinage, as is 'queenhood' (*MG*176). 'Queenly' *OED* 2 'resembling a queen, queenlike' see first 1832 version 'The Lady of Shalott': 'By the water stood the queenly / Lady of Shalott'. See also 'kinglike' *OED* B 'like, or in a manner befitting a king' only in *Becket* 4.2; 'Kingling' *Becket pro.* 'You could not see the King for the kinglings' (prev. Sylvester, Cleveland, Churchill, Southey). Other compounds in '-hood' are 'hardihood' (*GL*542, 546) first in *Comus* 650; 'youthhood' (*GL*566) prob. from Carlyle; 'lustihood' (*LE*202) from *ADO* 5.1.76. **20.** See Malory x 62 'falslier nor traitorlier'; Malory v 2 'royalest' (cp. 'royaller' *MV*106), Malory viii 4 'famousest and marvelloust', Malory ix 16 'most goodliest'. In T. note comparison of adverbs: 'making slowlier' (*GE*167), 'must keep it safelier' (*LE*217), 'breathed far purelier' (*Aylmer's Field* 459), 'my son will speak for me ablier than I can' (*Columbus* 216). Some of T.'s adverbs are rarities: 'unwaveringly' (*GL*139) prev. Coleridge; 'unmockingly' (*GL*288) T.'s

coinage; 'oilily' (*GL*796) T.'s
coinage; 'statelily' (*MG*175) prev.
1611, 1672, 1796; 'dissolutely'
(*GE*275) *OED* 3 'licentiously'
prev. 1530, 1611, 1711;
'delightsomely' (*BB*58) prev. 1576,
1600, 1603; 'weariedly' (*LT*156)
prev. 1681, 1815, 1865; 'cheerly'
('The Lady of Shalott' l. 30) from
Spenser, *T.M.* 321, *AYL* 2.6.14.
21. 'Princelike' *OED* B 'in a
princely manner; like a prince'
CYM 5.5.293. Baker's *Concordance*
lists 60 like compounds. In the
Idylls there is 'fool-like' (*GL*462),
T.'s coinage 'unknightlike'
(*GL*1122) – Pfordresher, p. 244
shows T. first had Malory's
'unknightly'; 'Lancelot-like'
(*GL*1270) analogous formation to
'Nestor-like' *1H6* 2.5.6, 'sunlike'
(*MG*789), 'gem-like' (*GE*198),
'brother-like' (*GE*884) from *3H6*
5.1.105; 'tusklike' (*BB*311) not in
OED; 'knightlike' (*BB*422) prob.
from Drayton, *Polyolb*. then *Prin*.
4, 577; 'eagle-like' (*BB*527),
'magnet-like' (*MV*573) *Prom. Unb*.
then T.; 'godlike' (*MV*837),
'dreamlike' (*HG*260), 'chasm-like'
(*HG*815) not in *OED*; 'catlike'
(*LT*516) from *AYL* 4.3.116;
'lionlike' (*G*107). T. also imitates
Malory in making compounds of
'-wise.' Malory has for example 'in
like wise', 'rightwise', 'in such wise',
'none otherwise but', 'in the richest
wise' (Malory i 1, 5, v 3, xi 7, xii 6).
In mimicry is 'in such-wise'
(*MV*640) and of the poet's creation
are 'mocking-wise', 'broken-wise',
'dropwise', 'earthlywise' and
'elsewise' (*BB*383, *MV*98, 272,
*HG*626, *LT*675). T.'s 'dropwise'
only has a single antecedent, as part
of a medical description; 'in
such-wise' is also Homeric, *Il*. 5,
274; 'earthlywise' is T.'s own nonce
word, prob. formed from Malory's
frequent use of 'earthly' in the Grail
sequence.
22. 'Knightly' Malory ii 8, iv 9, vi

11, ix 17; 'unknightly' Malory x 19,
70, which demonstrates that already
T. knew much more of Malory than
the final book.
23. cp. Cymochles v. Prince Arthur,
FQ II viii 49: 'Upon him lightly
leaping without heed / Twixt his
two mighty arms engrasped fast, /
Thinking to overthrowe and downe
him tred'.
24. 'Full knightly' Malory x 68, xx
14; 'knights-errant' Malory ix 12.
25. Suggested by Lancelot's actual
knighting of Gareth, Malory vii 5
'and then Sir Launcelot gave him
the order of knighthood'.
26. Based on Malory iii 8.
27. Malory xvii 23.
28. Malory viii 5.
29. See my study (1968) p. 95 ff.
30. 'Garlandage' is T.'s coinage.
Other compounds with this suffix
include 'embassage' (*BB*90),
'scaffoldage' (*BB*361, first version)
from *TRO* 1.3.156, 'rummage'
(*BB*410) from *HAM* 1.1.107,
'pupilage' (*MV*515) from
'pupillage' *FQ* II x 64, 'harbourage'
(*GL*813, 823, *MG*281, 290, 299)
from *JN* 2.1.234. T. also has
'cordage' (*Enoch Arden* 17),
'fruitage' (*Enoch Arden* 555) from
PL 10, 561, 'pasturage' (*Enoch
Arden* 17, 551, 671), 'flowerage'
(*Aylmer's Field* 203) from Carlyle.
31. Paralleled by Lynette's entry
(*GL*573–8) which sounds like a
piece of Renaissance blazon, and by
Gawain's entry (*LE*550–6) which
follows Malory iv 18 in ranking
Gawain after Lancelot and
Tristram, but substitutes Geraint
(from *Mabinogion*) in place of Bors,
and Gareth for Percivale, Pelleas
and Marhaus.
32. See Tacitus, *Germania* par. 6,
FQ v xi 52 for the disgrace of
discarding one's shield; *FQ* II viii 31
for the disgrace in making an
undeclared attack.
33. Vivien's 'Sir Boy' echoes *ADO*
5.1.83, *TIT* 4.3.2. In the same class

are Kay's mock-title for Gareth:
'Sir Fine-face', 'Sir Fair-hands',
answered in kind by Lancelot,
who terms Kay 'Sir Seneschal'
(*GL*451,465). Lynette refers
to Gareth as 'Sir kitchen knave' and
promotes him to 'Sir Knave'
(*GL*767, 993, 1166). The Lord of
Astolat half-humorously calls his
disabled son Torre 'Sir Churl'.
Ettarre refers to Pelleas as 'Sir Baby'
(*PE*183). Tristram calls Dagonet
'Sir Fool', 'Sir Dagonet' (*LT*9, 243,
273). In Malory x 12 Arthur
knights Dagonet; in T. Gawain 'in
his mood' (echoing *TGV* 4.1.51
'Who, in my moode, I stab'd unto
the heart') mock-knights Dagonet.
Pfordresher, pp. 83, 185, 235, 253,
503 shows the discarded variants
'Sir Stripling', 'Sir Scullion', 'Sir
Merlin', 'Sir Kitchen boy', 'Sir
Rebel', 'Sir Mark'.
34. Echoing *PL* 6, 236 'To . . . open
when, and when to close / The
ridges of grim Warr'.
35. Malory i 14, 15, 16, 17 etc. has
'Sir Arthur'.
36. Malory xiv 2 'Also Merlin made
the Round Table in tokening of
roundness of the world, for by the
Round Table is the world signified
by right'.
37. *Isa.* 14.13.
38. Field (1971) p. 41.
39. Malory xii opens with 'and' and
often chapters open with the
conjunction, e.g. i 7, 11, 12, 18, ii 5,
17, iii 8.
40. Malory i 4.
41. Malory xxi 5.
42. Malory ii 15. T. frequently shows
a similar freedom, e.g. the 18
examples of 'and' (*CA*338–55) to
suggest Arthur's and Bellicent's
shared childhood. *The Times* for
23rd Dec. 1869, p. 4 did not
approve: 'The writing is
commonplace and careless; the
word "and" is repeated *ad nauseam*;
there is an entire lack of that
ornament with which Tennyson can

produce an effect that is rich
without being florid'. Occasionally
T. mimics Malory's use of 'and':
e.g. Malory iv 1 'a fair lady and a
good' which in one case T.
develops to the full: 'Broad brows
and fair, a fluent hair and fine, /
High nose, a nostril large and fine,
and hands / Large, fair and fine!'
(*GL*454–6). See also Malory iv 7 'a
full fair manor and a rich' and 'All
in a full-fair manor and a rich'
(*GL*825). *ROM* 2.2.8 has 'Her
vestal livery is but sick and
green'.
43. 'The Image in Process' in *The
Modern Tradition*, ed. Ellmann and
Feidelson (1965) p. 168.
44. e.g. the second and tenth
sentences of Malory iii 1, the tenth
sentence of iii 2.
45. Malory i 2.
46. Malory's and Shakespeare's 'and
but' (e.g. Malory vii 14, xvi 14, xxi
5, *SHR* 4.4.2, *ROM* 2.2.76) is
occasionally reflected by T.
(*GL*603, *MG*11, *HG*746, 846,
*PE*71).
47. e.g. Malory i 2, 3, 4, 5, 8, 9, 14, 15,
19, 27.
48. *Morte d'Arthur* 13, 66, 82, 113,
133, 148, 193, 204, 226.
49. Malory iv, xviii, xix. Chapters
opening this way include Malory
i 10, 13, ii 11, 13, iii 4.
50. Imitated by Matthew Arnold
with the 'And' that opens *Sohrab and
Rustum*. Among small narrative
formulae 'There on a day' (*MG*147)
follows *FQ* iv ii 45, and 'for on a
day' (*HG*101) *FQ* i ix 12. 'Then on
a day' opens an episode in Malory i
21, 'So upon a day' Malory x 53, x
86, and 'Then upon a day' Malory
xii 1.
51. T.'s idiosyncratic use of 'so' is
Shakespearean ('so' equals 'if') in
Bedivere's 'but my belief / In all this
matter – so ye care to learn'
(*CA*183), in the words of
Ambrosius 'And this am I, so that

ye care for me / Ever so little'
(*HG*614) and in the plea of Pelleas,
'Content am I so that I see thy
face / But once a day' (*PE*235).
Shakespearean also are 'And so
there lived some colour in your
cheek' (*GE*620) where 'so' is *OED*
26a 'on condition that, provided
that' and Merlin's 'But, so thou
dread to swear' (*GL*268) where
'so' is *OED* 26b 'in the event that,
in case that.'

52. Malory i 1.

53. Suggested by G. C. Macaulay
(1897) p. 54.

54. T.'s Merlin echoes Malory's
Merlin in two forms: Malory i 25
'for an' and Malory iii 1 'but an'.
Merlin uses 'an' alone in Malory i
10, 20, 23, ii 8, iii 1, enough for T. to
consider this a special verbal trait
of the magician's.

55. Note Doorm's 'an if he live' and
Lavaine's equally redundant 'But,
father, give me leave an if he will'
(*GE*553, *LE*218) echoing Malory x
84, *AYL* 2.5.56, *TGV* 3.1.257.
The second element when Doorm
continues the figure: 'An if he
live . . . / And if he die . . .' echoes
TGV 1.1.75.

56. A study of the paragraph
'breaks' through the serial poem's
evolution is instructive. The *Morte
d'Arthur*, 1859 *Merlin and Vivien*,
and *The Marriage of Geraint* (i.e. the
first two thousand lines of the poem)
have none. The first break occurs at
Geraint and Enid line 556 (The way
T. makes this break shows Doorm's
values are inverted, a horse being
'noble' whereas its master is merely
human). *Guinevere* has six paragraph
breaks (*G*52, 144, 375, 577, 607,
656). *Lancelot and Elaine* has eleven,
The Holy Grail four only (*HG*563,
631, 644, 865), and *The Coming of
Arthur* one (*CA*62) just at that
epiphanic point where Arthur enters
the design. Clearly he is no ordinary
hero. *Pelleas and Ettarre* has nine
paragraph breaks, *Gareth and

Lynette thirty-six (illustrating how
much dialogue it contains, often
repartee), *The Last Tournament* four,
and *Balin and Balan* eight (T. has
this idyll set as a single verse unit,
with only indentations at each
paragraph head, not spacing
between paragraphs, as a mark of
where the paragraph begins, in the
manner of Milton). Omission of
customary spacing speeds up a poem
already rapid and compressed. In
the addition to *Merlin and Vivien*
(1875) T. added two breaks, to tie it
to *Balin and Balan* (*MV*61, 83).
Clearly speeches terminating with
half lines are modelled on
Shakespeare's last phase (e.g. with
fair consistency throughout *The
Tempest*). Paragraph breaks in
non-dramatic verse originate with
Coleridge's conversation poems,
the 1795 *The Aeolian Harp* l. 12,
Reflections . . . Retirement l. 26, *This
Lime Tree Bower* ll. 20, 43, *Frost at
Midnight* l. 23. See also Wordsworth's
The Old Cumberland Beggar l. 105,
Tintern Abbey ll. 22, 49, 111, *Michael*
ll. 255, 382 (in each case followed by
the indication: 'At this the old Man
paused'). In continuous narrative-
descriptive verse paragraph breaks
first occur in the 1850 version of
The Prelude.

57. Ricks (1972) p. 276. The
foundation image was first made at
Ballybunion, west coast of Ireland,
1842, according to *Memoir*, i, 218.

58. Shaw (1976) p. 199.

59. The colon and semicolon in
Milton are described by Cary and
Fowler, p. 427: 'The colon can be
much heavier than ours; so that we
often find it where we would have
put a full stop. But it also has a great
variety of uses of different
rhetorical weight: namely to mark
logical divisions and to introduce
alternatives, reasons, concessions,
comparisons, defining clauses, after
thoughts, interruptions, and direct
speech. The lighter semicolon often

separates stages in a narrative sequence or items in a catalogue.'
60. Or as a means of testing the echo which is so important for the series as a whole.
61. In that it is a self-containing and self-contained image, whereas the *Morte d'Arthur*, especially in the action of the three fair queens at the close, is like an invocation in reverse, a revocation, as indeed is the whole ritual act of giving up Excalibur.
62. 1 *Cor* 13.12 'now we see through a glass darkly'; in Malory i 20 Merlin has the premonition 'I shall die a shameful death to be put in the earth quick'.
63. T. is fond of extended images and metaphors. Note Vivien's arm curved round Merlin's neck (*MV*239) which 'tightens' over three hundred lines later (*MV*612–13), pressure constantly being applied, also Gawain likened to a leashed dog anxious to spring on a rat (*PE*274–8), one of several effective 'homely' images in the series, and almost thirty lines later, he 'sprang' and 'bounded forward to the castle walls' (*PE*307, 355). In Malory vii 4 Gareth's combat with Kay ends when Gareth 'with a foyne thrust (Kay) through the side'. In T. Gareth's master is simply 'shoulder-slipt' and his fate is left in suspense until comically the 'dislocated' Kay enters Camelot (*GL*740, 1182).
64. Peters (1965) p. 81.
65. The whole passage (*LE*426–88) has many heroic echoes. Arthur's dragon motif originates in Geoffrey of Monmouth's *Historia* xi 1. That Arthur is 'easily to be known' by the dragon motif on robes and throne, echoes *Od.* 6, 90 of Artemis 'easily may she be known' or *FQ* iii xi 7 'full easie to be known'; 'afield' is from *TRO* 5.3.67; 'stranger knight' is a Spenser term; 'overdo' is a Malory word; and the 'plumes driv'n backward' echo *PL* 1, 222–3:

'the flames / Drivn backward slope their pointing spires'. Ricks, p. 1634 quotes a letter of T.'s on a voyage to Norway: 'the green sea looking like a mountainous country, far-off waves with foam at the top looking like snowy mountains bounding the scene; one great wave, green-shining, past with all its crests smoking high up beside the vessel'.
66. See ch. 2 n 102. Homer's 'loud-sounding sea' and 'the sounding sea' lie behind 'the sad sea-sounding shores of Lyonnesse' and the 'ocean-sounding welcome' accorded Tristram (*MV*73, *LT*168). T.'s 'many a windy wave', 'windy walls' and 'waste sea' (*MG*337, *GE*164, *PA*92) are likewise Homeric.
67. Bowra (1952) p. 278.
68. Nash (1972) pp. 160–1. Was T.'s Red Knight who threatened 'To hang whatever knight of thine I fought / And tumbled' in Lewis Carroll's mind when in front of Alice 'the Red Knight's horse stopped suddenly: "You're my prisoner!" the knight cried, as he tumbled off his horse' (*Through the Looking Glass*, 1872, ch. viii)?
69. Saintsbury (1895) p. 35.

CHAPTER SIX
Songs
1. *Mythology and Rites of the British Druids* (1809) p. 77.
2. op. cit., p. 76.
3. Philosopher and physiologist, 6th century B C, *Ancilla to the Pre-Socratic Philosophers*, tr. Freeman. For the rainbow, see *Gen.* 9.13–16.
4. Malory iii 1.
5. 'The Great Deep or Lowest Point of Existence' is an expression of the Welsh *Triads*; in *Gen.* 7.11 it is the Deluge, in *Ps.* 36.6 'thy judgments are a great deep', in *Isa.* 51.10 it is the sea, and in *Amos* 7.4 quite obscure. 'And truth or clothed or

naked' cp. *1H6* 2.4.20 'The truth appears so naked on my side'.

6. For *The Coming of Arthur*'s inner structure see my article (1970) p. 142.

7. Geoffrey's *Historia* x 7 shows a unanimous response to Arthur before battle; the alliterative Layamon's *Brut* ll. 19, 925–9 has trumpets proclaim him king, and the most fervent battle anthem occurs ll. 22, 076–86.

8. 1 *Cor.* 11.1. Also 'he will lift us from the dust' echoes *Ps.* 113.7 'He raiseth up the poor out of the dust' and 'secret things' echoes *Deut.* 29.29 'Secret things belong to the Lord'.

9. 'Kingliest' linked with 'knightliest' (*GL*1129, *LT*706). For flowers that 'blow' *OED* 1 'to burst into flower, blossom, bloom' see *MND* 2.1.249, *PL* 7, 319, *GL*1003, 1042, *HG*668. T. also has 'blowing trees' (*GL*655). 'Warble' is gentle and melodious singing, espec. of birds, see Spenser, *SC June* 4. 'Warbling' in birdlike fashion announces Vivien, the perfect mimic (*BB*432).

10. Cp. *AYL* 3.5.83 'Who ever loved, that loved not at first sight'.

11. 'By God's grace' (*GL*707, *MG*344) from *R2* 1.3.37, *H5* 1.2.262 etc., 'By God's rood' (*MG*368, *MV*374) T.'s own, formed from 'Christ's rood'; 'God's curse' (*GE*616, 661, *LT*447) from *2H6* 4.8.33; Enid's 'By Heaven, I will not drink' (*GE*664) echoes her cry, *Mabinogion*, p. 257; 'God's mercy' (*LE*24) from *AWW* 1.3.155; Lancelot's cry 'For God's love, a little air' (*LE*504) echoes Percivale, Malory xiv 2; Gawain's 'Yea, by God's death' (*LE*675) seems T.'s expansion of ''sdeath'; see also Lynette's 'Good lord, how sweetly smells the honeysuckle' (*GL*1255) and *SHR* 4.5.2 'Good lord, how bright and goodly shines the moon'.

12. Note the swearing of vows, a monosyllabic weighting of every word, so that misunderstanding is impossible (*CA*132–3, 261, 467, 469, *GL*265–9, *G*247, 464, 469).

13. *LR* 2.2.80. The refrain also echoes *Inferno* xv 95–6: *Pero giri Fortuna la sua rota, | Come le piace*. In Malory xx 17 Lancelot says 'but fortune is so variant, and the wheel so moveable, that nys none constant abiding'. Fortune's wheel had taken another strange turn for T. during the poem's composition. 'In June (1856) news came that R.'s bank would probably break and that all my father's little savings might be lost. On July 2nd my mother wrote "A(lfred) showed a noble disregard of money, much as the loss would affect us"' (*Memoir*, i, 415).

14. Someone attempting to escape from Doorm 'made / The long way smoke beneath him in his fear' (*GE*532) echoing *FQ* 11 v 3 'But prickt so fiers, that underneath his feete / The smouldering dust did round about him smoke'.

15. W. Nash (1972) p. 361.

16. Echoing *FQ* 1 v 33 'And come to fiery flood of Phlegeton', *PL* 2, 580–1 'Fiery Phlegethon / Whose waves of torrent fire inflame with rage'.

17. Suggesting Plato's images of the lyre, harmony, love and the soul in *The Phaedo*.

18. *Tennyson's Style* (1976) p. 199. The song's last line 'And trust me not at all or all in all' is redolent of *SHR* 2.1.130 'That is, her love; for that is all in all'.

19. cp. Malory x 86 'And then (Palomides) began to make a rhyme of la Beale Isoud and him'. Lancelot's casual form 'by and by' (not recorded *OED*, but see *FQ* 11 viii 4 and frequent in Shakespeare) reveals the genuine lover.

20. *Bentley's Quarterly* 2 (Oct. 1859) pp. 181–2. Eventually, Merlin's voice becomes infected with the long ā (*MV*804–36).

21. In Malory x 27 Dinadan makes up a lay and arranges to have it sung before Mark.

22. Echoing *Il.* 6, 506–11, *Aen.* 11, 490. Both Paris and Gawain are handsome, vain philanderers.

23. 'He set himself to play upon her' (*LE*642) cp. *HAM* 3.2.381 'You would play upon me; you would seem to know my stops'. 'Sallying' (*LE*643) see *OED* 6 'a sprightly or audacious utterance'.

24. cp. the song 'welcome, sweet Death' in Dowland's *Go, Nightly Cares.*

25. *Isa.* 35.6 'Then shall the lame man leap as an hart, and the tongue of the dumb sing'.

26. 'House' echoing Malory xvii 15 'And with that he saw . . . that the house was as bright as all the torches of the world had been there'; 'A castle like a rock upon a rock' cp. the pun made by Jesus, *Matt.* 16.18 'And I say also unto thee, thou art Peter and upon this rock I will build my church'.

27. *Dan.* 3.19 'heat the furnace one seven times more than it was wont to be heated'.

28. cp. *FQ* 11 iii 41 'But easy is the way and passage plaine / To pleasures pallace: it may soone be spide, / And day and night her dores to all stand open wide'; and brambles symbolic of abandon, *Isa.* 34.13 'nettles and brambles in the fortresses'.

29. cp. Malory vii 15 'and blew so the horn eagerly that the siege and the castle rang thereof' and *FQ* 11 ix 11 'And wind his horne under the castle wall, / That with the noise it shooke as it would fall'.

30. 'Broken music' *AYL* 1.2.150. ' "Save for that broken music in thy brains, / Sir Fool," said Tristram, "I would break thy head" ' (*LT*267–8) echoing Malory ix 18 'Sir Tristram . . . gat Sir Dagonet by the head, and gave him such a

fall to earth that he bruised him sore so that he lay still'.

31. 'Tested gold' *MM* 2.2.149. When Tristram taunts Dagonet: 'Come, thou art crabbed and sour: but lean me down, / Sir Dagonet, one of thy long asses' ears' (*LT*272–3) T. combines the two Shakespeare allusions, *ERR* 4.4.30 'I am an ass, indeed; you may prove it by my long ears' and *WT* 1.2.102 'that was when / Three crabbed months had sour'd themselves to death'.

32. Nash (1972) p. 140.

33. 'Measure' *OED* 20 'a dance, espec. a grave or stately dance'.

34. Nash (1972) p. 188.

35. Ricks, p. 1723.

36. *Matt.* 25.1–13.

37. The setting: 'one low light betwixt then burn'd / Blurr'd by the creeping mist' (*G*4–5) cp. Satan's entry into paradise, *PL* 9, 180: 'Like a black mist low creeping'.

38. Note the fine visual reflection of the song-parable as Arthur prepares to depart: 'And near him the sad nuns with each a light / Stood' (*G*586–7).

39. 'Made answer' *FQ* vi xi 12, *PL* 5, 735 etc. In fact elves frame the series (see Ricks, p.1469) T. cites Layamon's *Brut*, which relates that elves were present at Arthur's birth. As smiths they also forged Excalibur, thus an element of its hilt is 'elfin Urim' (*CA*298), combining Spenser's word 'elfin' (*FQ* i iv 42) with 'Urim' (*Exod.* 28.30, *PL* 6, 761). 'Elvish emblemings' are on the gate at Camelot (*GL*229), 'elvish' being the Gawain poet's word (*Sir Gawain and the Green Knight* l. 681). Vivien calls Cupid a 'little elf-god' (*MV*247). 'The little elves of chasm and cleft / Made answer, sounding like a distant horn' at Arthur's coming, and Bedivere tells Arthur to disregard 'Elves, and the harmless glamour of the field' before the last battle (*G*248, *PA*52).

CHAPTER SEVEN
Dreams

1. Hair (1976) p. 296. In Malory i 19 Arthur dreams of griffins and serpents which 'burnt and slew all the people in the land', perhaps echoed when 'the rest slew on and burnt' (*CA*438) in Leodogran's dream. The phantom king who 'sent out at times a voice' (*CA*436) echoes *Ps.* 68.33 'he sendeth out his voice and that a mighty voice'. The divine will can only come to man through dreams.

2. 'Arthur's harp' (*GL*1281, *LT*333) T. gives as the constellation Lyra. Cp. 'A star shot: "Lo," said Gareth, "the foe falls!" / An owl whoopt: "Hark the victor pealing there"' (*GL*1284–5) and Byron, *Manfred* i i 197–8: 'When the falling stars are shooting, / And the answer'd owls are hooting'.

3. 'Beaten broad' cp. *Matt.* 7.13 'Broad is the way that leadeth to destruction' and *FQ* i i 11 'That path they take that beaten seemd most bare' (to the Wood of Error).

4. A perceptive analysis of the two poems is to be found in Wright (1929) 71–103, Reed (1969) 58–69, Eggers (1971) 23–35, Rosenberg (1973) 74–7, and Kincaid (1975) 171–7.

5. An analysis of the entire scene is in Nash (1972) pp. 40–4, 285–8, 335, 378–9. Balin's innocent witness of Lancelot and Guinevere with its tragic consequences suggested by a like incident in Malory ii 16 when Balin 'looked into a fair little garden, and under a laurel tree he saw her lie upon a quilt of green samite and a knight in her arms, fast halsynge either other, and under their heads grass and herbs'.

6. T. glossed this: 'The only real bit of feeling, and the only pathetic line which Vivien speaks'. Note the serpentine suggestions in her role and appearance. Mark first encourages her: 'Here are snakes within the grass; / And you, methinks . . . can stir them till they sting' (*MV*33–6) echoing Virgil, *Ecl.* ii 93 : *frigidus, o pueri, fugite hinc, latet anguis in herba* ('O boys, fly from here, a clammy snake lurks in the grass') and Milton's infernal serpent who, *PL* 1, 35 'stirr'd up with envy and revenge'. When the 'wily' Vivien stole from Arthur's court she is linked through the adjective with Milton's 'wily Adder' (see ch. 3 n 122). She shows 'faintly venom'd points / Of slander' to Merlin (*MV*170). Later 'there lay she all her length' with a 'twist of gold' in her hair, and her robe of 'red samite' (redolent of the scarlet whore of Babylon) 'clung' about her 'lissome limbs' (*MV*217, 219, 221). Then, attaching herself to the only vulnerable part of her Achilles, she 'holding by his heel, / Writhed toward him, slided up his knee and sat . . . curved an arm about his neck, / Clung like a snake' (*MV*236–40). Gladstone thought this a fine example of the poet's 'extraordinary felicity and force in the use of metaphor and simile' (*Quarterly Review* 106, 1859, p. 472). Vivien 'here combines the roles of Eve and Satan. She lusts for Merlin's forbidden knowledge and in grasping his heel, like the serpent in *Genesis* who bruises man's heel, she brings death into the world' (Rosenberg 1973, p. 114). At the end she becomes 'stiff as a viper frozen' and then envisages that she will 'in some low cave . . . crawl' (*MV*843, 882). Just as 'back to the thicket slunk / The guilty Serpent' after Milton's Eve had been seduced (*PL* 9, 784–5), so too 'the thicket closed / Behind her' (*MV*971–2) when Vivien left Merlin to his doom.

7. cp. *FQ* 11 ix 16 'As when a

swarme of Gnats at eventide / Out
of the fennes of Allan doe arise, /
Their murmuring small trompetts
sownden wide'.
8. Echoing *Aen.* 8, 432 *flammisque
sequacibus iras*, with an echo of
'rolling' fire, *Aen.* 4, 670 *flammae . . .
volvantur. Aen.* 2, 706, 758 Virgil
speaks of *aestus incendia volvunt . . .
ignis . . . volvitur.* See also 'rolling
year' (*PA*91) echoing *Aen.* 1, 234:
volventibus annis.
9. According to classical precedent
a man who sees nymphs becomes
'possessed by nymphs' (Theocr. 13,
44). Also even today the noonday
hour is considered a haunted time
in Greece, and it is dangerous to
disturb the sleeping Pan at this time
(Theocr. 1, 15 ff.).
10. Trumpets are emphatically
plural at the beginning, and Merlin
signifies their chivalric meaning:
'Such fire for fame, / Such trumpet
blowings' but at the end there is
ominously a single muted
instrument: 'The sudden trumpet
sounded as in a dream . . . Thro' the
thick night I hear the trumpet blow'
(*CA*481–96, *MV*415, *LT*151, *G*526,
566). 'Thick night' echoes *MAC*
1.5.51.
11. Nash (1972) p. 154. 'These
be . . .' (*LT*412), *Gen.* 36.43, *Exod.*
32.4.
12. Nash (1972) pp. 163–4.
13. ll. 80–1 interesting metrically.
Critics taxed T. for metrical licence
(e.g. Buxton Forman 1871,
pp. 67–8) but there is always
expressive purpose in every
deviation. Buxton Forman's
complaint (p. 67) against the line
'Ulfius, and Brastias, and Bedivere'
(*CA*135) for its 'formlessness' is
answered by F. J. Rowe (1891,
p. 39): 'Lines composed of proper
names often take license in their
scansion, cf. Verg. *Georg.* 1, 437'.
14. In Malory xxi 3 Gawain is
accompanied by ladies.
15. Gawain's 'lightness' stems from

Malory iii 8, iv 22. 'Light-of-love'
(*PE*353) stems from Shakespeare's
reference to a song of that name,
TGV 1.2.83, or to *ADO* 3.4.44, 47.
16. T. compares *Aen.* 6, 740–1:
*aliae panduntur inanes / suspensae ad
ventos* ('Some are hung stretched out
to the empty winds'). Rowe, p. 57
notes the image of Gawain's ghost
'Like wild birds that change / Their
season in the night and wail their
way / From cloud to cloud'
(*PA*38–40) is based on *Purgatorio* 5,
46–8 and that there are like effects
Il. 3, 3, *Aen.* 10, 264; also that T.'s
expression 'light upon the wind'
(*PA*46) recalls *Purgatorio* 5, 75:
e paion si al vento esser leggieri ('and
seem so light upon the wind').

CHAPTER EIGHT
Characterisation
1. Malory v 12, xvi 17, 9, xiv 9,
xviii 3.
2. Sp. Gorloïs (to rhyme with 'is')
FQ iii iii 27. T. changes another
minor character, Lot. In Malory ii
10 Lot is majestic, killed by
Pellinore while warring against
Arthur, a fate quite different from
the figure who 'lies like a log, and
all but smoulder'd out . . . A
yet-warm corpse, and yet
unburiable, / No more; nor sees,
nor hears, nor speaks, nor knows
(*GL*74–80). Swinburne's Lot is
also moribund, *Works* IV, p. 44:
'But cold as rains in autumn was
King Lot / And grey-grown out of
season'.
3. *Sir Gawain and the Green Knight*
l. 961.
4. Here Gawain briefly recalls Paris,
end of *Il.* 6 (T.'s trans. is in *Memoir*,
ii, 15). Gawain 'in his mood'
(*LT*1, echoing *TGV* 4.1.51 'Who,
in my moode, I stab'd unto the
heart') stems from Malory iii 4 and
vii 34 where he sat 'in great envy'
at seeing others given priority, and
where he is said to be 'vengeable'.
This no doubt accounts for

'scowling Gauwaine, like the night in day' of Morris ('King Arthur's Tomb') and T.'s knight who, when asked to leave the festivities on an errand 'with smiling face arose, / With smiling face and frowning heart' (*LE*550). Swinburne, *Works* IV 49, 178 takes a different view: 'gracious Gawain, scattering words as flowers, / The kindliest head of worldly paramours' and 'Gawain, sweet of soul and gay / As April ere he dreams of May'.

5. 'Fluent' *OED* 3 *transf.* 'Of hair: growing in abundant quantity and falling in graceful curves; flowing'. Lancelot's estimate of Gareth as if he were a horse: 'Broad brows and fair, a fluent hair and fine, / High nose, a nostril large and fine, and hands / Large, fair and fine!' (*GL*454–6) mimics *Venus and Adonis* l. 296: 'Broad breast, full eye, small head, and nostril wide, / High crest, short ears'. 'Hands / Large, fair and fine!' is based on Malory vii 1 'and the fairest and the largest handed that ever man saw'.

6. Other heroes who are fair include Odysseus during his transformation, *Od.* 13, 431, Menelaus, *Od.* 4, 332, *Il.* 17, 578, and Achilles, *Od.* 1, 197. Christ is frequently blonde in stained glass windows and Bible illustrations of the Victorian period. *Memoir*, i, 485 notes that Arthur Henry Hallam's eyes were blue, the same colour as King Arthur's (*LT*662, *PA*337).

7. Homer's Helen has 'fair hair' or is 'fair-tressed' and Virgil's Dido, Spenser's Una, Milton's Eve are all blonde, *Od.* 15, 58, *Aen.* 4, 590, *FQ* 1 x 28, *PL* 4, 305, 496. Guinevere is fair-haired in Owen Meredith's 'The Parting of Launcelot and Guenevere' and G. A. Simcox's *The Farewell of Ganore*.

8. Shunning evil is a characteristic of Malory's Gareth, see Malory vii 34, xx 1. In *The Beguiling of Merlin* (Lady Lever Gallery, Port Sunlight)

Burne Jones has made his Merlin beardless but very effectively elfin and half-devil.

9. Swinburne's Mark is also a 'swart lean man' with 'black streaked beard' (*Works*, IV, p. 60). Mark's 'long crane legs' (*LT*723) betoken lechery in medieval iconography, e.g. Chaucer's Reeve: 'ful longe were his legges and ful lene, / Ylyk a staf, there was no calf ysene', *General Prologue* 591.

10. Echoing Chaucer, *A. Mil.* 3745 'And on his lippe he gan for anger byte' or *SHR* 2.1.248 'Nor bite the lip, as angry wenches will'.

11. Lancelot has 'locks of auburn' and 'eyes of blue' in Reginald Heber's *Morte d' Arthur* III xxvii. In Morris's 'King Arthur's Tomb' he has 'red-golden hair'. T. preserves Lancelot's traditional courtesy. Malory viii 17 has Lancelot 'peerless of courtesy and of knighthood' and in Malory xv 4 he is told 'for of a sinner earthly thou hast no peer as in knighthood', echoed by T. in Lancelot being a knight 'peerless' (*LE*1084, 1274). Galahad 'the goodliest knight, and of the best men of the world come' in Malory xiii 8, and in Malory xx 13 'the tears brast out of (Arthur's) eyen, thinking on the great courtesy that was in Sir Launcelot more than in any other man'. T. reflects this exemplary courtesy (*BB*252, *LE*1352, *LT*703–4, *G*321). Lancelot's reluctance to fight Arthur in Malory xx 13 is reflected in Arthur's words: 'and he / That did not shun to smite me in worse way, / Had yet that grace of courtesy in him left, / He spared to lift his hand against the King / Who made him knight' (*G*431–4) Lancelot as Arthur's 'right arm' (*LT*202, *G*426) is heroic, *Aen.* 7, 472, 12, 24, *TIM* 3.5.76.

12. cp. Arnold's *Tristram and Iseult* i 119, 123 where Iseult has 'proud dark eyes' and 'raven hair'. Turnus

to Allecto and her reply, *Aen.* 7,
436–66 is imitated by T. for
Tristram and Isolt. Turnus says to
Allecto: 'But your great age,
exhausted and decayed, and past
the fertile time for truth, makes you
restless and anxious all to no
purpose' and the goddess ironically
echoes his words: 'See who I am,
whose great age, exhausted and
decayed and past the fertile time for
truth, deludes me with imaginary
dread' (trans. W. Jackson Knight).
In T. it is Tristram and Isolt:
   Then Tristram, ever dallying with
     her hand,
'May God be with thee, sweet,
     when old and gray,
And past desire!' a saying that
     anger'd her,
"May God be with thee, sweet,
     when thou art old,
And sweet no more to me!"'
(*LT*621–5)
13. Note *Sir Gawain and the Green
Knight* ll. 81–2 'the fair and flawless
queen / Glanced with her grey eyes'.
In *The Defence of Guenevere* 224–5,
Morris has his queen speak of 'My
eyes, / Wept all away to grey' as if
her weeping was so copious that the
original colour was lost. See also
Sebastian Evans, 'Arthur's
Knighting': 'Ginevra looked at
Arthur, but the gray / Of her bright
eyen knew nought of lover's fear'.
Guinevere's beauty is never
explicit in Malory. In Malory iii 1
Merlin admits 'she is one of the
fairest on live'. Geoffrey's *Historia*
ix 9 states quite clearly: *tocius insule
mulieres pulchritudine superabat* ('and
in beauty surpassed all the women
of the island') and also the Vulgate
*Merlin: ce estoit la plus bele feme qui
fust en toute bertaigne au tans de lors.*
T. follows this in making his queen
'fairest of all flesh on earth' (*CA*3).
14. cp. *Judg.* 14.19 'And his anger
was kindled' and *Aen.* 12, 237 'By
such words the soldiers' counsel
was kindled' (*incensa*).

15. Ricks, p. 1616 compares
Coleridge, 'The Raven' l. 25: 'His
brow, like a pent-house, hung over
his eyes'.
16. *Rev.* 1.15, 14.2, 19.6.
17. 'Shaken' from 'shake' *OED* 4c
'a tremor (in the voice)'.
18. A similar formula used
*MG*430–2, *LE*181–3.
19. Malory x 6.
20. Echoing *Job* 29.24 'if I laughed
on them, they believed it not'.
21. Geoffrey's *Historia* viii 12,
Malory ii 19.
22. cp. Jupiter, *Aen.* 12, 829: *Olli
subridens hominum rerumque repertor*
('To her smilingly the designer of
men and things').
23. Echoing Malory xviii 20 'and
she lay as though she had smiled'.
24. See Hallam Tennyson's
comment, *Eversley Edition*, p. 487:
'My father loved his own great
imaginative knight, the Lancelot of
the *Idylls*'. It is hard to understand
the complaint in *Quarterly Review*
128 (Jan. 1870) 8: 'Lancelot ought
to have been much more seriously
and fully drawn than he is'.
25. *Blackwood's Edinburgh Magazine*
86 (Nov. 1859) 626.
26. Another face that is 'marred' is
Satan's, *PL* 4, 116: 'which marred
his borrowed visage'.
27. *Bentley's Quarterly* 2 (Oct. 1859)
171; H. D. Traill, 'Aspects of
Tennyson', *The Nineteenth Century*
32 (1892) 962; Arthur Waugh
(1892) p. 161; W. Macneile Dixon
(1901) p. 101; H. L'A. Fausset
(1923) p. 261; W. B. Yeats,
intro. xxvii, *Oxford Book of Modern
Verse* (1936).
28. Malory i 20.
29. Malory i 27.
30. Malory xxi 4.
31. Malory xx 6. J. P. Eggers, p. 39,
makes an important distinction:
'Malory's king is a human member
of a society in which the chivalric
code has grown organically; Arthur
brings together the Order of the

Round Table but is not the founder of a whole way of life, as he is in the *Idylls*'.

32. Malory iii 15.

33. *Memoir*, ii, 520 has T.'s favourable comment on *PL* 4, 354 for attaining the same effect. The Malory items T. has incorporated in his list are traced in ch. 2 n 105.

34. e.g. 'half unwillingly' (*GL*565) from *FQ* 11 x 77 'halfe unwilling'; 'youthhood' (*GL*566), only other contemporary example, Carlyle; 'privily' and 'mayest' (*GL*567, 572) are Biblical; 'ta'en or slain' (*GL*572) from *R2* 5.6.4.

35. *Edinburgh Review* 110 (July 1859) 249.

36. e.g. 'taint in nature', 'pretext', 'law', 'suspicious that her nature had a taint', 'cause . . . cause . . . cause', 'Guilty', 'errs . . . fault' (*MG*31, 33, 37, 68, 87–9, 120, 132). Here syntax is often latinate, reinforcing the sense of legality, e.g. 'All flyers from the hand / Of Justice, and whatever loathes a law' (*MG*36–7).

37. *Sir Gawain and the Green Knight* l. 499 or Gower, *Conf.* i 30; also Wordsworth, *The Cuckoo and the Nightingale* l. 204. 'Afresh' (*GE*904) from *R3* 1.2.56.

38. Entries in Emily Tennyson's diary for June 15th, Sep. 10th, 11th, and 17th, 1856: 'A(lfred) reads Griselda to me . . . and Enid as far as it is done and we weed the garden . . . very fine that I take a holiday from letter writing to have a ride in the Rocking chair in the garden while A tears out Quitch . . . Quitch again tho' it is rainy . . . A with his Quitch again.'

39. Echoing *Gen.* 2.24 'Therefore shall a man leave his father and his mother, and shall cleave unto his wife: and they shall be one flesh'.

40. F. J. Furnivall, *Queste de Saint Graal* (1864), *pref.* vi.

41. The phrase is cited by R. H. Hutton in his fine defence of the *Idylls* (*Macmillan's Magazine* 27, Dec. 1872, 165).

42. In the 19th Century, twelve hundred young women were kept in enforced virginity in the harem of the great Zulu king, Shaka. Those who were caught with a lover were lucky to escape with a quick strangling. These examples could be multiplied almost indefinitely (Ritter 1978, pp. 297, 337).

43. These and other critical comments by T.'s literary contemporaries are supplied by Ricks, *Tennyson*, pp. 271–3.

44. Again note the delicacy of Arthur's diction. 'Footfall' (*G*504) stems from *TMP* 2.2.12. G. C. Macaulay cites as parallel Aeschylus, *Agamemnon* 419–24, which describes the desolation of Menelaus after Helen has gone from him.

45. 'For so the whole round earth is every way / Bound by gold chains about the feet of God' (*PA*422–3) is a Renaissance commonplace, cp. *FQ* 11 vii 46 'She held a great gold chaine ylincked well, / Whose upper end to highest heven was knitt'; *PL* 2, 1051 'Hanging in a golden chain / This pendant world'.

46. T.'s Avalon is a subtle blend of many heroic traditions. 'Where falls not hail, or rain, or any snow, / Nor ever wind blows loudly' echoes *Od.* 6, 42 'Not by winds is it shaken, nor ever wet with rain, nor doth the snow come nigh thereto, but most clear air is spread about it cloudless, and the white light floats over it' (trans. Butcher and Lang); 'deep-meadow'd' *Il.* 9, 151; 'happy' in Virgil's use, *laetas segetes* ('happy fields') *Georg.* 1.1; 'orchard lawns', 'orchard' attrib. *ROM* 2.2.63, 'lawns' a paradisal detail, *PL* 4, 252; 'bowery' first Pope, *Windsor Forest* 1. 262; 'island-valley . . . crown'd with summer sea' *Od.* 10, 195 'Round the island the sea lies like a crown'. T. himself identified the passages from the *Odyssey* (see Ricks, p. 596) and also added Pindar, *Pythian Odes* x 23 for 'deep-meadow'd' and Lucretius iii 18 ff. for the description of heaven.

47. T. S. Eliot, *Selected Essays*, p. 331.

48. *Memoir*, i, 453.

49. *Quarterly Review* 128 (Jan. 1870) 7.

50. 'One unpardonable fault, the fault of tediousness, pervades the whole of the *Fairy Queen* . . . Of the persons who read the first canto, not one in ten reaches the end of the first book, and not one in a hundred perseveres to the end of the poem. Very few and weary are those who are in at the death of the Blatant Beast. If the last six books, which are said to have been destroyed in Ireland, had been preserved, we doubt whether any heart less stout than that of a commentator would have held out to the end' (*Essay on John Bunyan*).

51. The *Idylls* were sarcastically criticised in this way by Frederick Harrison (1900) pp. 15–22. For a reply see Andrew Lang (1901) pp. 105–110.

52. *Memoir*, ii, 506.

Bibliography

Abbott, E. A. *A Shakespearian Grammar*. New York, Dover Publications, 1966.

Adler, T. P. 'The Uses of Knowledge in Tennyson's *Merlin and Vivien*' *Texas Studies in Language and Literature* 11 (1970) 1397–1403.

Alaya, Flavia M. 'Tennyson's "The Lady of Shalott": The Triumph of Art' *Victorian Poetry* 8 (1970) 273–89.

App, A. J. *Lancelot in English Literature*. Washington, D.C., Catholic University of America 1929.

Allingham, W. *A Diary*, ed. H. Allingham and D. Radford. London, Macmillan 1907

Alford, Henry. *Life, Journals and Letters of Henry Alford*. London, Rivington 1873.

Arthos, John. *On the Poetry of Spenser and the Form of Romances*. London, George Allen and Unwin 1956.

Altick, R. D. and Loucks, J. F. *Browning's Roman Murder Story*. Chicago, University of Chicago Press 1968.

Baker, A. E. *A Concordance to the Poetical and Dramatic Works of Alfred, Lord Tennyson*. London, Routledge & Kegan Paul 1965.

Baum, Paull F. *Tennyson Sixty Years After*. Chapel Hill, N.C., University of North Carolina Press 1948.

Bender, J. B. *Spenser and Literary Pictorialism*. Princeton, N.J., Princeton University Press 1972.

Boas, F. S. 'The *Idylls of the King* in 1921' *Nineteenth Century* 90 (1921) 819–30.

Bowden, Marjorie M. *Tennyson in France*. Manchester, University Press 1930.

Bowra, Sir Maurice. *Heroic Poetry*. London, Macmillan 1952.

— *From Virgil to Milton*. London, Macmillan 1945.

Brashear, William R. *The Living Will: A Study of Tennyson and Nineteenth-Century Subjectivism*. Mouton, The Hague 1969.

Brault, J. G. *Early Blazon: Heraldic Terminology in the Twelfth and Thirteenth Centuries with Special Reference to Arthurian Literature*. Oxford, Clarendon Press 1972.

Brewer, Derek S. *Essays on Malory*, ed. J. A. W. Bennett. Oxford, Clarendon Press 1963.

Brooke, Stopford A. *Tennyson: His Art and Relation to Modern Life*. London, Isbister 1894.

Buckley, Jerome H. *Tennyson: the Growth of a Poet*. Cambridge, Mass., Harvard University Press 1960.

Campbell, Nancie. *Tennyson in Lincoln: A Catalogue of the Collections in the Research Centre*. Lincoln, England, The Tennyson Society. vol. I, 1971. vol. II, 1973.

Christ, Carol T. *The Finer Optic: the Aesthetic of Particularity in Victorian Poetry*. New Haven and London, Yale University Press 1975.

Clark, Hugh, and Wormull, Thomas. *A Short and Easy Introduction to Heraldry*. 4th ed., London, Kearsley 1779.

Collins, J. Churton. *Illustrations of Tennyson*. London, Chatto and Windus 1891.

Cross, Tom Peete. 'Alfred Tennyson as a Celticist' *Modern Philology* 18 (1921) 485–92.

Crump, M. Marjorie. *The Growth of the Aeneid*. Oxford, Blackwell 1920.

— *The Epyllion from Theocritus to Ovid*. Oxford, Blackwell 1931.

Dahl, Curtis. 'A Double Frame for Tennyson's "Demeter"?' *Victorian Studies* 1 (1958) 356–62.

Davies, Edward. *The Mythology and Rites of the British Druids*. London, J. Booth 1809.

Dixon, W. Macneile. *A Primer of Tennyson*. London, Methuen 1894.

Dodsworth, Martin. 'Patterns of Morbidity: Repetition in Tennyson's Poetry' *The Major Victorian Poets: Reconsiderations*, ed. Isobel Armstrong. London, Routledge & Kegan Paul 1969.

Donington, Robert. *Wagner's 'Ring' and its Symbols*. London, Faber and Faber 1969.

Dyboski, Roman. *Tennysons Sprache und Stil*. Vienna and Leipzig, Wilhelm Braumüller 1907.

Eggers, J. Phillip. *King Arthur's Laureate: A Study of Tennyson's 'Idylls of the King'* New York, New York University Press 1971.

Eliot, T. S. *Selected Essays*. London, Faber and Faber 1932.

— *The Use of Poetry and the Use of Criticism*. London, Faber and Faber 1933.

Elliott, Philip L. 'Imagery and Unity in the *Idylls of the King*' *Furman Studies* 15 (1968) 22–8.

Elsdale, Henry. *Studies in the Idylls*. London, Henry S. King 1878.

Engelberg, Edward. 'The Beast Image in Tennyson's *Idylls of the King*' *ELH* 22 (1955) 287–92.

Fausset, Hugh L'A. *Tennyson*. London, Cape 1929.

Field, P. J. C. *Romance and Chronicle: A Study of Malory's Prose Style*. Bloomington, Indiana University Press 1971.

Foster, John. *A Shakespeare Word-Book*. London, George Routledge and Sons 1908.

Fowler, Alastair D. S. (ed.) *Paradise Lost*. London, Longman Group Limited 1971.

Fraser, G. S. 'Proper Names in Poetry' *Times Literary Supplement* 11 June 1970, p. 638.

Frye, Northrop. *Anatomy of Criticism: Four Essays*. Princeton, N. J., Princeton University Press 1957.

Furnivall, F. J. (ed.) *Seynt Graal, the History of the Holy Graal*. 2 vols., London, Roxburghe Club 1861.

— ed. *Quest de Saint Graal*. London, Roxburghe Club 1864.

Gardner, E. G. *The Arthurian Legend in Italian Literature*. New York, Octagon Books 1971.

Goslee, David F. 'The Stages in Tennyson's Composition of "Balin and Balan"' *The Huntington Library Quarterly* 38 (1975) 247–68.

Geoffrey of Monmouth. *Historia Regum Britanniae* in *Six Old English Chronicles*, ed. J. A. Giles. London, Bohn 1848.

Geoffrey of Monmouth. *History of the Kings of Britain*, ed. Lewis Thorpe. Harmondsworth, Penguin Books 1968.

Gray, J. M. 'Fact, Form and Fiction in Tennyson's "Balin and Balan"'
Renaissance and Modern Studies 12 (1968) 91–107.
— 'A Study in Idyl: Tennyson's "The Coming of Arthur"' *Renaissance and Modern Studies* 14 (1970) 111–50.
Grose, Francis. *A Provincial Glossary.* 2nd. ed. London, Hooper 1790.
Gurteen, S. Humphreys. *The Arthurian Epic: A Comparative Study of the Cambrian, Breton and Anglo-Norman Versions of the Story and Tennyson's Idylls of the King.* New York and London, G. P. Putnam's Sons 1895.
Haight, Gordon S. 'Tennyson's Merlin' *Studies in Philology* 44 (1947) 549–66
Hair, Donald S. 'Tennyson's *Idylls of the King*: Truth "In the Fashion of the Day"' *English Studies in Canada* 2 (1976) 288–98.
Halperin, M. *Le Roman de Tristan et Iseut dans la littérature anglo-américaine au XIX at au XXe siècles.* Paris, Jouve et Cie 1931.
Haderlein, K. G. J. 'Doubleganger: The Hero and his Double, A Phenomenological Study' Unpub. diss. Edmonton, Alberta, 1971.
Harrison, Frederick. *Tennyson, Ruskin, Mill and Other Literary Estimates.* New York, Macmillan 1900.
Havens, R. D. *The Influence of Milton on English Poetry.* New York, Russell and Russell 1961.
Heath-Stubbs, J. *The Darkling Plain.* London, Eyre and Spottiswoode 1950.
Hoge, James O. (ed.) *The Letters of Emily, Lady Tennyson.* University Park and London, The Pennsylvania State University Press 1974.
— 'Tennyson on Shakespeare: His Talk about the Plays' *Texas Studies in Language and Literature* 18 (1976) 147–70.
Honan, Park. *Browning's Characters.* New Haven, Yale University Press 1961.
Howie, J. G. 'Sappho Fr. 94' pp. 299–342 *Papers of the Liverpool Latin Seminar*, second series, ed. Francis Cairns 1979.
Johnson, E. D. H. *The Alien Vision of Victorian Poetry.* Princeton, N. J., Princeton University Press 1952.
Johnson, Wendell Stacy. *Sex and Marriage in Victorian Poetry.* Ithaca, Cornell University Press 1975.
Jones, Richard. *The Growth of the 'Idylls of the King'.* Philadelphia, Lippincott 1895.
Joseph, Gerhard. *Tennysonian Love: the Strange Diagonal.* Minneapolis, University of Minnesota Press 1969.
Kaplan, Fred. *Miracles of Rare Device.* Detroit, Wayne State University Press 1972.
Keightley, Thomas. *The Fairy Mythology.* 2 vols., London 1828.
Killham, John (ed.) *Critical Essays on the Poetry of Tennyson.* London, Routledge and Kegan Paul 1960.
Kincaid, James R. *Tennyson's Major Poems.* New Haven, Conn., Yale University Press 1975.
Knowles, Sir James T. 'Aspects of Tennyson' *Nineteenth Century* 191 (1893) 164–88.
Kozicki, Henry. 'A Dialectic of History in Tennyson's *Idylls*' *Victorian Studies* 20 (1977) 141–57.
Landow, G. P. 'Closing the Frame: Having Faith and Keeping Faith in Tennyson's "The Passing of Arthur"' *Bulletin of the John Rylands University Library* 56 (1974) 423–42.

Lang, Andrew. *Alfred Tennyson*. Edinburgh, Blackwood 1901.
Lauvrière, Emile. *Repetition and Parallelism in Tennyson*. London, Henry
   Frowde 1910.
Layard, G. S. *Tennyson and His Pre-Raphaelite Illustrators*. London, E. Stock
   1894.
Littledale, H. *Essays on Lord Tennyson's 'Idylls of the King'*. 2nd ed., London,
   Macmillan 1912.
Longinus. *On the Sublime*. ed. and trans. W. Rhys Roberts, Cambridge
   University Press 1899.
Loomis, Laura Hibbard. *Adventures in the Middle Ages*. New York,
   Burt Franklin 1962.
Loomis, R. S. (ed.) *Arthurian Literature in the Middle Ages*. Oxford,
   Clarendon Press 1959.
Lucas, F. L. *Ten Victorian Poets*. 3rd ed. Cambridge University Press 1948.
Luce, Morton. *A Handbook to the Works of Alfred, Lord Tennyson*.
   London, Bell 1895.
MacCallum, Sir M. W. *Tennyson's 'Idylls of the King' and Arthurian Story from
   the Sixteenth Century*. Glasgow, Maclehose 1894.
MacCaffrey, Isabel G. *'Paradise Lost' as "Myth"*. Cambridge, Mass.,
   Harvard University Press 1959.
Madden, Sir Frederick (ed.) *Sir Gawayne*. Edinburgh, Bannatyne Club
   1839.
— (ed.) *Layamon's Brut*. 3 vols. London, Society of Antiquaries 1847.
Malory, Sir Thomas. *The History of the renowned King Arthur, King of
   Britain*. 2 vols., London, Walker and Edwards 1816.
— *La Mort D'Arthur. The most ancient and famous history of the renowned
   Prince Arthur and the knights of the Round Table*. 3 vols., London,
   Wilks 1816.
— *The Byrth, Lyf and Actes of Kyng Arthur*. 2 vols., London, Longman &
   Co. 1817.
— *La Mort d'Arthur. The history of King Arthur and of the knights of the
   Round Table*. ed. T. Wright. 3 vols., London, Smith 1858.
— *Le Morte D'Arthur*. 2 vols., London, Dent 1906.
— *The Works of Sir Thomas Malory*. ed. Eugene Vinaver. 2nd ed., Oxford,
   Oxford University Press 1968.
Mabinogion. With trans. and notes by Lady Charlotte Guest. 3 vols.,
   London, Longman 1849.
— With trans. and notes by Lady Charlotte Guest. London, Dent 1906.
Marshall, George O. *A Tennyson Handbook*. New York, Twayne 1963.
Maynadier, Howard. *The Arthur of the English Poets*. Boston, Mass.,
   Houghton Mifflin 1907.
McCullough, Joseph B., and Brew, Claude C. 'A Study of the Publication
   of Tennyson's *Idylls of the King*' *PBSA* 65 (1971) 156–69.
McLuhan, H. M. (ed.) *Alfred Lord Tennyson: Selected Poetry*. New York,
   Holt, Rinehart and Winston 1956.
Meinhold, George D. 'The *Idylls of the King* and the *Mabinogion*' *Tennyson
   Research Bulletin* 1:3 (1969) 61–3.
Merriman, James Douglas. *The Flower of Kings: A Study of the Arthurian
   Legend in England between 1485 and 1835*. Wichita, Kans., The
   University Press of Kansas 1973.
Millard, Charles W. 'Julia Ward Cameron and Tennyson's *Idylls of the
   King*' *Harvard Library Bulletin* 21 (1973) 187–201.

Mustard, W. P. *Classical Echoes in Tennyson*. New York, Macmillan 1904.
Nash, Walter. 'The Poetics of Idyll'. Unpub. diss. Nottingham, 1972.
— 'Tennyson: "The Epic" and the Old "Morte"' *The Cambridge Quarterly* 6 (1975), 326–49.
Nicoll, Sir W. R. and Wise, T. J. *Literary Anecdotes of the Nineteenth Century*. 2 vols., London, Hodder and Stoughton 1896.
Nicolson, Sir Harold. *Tennyson: Aspects of his Life, Character and Poetry*. London, Constable 1923.
Paden, W. D. *Tennyson in Egypt: A Study of the Imagery in His Earlier Work*. Lawrence, Kans., University of Kansas Press 1942.
Palgrave, F. T. *Landscape Poetry from Homer to Tennyson*. London, Macmillan and Co. 1897.
Pallen, Conde Benoist. *The Meaning of the 'Idylls of the King'*. New York, American Book Co. 1904.
Peacock, Edward. *A Glossary of Words used in the Wapentakes of Manley and Coningham*. 2nd ed., London, Trübner and Co. 1889.
Peake, Arthur S. (ed.) *A Commentary on the Bible*. London, T. C. and E. C. Jack 1919.
Peters, Robert L. *The Crowns of Apollo*. Detroit, Wayne State University Press 1965.
Pfordresher, John. *A Variorum Edition of Tennyson's 'Idylls of the King.'* New York, Columbia University Press 1973.
— 'A Bibliographical History of Alfred Tennyson's *Idylls of the King*' *Studies in Bibliography* 26 (1973) 192–218.
Pitt, Valerie. *Tennyson Laureate*. London, Barrie and Rockliff 1962.
Poston, Lawrence. '"Pelleas and Ettarre": Tennyson's "Troilus"' *Victorian Poetry* 4 (1966) 199–204.
Priestley, F. E. L. 'Tennyson's *Idylls*' *University of Toronto Quarterly* 19 (1949) 35–49.
— *Language and Structure in Tennyson's Poetry*. London, Deutsch 1973.
Pyre, J. F. A. *The Formation of Tennyson's Style*. Madison, Wisconsin, University of Wisconsin Press 1921.
Quinn, Kenneth. *Virgil's Aeneid: A Critical Description*. Ann Arbor, University of Michigan Press 1969.
Rader, R. W. *Tennyson's 'Maud': the Biographical Genesis*. Berkeley, University of California Press 1963.
Rawnsley, H. D. *Memories of the Tennysons*. Glasgow, Maclehose 1900. 2nd. ed., 1912.
Reed, John R. *Perception and Design in Tennyson's 'Idylls of the King'*. Athens, Ohio, Ohio University Press, 1969.
Ricks, Christopher (ed.) *The Poems of Tennyson*. London, Longmans 1969.
— *Tennyson*. London, Macmillan 1972.
— 'Tennyson's Methods of Composition' *Proceedings of the British Academy* 52 (1966) 209–30.
Richardson, Joanna. *The Pre-Eminent Victorian: A Study of Tennyson*. London, Cape 1962.
Ritter, E. A. *Shaka Zulu*. Harmondsworth, Penguin Books 1978.
Robinson, Edna Moore. *Tennyson's Use of the Bible*. New York, Gordian Press 1968.
Rogers, David. *Tennyson's 'Idylls of the King' and Other Poems*. New York, Monarch Press 1965.

Rosenberg, John D. *The Fall of Camelot: A Study of Tennyson's 'Idylls of the King'.* Cambridge, Mass., Harvard University Press 1973.

Ryals, Clyde de L. *From the Great Deep: Essays on 'Idylls of the King'.* Athens, Ohio, Ohio University Press 1967.

Saintsbury, George. *Corrected Impressions.* London, Heinemann 1895.

Shannon, E. F. *Tennyson and the Reviewers.* Cambridge, Mass., Harvard University Press 1952.

Shaw, W. David. *Tennyson's Style.* Ithaca, London, Cornell University Press 1976.

Slinn, E. Warwick. 'Deception and Artifice in *Idylls of the King'* *Victorian Poetry* 11 (1973) 1–14.

Smalley, Donald. 'A New Look at Tennyson – and especially the *Idyll* *Journal of English and Germanic Philology* 61 (1962) 349–57.

Smith, Elton E. *The Two Voices: A Tennyson Study.* Lincoln, Nebraska, University of Nebraska Press 1964.

Solomon, Stanley J. 'Tennyson's Paradoxical King' *Victorian Poetry* 1 (1963) 258–71.

Stange, G. Robert. 'Tennyson's Mythology: A Study of "Demeter and Persephone"' *ELH* 21 (1954) 67–80.

Staines, David. 'The Prose Drafts of Tennyson's *Idylls of the King'* *Harvard Library Bulletin* 22 (1974) 280–308.

— 'Tennyson's "The Holy Grail": The Tragedy of Percivale' *Modern Language Review* 69 (1974) 745–56.

Swinburne, A. C. *Under the Microscope.* London, White and Co. 1871.

— *The Complete Works.* New York, Russell and Russell 1968.

Tatlock, J. S. P. *The Legendary History of Britain.* Berkeley, University of California Press 1950.

Tennyson, Alfred Lord. *The Works of Alfred, Lord Tennyson,* Eversley Edition, 9 vols., annotated by Alfred, Lord Tennyson, ed. Hallam, Lord Tennyson. London, Macmillan 1907–08.

— *Idylls of the King,* ed. J. H. Fowler. London, Macmillan 1930.

— *Gareth and Lynette. The Marriage of Geraint. Geraint and Enid. The Holy Grail. Guinevere.* ed. G. C. Macaulay. London, Macmillan 1892, 1893.

— *The Coming of Arthur. Lancelot and Elaine. The Passing of Arthur.* ed. F. J. Rowe. London, Macmillan 1902.

— *The Poems of Tennyson,* ed. Christopher Ricks. London, Longmans 1969.

Tennyson, Sir Charles. *Alfred Tennyson.* London, Macmillan 1950.

— *Six Tennyson Essays.* London, Cassell 1954.

— 'The Dream in Tennyson's Poetry' *Virginia Quarterly Review* 40 (1964) 228–48.

Tennyson, Emily, Lady. *Letter Diary.* Unpublished, no date. *The Letters of Emily, Lady Tennyson.* ed. J. O. Hoge. University Park and London, The Pennsylvania State University Press 1974.

Tennyson, Hallam, Lord. *Alfred Lord Tennyson: A Memoir.* 2 vols., London, Macmillan 1897.

— *Tennyson and His Friends.* London, Macmillan 1911.

Thomson, J. A. K. *Classical Influences on English Poetry.* London, George Allen and Unwin 1951.

Tillotson, Kathleen. 'Tennyson's Serial Poem' *Mid-Victorian Studies,* by Geoffrey and Kathleen Tillotson, pp. 80–109. London, University of London Athlone Press 1965.

Trenkner, Sophie. *Le Style kai dans le récit attique oral.* Assen 1960.

Turner, Paul. *Tennyson*. London, Routledge and Kegan Paul 1976.
— 'Some Ancient Light on Tennyson's "Oenone"' *Journal of English and Germanic Philology* 61 (1962) 57–72.
Waterston, Elizabeth H. 'Symbolism in Tennyson's Minor Poems' *University of Toronto Quarterly* 20 (1951) 369–80.
Wilkenfeld, R.B. 'Tennyson's Camelot: The Kingdom of Folly' *University of Toronto Quarterly* 37 (1968) 281–94.
Wilkie, Brian. *Romantic Poets and Epic Tradition*. Madison, University of Wisconsin Press 1965.
Wright, H.G. 'Tennyson and Wales' *Essays and Studies* 14 (1929) 71–103.
Yeats, W.B. (ed.) *Oxford Book of Modern Verse*. Oxford, University Press 1936.

Index

integral or planned from outset,
3–7, 20, 23, 75, 76–89, 105–6;
landscape in 62–75; literary
allusion (Biblical, *see* Biblical;
classical, *see* Homer, Virgil;
English, *see* Chaucer, Malory,
Milton, Shakespeare, Spenser);
metaphor, 89–94; plot summary,
6–9; prefixes and suffixes, 76–80,
152n1, 153n7, 154n9, 155n16
n18, 156n21; second person
singular, 146n74; songs, 96–108;
sources, major Arthurian, 10–
42, 48–50, 63–4
Isolt, the Irish, 7, 37, 52, 56, 75,
77, 78, 81, 115, 121, 164n12
Isolt, the Breton, 52, 116

James, Henry, 134
Joseph of Arimathaea, 54, 146n75
Jung, Carl Gustav, 37

Kaplan, Fred, 139n15
Kay, 57, 77, 89, 159n63
Kincaid, James, 162n4
Knowles, Sir J. T., 43

Lady of the Lake, 13, 53, 64, 121,
139n17
'Lady of Shalott, The', 21, 124,
142n98, 145n27, 147n81, 149
n119, 153n7, 155n19
Lancelot, 27, 33, 44, 48–50, 51, 54,
58, 71–2, 77, 79, 82–3, 89, 91–3,
110, 123, 142n98, 144n11n27,
164n11, 165n24; and Guinevere,
7, 14, 19–20, 58, 97, 102, 103,
112, 113, 120, 124–6
Lancelot and Elaine, 21–4, 52, 91,
113, 140n53n56, 143n102, 151
n32n33, 154n8, 159n65
Lancilotto Panciatichiano, 151n33
landscape, 62–75
Lang, Andrew, 167n51
Last Tournament, The, 4–6, 34–7,
78, 96, 97, 115, 141n69, 143
n102n104, 159n68, 161n30n31
Lavaine, 22, 45–6, 48, 71, 91, 120,
140n53, 158n55
Layamon, 145n47, 160n7, 161n39
Leodogran, 53, 96, 109–10, 162n1
Leodogran's chamberlain, 53

Limours, 18–19, 111, 140n41
Longinus, 50, 51, 145n45
Lord of Astolat, the, 22, 157n33
Lot, 47, 163n2
Lucretius, 142n89
Lynette, 32–3, 57, 77, 79, 80, 89,
98, 110, 156n31, 157n33
Lyonnesse, 78, 115
Lyonors, 33, 80

Mabinogion, 14–19, 32, 59, 62–4,
69, 139n25
Macmillan's Magazine, 166n41
maimed churl, the, 84
Malory: in *Balin and Balan*, 37–42,
45, 85, 146n74, 162n5; in *The
Coming of Arthur*, 29–30, 47, 84,
87, 141n83; in *Gareth and Lynette*,
32–4, 57, 77, 81, 84, 89, 128,
142n91, 143n105, 144n23n24,
153n7, 156n25, 158n54, 164n8;
in *Guinevere*, 19–20, 44, 60, 127;
in *The Holy Grail*, 24–9, 141n78;
in *Lancelot and Elaine*, 21–4, 45–
46, 50, 143n102, 154n9; in *The
Last Tournament*, 34–7, 82, 143
n104, 146n74, 161n30, 163n4; in
Merlin and Vivien, 12–14, 61, 139
n15; in *Morte d'Arthur*, 10–12,
156n22; in *The Passing of Arthur*,
30–1, 163n15; in *Pelleas and
Ettarre*, 31–2, 161n29
Mark, 7, 9, 37, 65–6, 75, 77, 116,
120, 143n105, 164n9
Marriage of Geraint, The, 4–5, 15–
18, 99–100, 110, 153n3, 158n55
n56
Memoir, 1, 2, 10, 34, 151n34, 160
n13
Merlin and Vivien, 3–6, 9, 12–15,
53, 71, 78, 84, 102, 130, 139n15
n16, 144n14, 158n57, 162n6
Merlin, 7, 13–14, 51, 53, 55, 77,
78, 79, 89, 96, 113, 114, 120,
123, 153n7, 158n54, 159n62,
160n20, 164n8
metaphor, 89–95, 130, 143n102,
162n6
Milton, John, 2, 11, 24, 44, 45,
58–61, 66, 74, 76, 79, 95, 138
n7, 142n90, 149n120n123,
153n7

Index of passages analysed (page references in italic)